AMERICAN COMMON LAW AND THE PRINCIPLE NULLUM CRIMEN SINE LEGE

AMERICAN COMMON LAW AND THE PRINCIPLE NULLUM CRIMEN SINE LEGE

by

STANISŁAW POMORSKI

Second, revised and enlarged edition

1975

MOUTON
THE HAGUE · PARIS

PWN—POLISH SCIENTIFIC PUBLISHERS
WARSZAWA

Graphic design: *Zygmunt Ziemka*

This translation has been made from
Amerykańskie common law a zasada nullum crimen sine lege
published in 1969 by Państwowe Wydawnictwo Naukowe
Warszawa

Translated by *Elżbieta Chodakowska*

ISBN 90 279 3184 4

Printed in Poland
(D.R.P.)

To KRZYSIA and ROMAN

ACKNOWLEDGEMENTS

This book is a result of basic research carried out during the two academic years 1964–1965 and 1965–1966 at the Harvard Law School in Cambridge, Mass., with which I was affiliated as a Visiting Scholar. The preparation of the present, new enlarged and revised English edition was accomplished during the summer of 1972, when the Harvard Law School, through its International Legal Studies, again extended its hospitality to me.

Naturally enough my gratitude goes first of all to the Harvard Law School, its faculty, its library and administrative staff generally, and to its International Legal Studies in particular.

My special personal feelings of gratitude and affection go to persons whom I owe, above all, this extraordinarily valuable scholarly opportunity, Professor Harold J. Berman and Professor Milton Katz, Director of the International Legal Studies.

During my two visits to the Harvard Law School I had an opportunity to attend many classes and seminars and to have numerous informal discussions with HLS faculty members. All of them were most valuable and useful in the process of my studies, research and writing. I am much obliged to my teachers of American and comparative law, to persons who drew my attention to important legal problems and questions and who helped me in finding solutions. I would like to express my best thanks particularly to Harvard Law School Professors Richard R. Baxter, Harold J. Berman, Jerome A. Cohen, Alan M. Dershowitz, Paul A. Freund, Charles Fried, and Livingston Hall.

I owe special gratitude to Professor Livingston Hall for his gracious assistance during the preparation of the present edition of this book. His careful reading of the manuscript resulted in numerous critical remarks which were of great value and importance. Due to Professor Hall's criticism many mistakes have been eliminated. It is also Professor Livingston Hall who drew my attention to important sources concerning the revision of American penal systems in recent years. May I also express my gratitude to Dr. Jan Stèpăn, Foreign Law Librarian at HLS for his numerous valuable suggestions.

I am also very much indebted to Dr. Krzysztof Poklewski-Koziełł for his careful reading of the manuscript in English and comparing it with the Polish original; his numerous remarks have been of great value to me.

This book benefited greatly from comments and criticism made during the preparation of its first edition, and after its publication in Poland, by Polish legal scholars. I should mention among them first of all Professor Arnold Gubiński, as well as Professor Igor Andrejew, Professor Tadeusz Cyprian, Dr. Stanisław Frankowski, Dr. Leszek Kubicki, Professor Leszek Lernell, late Professor Jerzy Sawicki, Professor Mieczysław Siewierski and Professor Wacław Szyszkowski.

My work on this book has been constantly encouraged by my sister Professor Krystyna Pomorska-Jakobson and her husband Professor Roman Jakobson. I would like to express here my warmest gratitude and affection to them.

I would also like to express my gratitude to the American Philosophical Society and to the Ford Foundation, whose grants helped me considerably in carrying out my research in 1965/1966 and 1972 respectively.

My best thanks go finally to Dr. Elżbieta Chodakowska for her excellent work on the translation of this book from Polish into English and to my research assistant, a third year student at Rutgers University School of Law at Camden, Mr. Timothy J. O'Leary.

TABLE OF CONTENTS

INTRODUCTORY REMARKS

THE SUBJECT AND THE METHOD

In order to understand the American legal systems in general and its criminal law systems in particular it is essential to get an over-all notion of the fundamental concepts and functions of the common law. Since the term "common law" itself is ambiguous let us introduce at the outset its various meanings and designate which of them will be used in this work.

The English adjective "common" is derived from the Latin, *communis*, the Old French *commun*, the Old English *commun*, meaning "belonging equally to more than one",* or belonging to the community, free to be used by everyone, public. Historically, the original meaning of the term "common law" was most probably "communal law", i.e., a law binding on the whole kingdom, common to the country at large, distinct from the customary law binding, for instance, on one county or on one territory.

This uniform law, common to the whole kingdom, was laid down and employed by the central Royal Courts, i.e. the common law courts which were powerful enough to impose on the country at large the legal system they themselves created. Hence the common law, contrary to a rather popular notion, is not the customary law. I t i s t h e l a w c r e a t e d b y t h e C o u r t s.[1]

---

* Johnson's Dictionary—translator's note.

[1] Some writers suggest that the common law is the customary law of the courts. It is difficult to agree even with this formulation. The common law is binding at present not because the courts used to apply it but because

With the emergence of the Court of Chancery[2] (an institution which tried some categories of civil cases under the equity jurisdiction) a competition between the common law and the equity system developed. With passage of time the latter became a separate, broad civil law system based on the precedents of the Court of Chancery, presently administered by the Chancery Division of the High Court. The canon law employed by the ecclesiastical courts was another rival of the common law. In comparative law literature the term "common law" is used as opposed to "civil law" or "Roman law", in order to distinguish the systems based on the English tradition from systems based on the continental European tradition.[3]

Finally, the law created by the courts is called common law to distinguish it from statutory law, i.e. the law laid down by the legislature.[4] In this work I will use the term common law principally in this sense since criminal responsibility under the common law, as thus defined, is the fundamental and most glaring form of the violation of the principle, *nullum crimen sine lege*. (Where "common law" is used in a different meaning it will be indicated in case the context itself does not make it clear.)

It should not be concluded, however, that "common law" and "statute law" are two isolated phenomena even if they

---

it became the law by virtue of binding decisions. In the past (more or less until the 19th century) the common law was indeed the customary law of the courts (Compare Chapter 1).

[2] The first decisions of the Court of Chancery appeared in the collections of judicial decisions at the end of the 15th century. T.F.T. Plucknett, *A Concise History of the Common Law*, 5th ed., Boston, 1956, p. 693.

[3] Compare: R. David, *Les Grands Systèmes de Droit Contemporain (Droit Comparé)*, Quatrième Édition, Dalloz 1971; R. B. Schlesinger, *Comparative Law. Cases-Texts Materials*, Mineola, New York, 1970, pp. 188ff.; A. T. von Mehren, *The Civil Law System. Cases and Materials for the Comparative Study of Law*, Englewood Cliffs, New Jersey, 1957, pp. 3ff.

[4] H. C. Black, *Black's Law Dictionary*, Revised Fourth Edition. St. Paul, 1968.

are distinguished from or opposed to each other. On the contrary: since they constitute the two fundamental components of the legal systems within the common law group they remain closely interrelated. The relation of the common law and statute law is discussed in greater detail in Chapter 2; however, to explain fully the terminology used in this work it seems desirable to present at this point the specific interrelation of these two concepts.

Beside the precedents made by the courts when functioning as creators and guards of the common law, there is another, no less important category of precedents established in the course of judicial interpretation of legislation. This category is a very important source of law. The judicial construction of a statute incorporated in a precedential decision becomes an integral part of the statute and is binding on equal footing with the statute itself.[5] Should this category of precedents also be considered as a component of the common law because it constitutes a source of law which does not come from the legislator but from the court? Some authors are in favor of such an extensive interpretation,[6] others use the term "judge-made-law", "decisional law", or "case law" as a descriptive of the whole institution of the precedential law. It seems that the second solution offers more terminological and conceptual clarity. Therefore the term "precedential law" will be used equivalent to "case law". The concept of precedent discussed in Chapter 1 applies both to common law precedents and to precedents established through judicial interpretation of statutes, for the general rules governing the structure of precedents embrace all their categories. The common law is the source of those extra-legislative rules which define the scope and the contents of a precedent and the mode of its application.

---

[5] *Gulf S.F. Ry Co.* v. *Moser*, 275 US 133 (1933): "Interpretation placed upon statute by Supreme Court becomes an integral part thereof". See also: *Winters* v. New York, 333 US 507 (1948).

[6] R. M. Perkins, *Criminal Law*, Brooklyn, 1957, p. 23.

This is so because these rules were created by the courts and the legal doctrine without any legislative interference.

The common law is not only one of the essential sources of law of the fifty-three American legal systems[7] but also a means to understand the legislative and constitutional sources. The influence of the common law upon the whole body of the American systems is manifold and many sided and for this reason difficult to present in a concise way. To put it in more general terms the common law created a certain habit of legal thinking and of formulating legal rules quite different from the Continental one. The rules of the common law derive from decisions in individual cases and at the same time are adjusted to the existing precedents. The effect of this is an extensive system of casuistry in which the legal rules sometimes reach down to the smallest detail. Although casuistic regulations are seldom exhaustive, common law systems are very dynamic due to the law-making role of the court which, when the need arises, can bridge the legal gaps. The common-law judges who not only apply the law but also act as law-makers betray a definite inclination toward pragmatic and instrumental thinking. In the absence of a binding precedent, the common-law judge, following teleological premises, will first look for the most practical or proper solution and then make new law. Seeking solutions by way of deduction from an abstract legal norm is alien to the mode of thinking shaped by the common law. One may venture the opinion that this is a non-academic way of thinking. The common law is a product of activities of courts, not of universities. In England as well as in a number of North American states one can still become a lawyer without a law degree. All this proves the pragmatism and anti-conceptualism of the common law.

---

[7] Formally both in Louisiana and in Puerto Rico, the common law neither was nor is binding. Since 1938 the binding force of the common law is restricted in the federal jurisdiction. For a fuller treatment see Chapter 1.

Hence, according to Roscoe Pound, the common law is not only a fixed body of definite rules but above all, "a mode of judicial and juridic thinking, a mode of treating legal problems".[8] Sometimes this "mode of treating legal problems" emphasized by Pound assumes the more concrete shape of meta-legal rules as, for instance, the rules of construing and applying precedents, or the rules governing statutory construction.[9]

This is by no means the extent of the common law influence on the statute law. Statute law in American jurisdictions does not constitute a well-knit system; rather an uncodified, uncoordinated, even tangled mass of legislation, more often than not segmental and fragmentary. It is of no avail to seek some general or guiding principle: it is the common law itself which organizes the system, putting it into a certain shape; it is the common law where the "general part" of the system can be discovered. Finally, statute law has borrowed much from the common law. Frequently the whole conceptual and terminological apparatus, the doctrines and constructs of the common law *are* promulgated in the form of statutes.

In the light of these facts it may be suggested, with no exaggeration, that the common law is the key to understanding the structure and means of operation of the American law.

In the realm of the criminal law, the common law performs a treble function: it constitutes an independent basis for imposing criminal responsibility for an act; it exerts an influence in determining responsibility under a criminal statute; it is a source of the "general part" of the criminal law.

This work is designed to consider the common law in its role as an independent basis for imposing criminal punishment

---

[8] "...The strength of the common law is in its treatment of concrete controversies—Pound says further—as the strength of its rival, the modern Roman law, is in its logical development of abstract conceptions". R. Pound, *The Spirit of the Common Law*, Boston, 1963, pp. 1–2.

[9] For a more penetrating analysis see Chapter 1 and Chapter 2.

in the light of the principle *nullum crimen sine lege* and, in particular, its safeguarding function. The reasons for choosing this topic are as follows:

1. It allows consideration of the system in its entirety (although from only one vantage point), whereas a description and analysis of the particular institutions or principles comprising the American criminal law would necessarily narrow the perspective.

2. The topic under discussion reveals the characteristic contradiction, from which the common law systems seem unable to rid themselves, between the principle of legality in the criminal law and the law-making role of the courts; it also shows the various repercussions of this contradiction.

Some aspects of the principle *nullum crimen sine lege* are even elevated to the rank of constitutional principles. For instance, a punishable act must be described with sufficient clarity by a statute lest it be voided as unconstitutional.[10] The Federal Constitution explicitly forbids the promulgation of retroactive penal statutes. Characteristically the aforementioned doctrines are applied in a very limited scope, if at all, where judicial precedents are involved.

3. Against the background of the issues discussed in this work it becomes clear that the codification movement in the United States is of considerable importance. In recent years, due to the efforts of the American Law Institute, it has gathered some momentum. The codification of the criminal law usually means the elimination of the common law of crimes. The Model Penal Code and several modern state codifications (Wisconsin, 1955, Illinois, 1961, Connecticut, 1969, New Hampshire, 1971, Kentucky, 1972, Pennsylvania, 1972, Delaware, 1973) bear witness to this fact.[11] So, we are actually

---

[10] For a fuller analysis see Chapter 2.

[11] The "common law of crimes" designates this part of the common law which provides an independent basis for an imposition of penal sanctions. See also *Proposed Criminal Code of Massachusetts* (1972), § 6.

dealing with a phenomenon which in spite of a gradual shrinking, is of considerable dimension but is dissolving at a slow pace.

The function of the common law as an independent basis of criminal responsibility is a ramification of the normative character of judicial precedent, unknown to the Continental law. The very notion of precedent, the way in which it functions in the American systems, the relation of these systems to the English legal tradition, and finally the interrelation between the common law and the statutory law—are general issues which must be examined before we may go deeper into the penal law problems. Chapters 1 and 2 are therefore largely introductory and deal with problems of a more general nature.

To a large extent the American law also constitutes a continuation of the English legal tradition in the area of the criminal law. In particular, criminal responsibility under the common law in the absence of legislation and the judicial creation of offenses are institutions stemming from the English common law of crimes. Chapter 3 seeks to establish the outlines of the English judge-made law in order to introduce the reader to the general background of criminal responsibility under the American criminal law.

Chapter 4 considers criminal responsibility within the framework of the common law. There the scope of the common law as the basis of criminal responsibility is considered from three points of view: the process through which the common law of crimes is gradually abrogated by the statute law; the competition between the common law and the statutory law in jurisdictions where the common law remains an independent

---

However not every codification of criminal law derogates the common law of crimes. Compare *New Mexico Criminal Code* (1963), § 40A-I-3; the 1974 *Florida Criminal Code*; the 1975 *Virginia Criminal Code*. Codification of substantive criminal law in the American jurisdictions is discussed as of April 1975, Compare: The American Law Institute, *1974 Annual Report*. The new criminal codes of Arkansas (1945) and Puerto Rico (1974), however, have not been available to this writer at the time the book was sent to print.

basis of responsibility; the survey of typical offenses punishable under the American common law.

The possibility of a conviction on the basis of a precedent for a common law offense is doubtless a departure from the principle *nullum crimen sine lege* because the punishment is inflicted without underlying legislation. However, this is not a serious violation of the principle of legality because the criminal character of the punished act was known earlier.

Chapters 5 and 6 deal with more drastic forms of violation of *nullum crimen sine lege* under the American systems. Criminal conspiracy, which is widely applied, adequately illustrates our point. Conspiracy creates enormous possibilities for the judges to expand the criminal law by creating new crimes where collective action is involved.

Another method of violating *nullum crimen sine lege* is the common law misdemeanor doctrine for it allows the court to make criminal any act injurious to public order, public morals, etc.

Chapter 7 deals with one of the ultimate results of the clash between two conflicting tendencies within the common law: the safeguarding function of criminal law and the law-making function of the court. Judge-made law, retroactive in its nature, makes some exceptions in order to mitigate the painful consequences in cases when acts formerly innocent are declared punishable.

The above remarks disclose the existence of two contradictory, conflicting trends within the American law. On the one hand we observe the tendency to preserve the common law of crimes (and thus the law-making function of the court in the field of criminal law) where criminal statutes are inadequate. This tendency is supported by a long tradition and the mores of various legal groups, in particular the judges, as well as by a certain intellectual conservatism and by a spirit of parochialism in the individual states. Needless to say these factors do not accelerate the process of legal reform in the United States.

It is not difficult to see that the existence of the common law of crimes and the right of courts to create new offenses may play into the hands of the reactionary forces which may at an opportune time use them for their own political ends.

On the other hand there is also a movement toward a more extensive application of *nullum crimen sine lege* through abolition of the common law of crimes and its replacement by statute.

Against this background the movement for codification of the criminal law in the United States attains great significance. Both the Model Penal Code drafted by the American Law Institute and several state codifications modeled on the MPC declare the statute to be the sole basis of criminal responsibility. Furthermore, some of these codifications restrict the possibility of creating new offenses in the area of conspiracy by requiring that the object of conspiracy be only an act criminal *per se*.

It should not be forgotten, however, that in twenty-three jurisdictions the common law of crimes still exists and that, in a great number of the remaining jurisdictions, the wording of the criminal statutes is as vague as the common law doctrines. Thus ample room is left for the judge to create new crimes.

Therefore there is still a long way to go before the principle *nullum crimen sine lege* will be fully implemented in all American jurisdictions.

GENESIS AND FUNCTION OF THE PRINCIPLE *NULLUM CRIMEN SINE LEGE*

The question now arises as to how it happened that the principle of *nullum crimen sine lege*, the stronghold of the rule of law in Continental Europe, is so drastically violated under many of the common law systems. What were the historical factors which led to this fundamental discrepancy?

In order to answer these questions we must take a closer look at the socio-political structure which generated the demand for *nullum crimen sine lege* and advanced its implementation in Europe. Next, we will seek to establish whether and to what extent an analogous structure developed in England whose legal system played the role of a model for other legal systems of the common law group.

It is common knowledge that the primary objective of the bourgeoisie, when it arose against feudalism, was to obtain legal protection and safety under the law. The protection of individual freedom within the framework of the "social contract" was the ultimate goal of the leading intellectuals of the Enlightenment. The feudal absolute state, however, threatened this freedom in many walks of life. The existing legal system was the natural enemy of the individual's rights. The substantive criminal law was in a state of chaos intensified by the feudal parochialism.[12] Regulations issued by the head of the state, local-customs and the Roman law provided the grounds for fixing penalties. As a matter of common practice judges created new crimes and inflicted punishments in an arbitrary manner. The notoriety of this practice is reflected in the words of the famous Carpzov: "At present almost all crimes are arbitrary and punishable on extra-legislative grounds".[13]

In France there also raged an extra-judicial repression. It was bred by the sinister institution *lettres de cachet*. The peasantry was subjected to the arbitrary patrimonial judicature.

---

[12] See for general discussion: C. L. von Bar and others, *A History of Continental Criminal Law*. Translated by T. S. Bell and others. Boston, 1916, particularly pp. 243–312; A. Esmein, *A History of Continental Criminal Procedure*. Translated by J. Simpson. Boston, 1913, pp. 211–322. Comp. also: O. Fischl, *Der Einfluss der Aufklärungsphilosophie auf die Entwicklung des Strafrechts*, Scientia Verlag. Aalen, 1973, pp. 1–11; M. T. Maestro, *Voltaire and Beccaria as Reformers of Criminal Law*. New York, 1942, pp. 1–13; L. Radzinowicz, *Crime and Ideology*. New York, 1966, pp. 2ff. I. Andrejew, L. Lernell, J. Sawicki, *Prawo Karne Polski Ludowej* (The Criminal Law of People's Poland), Warszawa, 1954, pp. 27ff.

[13] Andrejew, Lernell, Sawicki, op. cit., p. 38.

The existing codifications of the criminal law generally allowed the use of analogy.[14]

The irrational trial system with its formal theory of proof and the use of torture completes the picture. The arbitrariness and whim of the judges, the eager servants of the monarchy, flourished under these circumstances. No wonder that a Continental judge, the personification of the irrational and cruel system, became the most hated and compromised figure in the eyes of the generation of the Enlightenment.[15] Suffice it to mention the bitter fights Voltaire fought for years against the French courts.

Understandably, the chief demands of legal humanitarians—to declare the statute as the sole ground of penalization and to prohibit retroactive penalization (*nullum crimen, nulla poena, sine lege poenali anteriori*) reflected primarily the bourgeois' pursuit of legal certainty and protection. The demands had thus a political, anti-feudal, anti-absolutist character.

On the wave of mistrust and hostility toward the judges born during the Enlightenment and furthered by the French Revolution, the principle *nullum crimen sine lege* was stretched to its extreme so as to restrict the judge to the "literal" application of the law without even the right to interpret it.[16]

---

[14] Article 105 of the *Constitutio Criminalis Carolina* allowed the application of analogy. Analogy was also allowed by the Prussian Code of 1721, the Bavarian Code of 1751 and the Austrian Code of 1768. See: J. Hall, *General Principles of Criminal Law*, 2nd ed., Indianapolis, 1960, p. 32.

[15] S. Salmonowicz, *Prawo Karne Oświeconego Absolutyzmu* (The Criminal Law of Enlightened Absolutism), Toruń, 1966, p. 35; comp. also: M. T. Maestro, *Voltaire and Beccaria as Reformers of Criminal Law*, New York, 1942.

[16] In this connection we find in Beccaria's work the following statement: "Judges in criminal cases cannot have the authority to interpret laws, and the reason, again, is that they are not legislators [...] For every

The extensive codification movement which started in Europe at the end of the 18th century doubtlessly fostered the formulation and the realization of the demands of the humanitarians. The driving forces of the movement, apart from the need of restoration and reform in the realm of the law, were the unification tendencies.

Codification reflected the process of the eradication of feudal parochialism when the establishment and growth of national states was in progress. Hence the recognition of the principle *nullum crimen sine lege* was an essential part of the more general anti-parochial, and in this sense anti-feudal, tendency. Consequently the outstanding luminaries of the Enlightenment became the chief and most articulate spokesmen of *nullum crimen sine lege*. Also, the maxim was supported by lawyers who hardly fitted into the humanitarians' camp but who still considered this principle as a means toward the unification of the law.[17]

The forerunner of the principle *nullum crimen sine lege* was Montesquieu. He "requested that a precise statutory definition of criminal offences be introduced, that ambiguity be removed and no chance be left to the courts for an arbitrary use of stat-

---

crime that comes before him, a judge is required to complete a perfect syllogism in which the major premise must be the general law; the minor, the action that conforms or does not conform to the law; and the conclusion, acquittal or punishment [...] Nothing can be more dangerous than the popular axiom that it is necessary to consult the spirit of the laws. It is a dam that has given way to a torrent of opinions." C. B. Beccaria, *On Crimes and Punishments.* Transl. by H. Paolucci, Indianapolis and New York, 1963, pp. 14–15.

For Anselm Feuerbach's opinion see S. Salmonowicz, "Feuerbach: narodziny nowoczesnej doktryny prawa karnego" (Feuerbach: the father of the modern doctrine of criminal law), *Czasopismo Prawno-Historyczne*, 1964, Vol. 16, p. 335.

[17] S. Salmonowicz, *Prawo karne*...; op. cit., p. 55.

utory provisions".[18] The originality of Montesquieu's ideas is also striking because of the fact that *nullum crimen, nulla poena sine lege* seems to be a direct consequence of the theory of the separation of powers. Since the legislature determines both the criminal character of an act and the penal sanction it must be independent from the other two powers. Should a judge resort to the use of analogy or of the customary law he would then invade the legislator's territory.[19]

Beccaria, a zealous supporter of *nullum crimen, nulla poena sine lege*, strongly emphasized its importance in his work.[20] Other famous writers of this time also took a part in the discussion.[21]

---

[18] Ibidem, p. 35. Compare also: S. Pławski, "Zagadnienia prawa karnego w dziełach Monteskiusza" (Problems of Criminal Law in Montesquieu's Works), in: *Monteskiusz i jego dzieło* (Montesquieu and His Work). Symposium on 200th anniversary of his death, Wrocław, 1955; M. T. Maestro, *Voltaire and Beccaria...*, op. cit., pp. 22ff.; O. Fischl, op. cit. p. 32, M. T. Maestro, *Cesare Beccaria and the Origins of Penal Reform*, Philadelphia, 1973, p. 17.

[19] "In despotic governments there are no laws, the judge himself is his own rule. There are laws in monarchies; and where these are explicit, the judge conforms to them; where they are otherwise, he endeavors to investigate their spirit. In republics, the very nature of the constitution requires the judges to follow the letter of the law; otherwise the law might be explained to the prejudice of every citizen, in cases where their honor, property, or life is concerned." *The Spirit of the Laws*, by Baron Montesquieu. Transl. by Thomas Nugent, New York, 1949, Vol. I, p. 75. Montesquieu expresses also a firm opinion against the use of the analogy in the criminal law. Ibidem, p. 190ff.

[20] C. B. Beccaria, *On Crimes and Punishments*, op. cit., pp. 13–14; I. Andrejew, "Beccaria czytany dziś" (Beccaria Today), *Nauka Polska*, 1965, No. 3, p. 65; O. Fischl, op. cit., p. 39; M. T. Maestro, *Cesare Beccaria...*, op. cit., p. 22.

[21] "Si la loi n'a point prononcé de peine contre un délit, que celui qui l'a commis ne subisse aucune peine". *De La Législation ou Principes Des Lois*. Par M. L'Abbé De Mably, Amsterdam, 1776, Seconde Partie, p. 123. In the same work on p. 118 we find the following statement: "Ce n'est pas assez que les Lois soient douces et humaines pour être aimées des citoyens; il faut qu'on sache qu'on n'en a rien à craindre en remplissant ses devoirs, et qu'elles accordent une protection certaine à l'innocence".

The advancement of *nullum crimen, nulla poena sine lege poenali anteriori* was also justified by the humanitarian and utilitarian concept of punishment. According to this theory punishment as such was an evil justified only if it succeeded in preventing a greater evil, that is, the harm caused by the crime. By the nature of things a punishment enacted after the commission of the act, either on grounds of a retroactive law or by the judge who made a new law, could not prevent the harm. Therefore such a punishment was considered purposeless and, in effect, harmful.[22]

A. Feuerbach is credited with the famous formulation given to the principle *nullum crimen, nulla poena sine lege* in his Lehrbuch of 1801.[23]

It was in the Code of the Austrian monarch, Joseph II (1787), that the principle first entered the criminal law. The first paragraph of the first part of the Code introduced the formal definition of the crime, while the first paragraph of the second part also extended the principle to offenses punishable in administrative proceedings. Joseph's penal code was a typical codification of enlightened absolutism, a compromise between two social strata: the bourgeoisie and the feudality.

[22] J. Bentham, *Introduction to the Principles of Morals and Legislation*, New York, 1948, pp. 172–173. Similarly Feuerbach. Compare: S. Salmonowicz, "Feuerbach...", op. cit., p. 334; O. Fischl, op. cit., p. 147f. See also S. Glaser, *O mocy obowiązującej ustawy karnej pod względem czasu* (The Legal Force of a Penal Statute in Terms of Time), Lublin, 1921, p. 24. Retroactive penalization was already opposed by Hobbes in his philosophical writings; in particular, he stressed its obnóxiousness in regard to the deterrent aim of punishment. Compare: G. Williams, *Criminal Law, The General Part*, 2nd ed., London, 1961, pp. 580–581. The study of M. Borucka -Arctowa, *Prawo natury jako ideologia antyfeudalna* (The Law of Nature as an Anti-Feudal Ideology), Warszawa, 1957, contains some interesting remarks concerning the legal and philosophical ideas in this respect.

[23] Compare: H. Welzel, *Das deutsche Strafrecht*. Elfte Auflage, Berlin, 1969, p. 20; *Encyklopedia podręczna prawa karnego* (Small Encyclopedia of Criminal Law), W. Makowski, ed., Issue XVIII, p. 1143; S. Salmonowicz, "Feuerbach...", op. cit., p. 83.

It did not satisfy fully the humanitarian advocates of the reform whose demands were respected only inasmuch as they did not interfere with the interests of the absolute monarchy.[24] In the preamble the monarch emphasized that the ultimate goal of the reform was to guarantee to one and all an administration of justice based upon a uniform law, unambiguously defining punishable acts and preventing the arbitrariness of the judges.[25] The incorporation of *nullum crimen sine lege* was thus added emphasis in the preamble. The wording of the preamble indicates that the enactment of this principle was prompted both by the desire to adopt penal treatment based on humanitarian and rational premises and to have a uniform administration of justice all over the country. What is clearly evident here is not only a concession to the reform camp, which represented the interests of the bourgeoisie, but also a centralizing tendency of an absolute monarch who opposed the arbitrariness of the judges because of their parochial deviations.[26]

Two years after the publication of the Austrian Code the French Declaration of the Rights of Man (Arts. 7–8) followed by the French Constitution of September 3, 1791, Code pénal of September 25, and the Military Code of September 30 of the same year,[27] proclaimed the implementation of this principle.

The next codification which sanctioned the principle *nullum crimen sine lege* was the Prussian Landrecht of 1794.[28]

Subsequently all Continental nineteenth century codes

---

[24] S. Salmonowicz, *Prawo karne...*, op. cit., p. 221. See also O. Fischl, op. cit., p. 192ff.

[25] S. Salmonowicz, op. cit., p. 88; O. Fischl, op. cit., p. 199.

[26] S. Salmonowicz, op. cit., p. 117 and p. 136.

[27] A. Schottlaender, *Die Geschichtliche Entwicklung des Satzes: Nulla poena sine lege*, Wrocław, 1911; O. Fischl, op. cit., p. 210.

[28] S. Salmonowicz, *Prawo karne...*, op. cit., p. 221; O. Fischl, op. cit., p. 203.

adopted the principle.[29] England, however, as we know, did not. Until now the English criminal law accepts as the basis of criminal responsibility not only statute law but also the common law, that is, judge-made law. Furthermore, the English model was transplanted to the non-British systems, which belong to the common law group, the United States included.

How did it happen that a country proud that it had been governed by the rule of law longer than any country in Europe let herself be outdistanced by the absolute monarchies of Austria and Prussia?

There are various reasons and they can be explained on grounds of the differences in the socio-political structure in England and in the Continental countries and on grounds which belong within the realm of legal phenomena.

England ran far in advance of the Continent in her economic, social and political development. The bourgeois revolution succeeded in England over one hundred years before the French Revolution took place. The two revolutions developed in entirely different ways. The English was not as violent as the French, nor were its effects as deep and far-reaching, particularly in the sphere of law and government. The socio-political set-up and the role of the English judiciary differed widely from those of their Continental counterparts.

Government based on law was an English tradition with age old roots. It was expressed in the legal limitation of the royal power and affirmed by the Magna Charta. In Bracton's thirteenth century treatise it was put in these spectacular words: "The king ought not to be under any man, but under God and under the law, because the law makes him king... he

---

[29] For exceptions concerning the principle *nulla poena sine lege* see: *Encyklopedia podręczna prawa karnego*, op. cit., Issue XVIII, p. 1144. The following codes which allowed punishment by analogy are listed there: the Russian of 1845, the Austrian of 1852 and the Danish of 1866.

is no king if his will rules and not the law".[30] This law binding on all the inhabitants of the kingdom, including the king himself, was the common law. It was personified, made and executed by the central King's Courts. Needless to say, the functioning of a government based on law was conditioned on the independence of the law's founders and executors. The common law courts were independent of the Crown due to the influence of the social forces interested in the restriction of the royal prerogatives. They were the same forces which made King John (called John Lackland) put his seal to the Magna Charta Libertatum. In order to control effectively the executive branch the common law courts gradually developed a number of legal principles of a procedural nature which successfully safeguarded the individual's rights. It cannot be denied that throughout their history the common law courts often opposed the executive power in defense of the citizen.[31]

The era of absolutism, and rulers increasingly indignant of the legal restrictions tying them down, culminated in an open conflict between the Crown and the courts. Unable to break the resistance of the courts, long used to independence, the kings established a number of special institutions operating outside the common law. The best known is the Court of Star Chamber created in the sixteenth century, which soon became notorious for its hostility toward civil liberties. The policy adopted by another special tribunal—the High Commission—resulted in an open conflict with the Court of Common Pleas. When the High Commission issued warrants for arrest, thus exceeding its jurisdiction, the Court of Common Pleas stopped the proceeding with a writ of prohibition (an order prohibiting

[30] Quoted after J. Hall, *General Principles...*, op. cit., p. 31. ft. 21.

[31] See R. Pound, *The Spirit...*, op. cit., in particular the chapter "The Courts and the Crown"; T. F. T. Plucknett, *A Concise History...*, op. cit., pp. 191ff.

that further action be taken).[32] The judges of the Court of Common Pleas were summoned by the angry King James I. What followed was a confrontation of two ideas of rulership: one was a government based on law, the other a government based on the royal despotism. In the course of a stormy dispute, with the King resorting to the accusation of treason, the uncompromising Chief Justice Coke quoted Bracton. The judges did not yield[33] and the final victory was theirs.

The special courts which were established in the era of absolutism and which undermined the function of the common law courts were eventually abolished. The Long Parliament abolished the deeply hated Star Chamber in 1641. The rest was accomplished by the revolution. The common law courts, the bearers of the long-standing tradition of the rule of law emerged with greater strength from the struggle against the Stuarts. Coke's concept of the law, presented in the dispute with King James I, became the key-principle of the victorious bourgeoisie.

Therefore while the Continental judge of the eighteenth century, the obedient tool of the absolute monarchy, was considered a natural foe of liberty, and the maxim *nullum crimen sine lege* was designed chiefly to defend the individual against him, the independent common law courts in England enjoyed the fame of the natural defenders of civil liberties.[33a]

---

[32] The High Commission was an administrative tribunal established for deciding certain cases concerning church administration. It decided according to no fixed rules and was subject to no appeal. When it sought to arrest lay subjects in excess of its jurisdiction it collided with the Court of Common Pleas. R. Pound, *The Spirit...*, op. cit., p. 60.

[33] This memorable dispute took place on the 10th of November, 1612. See: R. Pound, *The Spirit...*, op. cit., pp. 60–61.

[33a] As Professor Parsons indicated: "...the crucial period was the early seventeenth century, when Justice Coke asserted the independence of the Common Law from control by royal prerogative. With this, the establishment of the organizational independence of the Judiciary was the crucial symbolic development. Substantially, the Common Law came

Furthermore, as Grünhut rightly observed, procedural protections were and still are dominant in the English legal system while the substantive protections carry less weight.[34] The intellectuals of the Enlightenment were deeply interested in the English procedural institutions. While a struggle was raging on the Continent led by Voltaire and other spiritual leaders of the bourgeois revolution against the feudal administration of justice with its secret trials, monstrous evidenciary rules and tortures, a defendant in England enjoyed numerous procedural safeguards. The burden of proof was on the prosecution, and the jury returned its verdict in open court after hearing the parties and their evidence. The admissibility of evidence was subject to numerous restrictions, and the use of torture forbidden. No wonder the Continental humanitarians thought highly of the English judicial system when comparing it with its severely criticized Continental counterparts.[35]

However, substantive legal safeguards were not wholly unknown to the English law. We will discuss here only those

---

to emphasize the protection of personal rights, the institution of property in private hands, and both freedom of contract and protection of contractual interests far more strongly than did the Continental Law". T. Parsons, "Evolutionary Universals" in: *Sociological Theory and Modern Society* (1967), p. 513.

See also: H. Lauterpacht, *International Law and Human Rights*. London, 1950, Chapter 8: "The English Sources of the Doctrine of Fundamental Rights".

[34] M. Grünhut, *Das Englische Strafrecht*, in: *Das ausländische Strafrecht der Gegenwart*. Herausgegeben von E. Mazger, A. Schönke, H. H. Jescheck. Dritter Band. Berlin, 1959, p. 179.

[35] Montesquieu, *The Spirit of the Laws*, op. cit., Vol. I, p. 91; Vol. II, p. 161; Mably, *De La Législation ou Principes Des Lois*. Seconde Partie, op. cit., pp. 119–122; F. M. Voltaire, *Letters Concerning the English Nation*, London, 1760, pp. 42ff., 48ff.; Compare also: A. Esmein, *A History of Continental Criminal Procedure*, op. cit., p. 322ff; M. T. Maestro, *Voltaire and Beccaria as Reformers of Criminal Law*, op. cit. The writers of the French Enlightenment expressed similar opinions concerning the American legal system. Compare: G. B. Mably, *Remarks Concerning the Government and the Laws of the United States of America*, London, 1784.

which are clearly related to though not identical with the Continental *nullum crimen sine lege poenali anteriori.*

These safeguards were by and large half-measures only; as a rule they were directed toward the Parliament, never toward the judge.

The first of these safeguards, probably the closest to the Continental *nullum crimen sine lege*, prohibited Bills of Attainder, that is, special acts of the legislature inflicting punishments upon specified persons, for acts which were not declared punishable before. This prohibition was first established in 1696 statute and concerned only the death penalty. Afterwards it was extended to include all kinds of punishment.[36] A canon of construction forbidding the retroactive application of statutes creating new crimes or inflicting heavier penalties for old ones performed a similar role.[37]

The rule of strict construction[38] of penal statutes became firmly established in the common law at the beginning of the eighteenth century. The common law courts used it in order to mitigate the extremely harsh penal legislation of the period of the primitive accumulation of capital.[39] The rule underwent some evolution but essentially remains the binding law in

[36] M. Grünhut, *Das englische Strafrecht*, op. cit., p. 180. The prohibition on acts of attainder sought not only to protect the accused against retroactive punishment but also safeguarded the power of the courts as sole administrators of justice.

On application of the bills of attainder comp.: T. F. T. Plucknett, *A Concise History...*, op. cit., p. 205.

[37] G. Williams, *Criminal Law*, op. cit., p. 580; J. Hall, *General Principles...*, op. cit., p. 58. Great Britain is also a signatory of the European Convention on Human Rights (1950); Article 7 of the Convention prohibits retroactive penalization. The Constitution of the United States (Article I, Sections 9 and 10) prohibits both Bill of Attainder and *ex post facto* laws which enact or increase penalties.

[38] Strict construction severely restricted the application of penal statutes. For a fuller treatment see Chapter 2.

[39] Compare: L. Hall, "Strict or Liberal Construction of Penal Statutes", *Harvard Law Review*, 1935, Vol. 48.

England.[40] As previously mentioned the incorporation of *nullum crimen sine lege* into the Continental law was connected with a strong movement for codification in Continental Europe in the eighteenth and nineteenth century. The nineteenth century witnessed recurrent but futile attempts to codify the criminal law in England too.[41] The failure was doubtless due to the peculiarity of the English legal mind, prone to casuistry and mistrustful of vague abstract language. Another serious obstacle in the way of codification was the enormous authority of the common law. It seems, however, that the factor which weighed most heavily in defeating attempts to codify the criminal law and which accounts for the absence of such attempts in other spheres of law, was the fact that there was no social need in England for unifying legislation. England has had a uniform, firmly entrenched common law for centuries. It was precisely the universality of this law which distinguished it from the marked parochialism known everywhere else under the feudal system.

It is noteworthy to mention another peculiarly English phenomenon which accounts for the fact that the law was uniform although not codified: it is the elite character of the English judiciary and its concentration. Both in the past and at present the judges of all the higher courts constitute a small group tied to the tradition of their profession. From time immemorial London was the site of these courts.

The reasons for this seemingly paradoxical disparity in attitudes toward the principle *nullum crimen sine lege*, setting apart the Continental Europe and England famous for her tradition of the rule of the law, may be summarized as follows:

At the time when the Continental bourgeoisie reached for *nullum crimen sine lege* as a means of legal protection their victorious English counterpart had long enjoyed security under

[40] The doctrine is discussed in Chapter 2.

[41] The attempts to codify the criminal law in England are amplified in Chapter 3.

English legal institutions. No influential social forces, interested in the abridgement of the privileges of the courts existed in England.

It should be remembered that it was a tradition of a uniform, universal law for the country at large; consolidation and unification were not needed to achieve what was alreadv achieved.

The law-making power of the court certainly ran counter to the interests of the unpropertied classes, above all the interests of the industrial proletariat. Facts bear witness to this; especially the conspiracy doctrine which was repeatedly used by the judges against the workers' coalitions.[42] The working class, unorganized and politically immature, could hardly have any influence upon the reform of the legal system at that time.

Thus the social structure was the determining factor which led to different treatment of the principle *nullum crimen sine lege* in the English and the Continental law. The reception of the English common law in America included the English disregard of *nullum crimen.*

In America too, especially in the eighteenth century, the common law was conceived as a guarantor of civil liberties, indeed as an embodiment of the law of nature founded upon principles "that are permanent, uniform and universal";[42a] therefore, the common law was conceived at that time as a unitary body of fixed doctrine existing from "time immemorial" and not susceptible to modifications by judges.[42b] If there was a feeling of apprehension it was the legislature, prone to political fluctuations, that was suspect. Subsequently the American constitutions contained substantive guarantees

---

[42] K. Marx, *Das Kapital,* Erster Band, Berlin, 1968, p. 769; G. Williams, *Criminal Law,* op. cit., pp. 669–701.

[42a] M. J. Horwitz, "The Emergence of an Instrumental Conception of American Law", in: *Law in American History,* 1971, pp. 287, 295ff.

[42b] Ibidem.

applying to criminal legislation but not to the common law.[43] Misgivings concerning judicial discretion were not foreign to the American legal mind and legal ideology of that period; characteristically enough, however, those misgivings were related to the judicial application of statutory law, not to the common law of crimes.[43a]

The later evolution of the common law and its transformation into an instrument of social policy and social change[43b] brought about the emergence of an instrumental conception of American law, i.e. the realization that common law factually is susceptible to changes and manipulations by judges. An instrumental conception shed new light on the judicial power under the common law: it now appeared to many, that indeed the courts exercise here a broad discretionary power which brings with it uncertainty and unpredictability, dangerous for civil liberties and incompatible with democratic principles of government. Such a broad discretionary power seemed particularly undesirable in criminal cases with a citizen's life, liberty and property at stake.[43c]

Therefore the breakdown of a unitary conception of the common law—as Professor Horwitz indicated in his excellent article—resulted in a "remarkable attack" on the doctrine of common law crimes and ultimately led, along with other, often political factors, to its rejection in many American jurisdictions.[43d] The process of gradual abrogation of common

---

[43] Ibidem, p. 295ff. For further explanation and substantiation the reader is referred to Chapters 4, 5, 6, and 7.

[43a] M. J. Horwitz, op. cit., pp. 292f., 303.

[43b] "What dramatically distinguished nineteenth century law from its eighteenth century counterpart is the extent to which common law judges came to play a central role in directing the course of social change... by 1820 the process of common law decision making had taken on many of the qualities of legislation". M. J. Horwitz, op. cit., p. 287.

[43c] Ibidem, pp. 301, 305.

[43d] Ibidem, p. 299.

law crimes commenced in the federal jurisdiction and went on throughout the nineteenth century.[43e]

It should be pointed out here, however, that a modern, instrumental conception of the common law was by no means universally accepted in the United States. On the contrary, it existed side by side with a traditional, unitary, Blackstonian conception which was supported by many influential American jurists, especially judges.[43f] The competitive coexistence of these two conceptions of the common law may explain, in part at least, why common law crimes were abolished and superseded by criminal statutes in some of the American jurisdictions, whereas they were retained in those remaining.

The term *nullum crimen, nulla poena sine lege poenali anteriori* contains four independent, though strictly connected rules—which are the pillars on which the principle of legality is based.

The principle *nullum crimen sine lege* comes to the forefront; at its core is the understanding that the legislative act is the only force determining the elements which constitute a punishable act.[44] It guarantees impunity to anyone who does not cross the line drawn by the statute defining punishable offenses; in effect, it marks the boundaries of the individual's freedom.[45]

[43e] See Chapter 4.

[43f] See Chapter 1.

[44] F. Von Liszt, *Lehrbuch des Deutschen Strafrechts*, Berlin, 1900, p. 73; H. Welzel, *Das Deutsche Strafrecht*, Elfte Auflage, Berlin 1969, p. 19; R. Maurach, *Deutsches Straftrecht. Allgemeiner Teil.* 4. Auflage, Karlsruhe, 1971, p. 107f.

[45] This principle of legality is aptly formulated by Radbruch: "...so ist das Strafrecht noch heute nicht nur gegen den Verbrecher gewendet sondern auch für ihn besorgt; es bezweckt, das Recht des Staates auf Strafe nicht nur zu begründen sondern auch zu begrenzen; es ist nicht nur die Quelle, sondern auch die Schranke der Strafbarkeit". G. Radbruch, *Einführung in die Rechtswissenschaft*, II Durchgearbeitete Auflage, Stuttgart, 1964, p. 150.

Under this principle the criminal law protects the citizen, as Liszt said, "not only against the offender but also against the prosecutor".[46]

Nullum crimen sine lege, determining the boundaries of the individual's freedom, simultaneously restricts the prerogatives of the state officials appointed to prosecute and punish. It institutes uniform, universally binding criteria and bars an arbitrary administration of justice.[47]

Under *nullum crimen sine lege* punishment on the grounds of the customary law or on the grounds of the general principles of justice or by analogy is forbidden.[48] A clear formulation of the criminal laws is rigorously observed. Vague words and phrases which fail to clearly define the elements of a punishable act do nothing but obscure the line dividing legal and illegal acts. A judge interpreting a vague law may easily create a new offense under the pretext of applying the law.[49]

---

[46] Cited after Radbruch, ibidem.

[47] This very aspect was strongly emphasized by the Permanent Court of International Justice in the Hague in advisory opinion of 1935 passed in connection with the introduction of punishability on grounds of analogy in the Free City of Gdańsk. See: J. Hall, *General Principles...*, op. cit., p. 28.

[48] G. Radbruch, *Einführung...*, op. cit., p. 150; H. Welzel, *Das Deutsche Strafrecht*, op. cit., p. 19; E. Mezger, *Strafrecht. Ein Studienbuch. Allgemeiner Teil*, Achte Auflage, München und Berlin, 1959, pp. 30–33; R. Maurach, op. cit., pp. 94, 108. Because it is difficult to draw a clear line between liberal construction and analogy, some authors advocate the inadmissibility of liberal construction. Compare: *Encyklopedia podręczna...*, op. cit., Issue VIII, p. 1145; J. Nowacki, *Analogia Legis*, Warszawa, 1966, p. 90. The prohibition on the usage of customary law and analogy applies, of course, only to the definition of offenses, not to the general principles of criminal liability. H. Welzel, *Das Deutsche Strafrecht*, op. cit., p. 19; F. Liszt, *Lehrbuch...*, op. cit., p. 75.

[49] The philosophers of the Enlightenment, and above all Montesquieu, emphasized strongly the need of clear, unambiguous laws. "It is an essential article that the words of the laws should excite in everybody the same

The prohibition of retroactive penalization is a distinct and independent category. Many authors suggest that *nullum crimen sine lege* also covers the prohibition of retroactive laws which declare an act punishable.[50] This opinion however seems inaccurate. Granted that crimes may be defined only by statute, it does not follow that some legislation cannot retroactively declare some acts punishable.[51]

It should be emphasized however that there is a close functional connection between the prohibition of retroactivity and the principle *nullum crimen sine lege*: they compliment each other. The principle of legality inherent in *nullum crimen sine lege* could not properly function if not followed by the prohibition of retroactivity; a person committing an act not prohibited by law could never be sure that in the future he or she would not be held responsible on grounds of a retroactive

---

ideas." Montesquieu, *The Spirit of the Laws*, op. cit., Vol. II, p. 165. "If the crime of high treason be indeterminate, this alone is sufficient to make the government degenerate into arbitrary power." Montesquieu, *The Spirit of the Laws*, op. cit., Vol. I, p. 190. Also compare C. Beccaria, *On Crimes and Punishments*, op. cit., pp. 17–18. In modern literature on the subject compare: *Leipziger Kommentar*, 9. Auflage, W. de Gruyter, Berlin, 1974, Vol. I, Comments to Article 2; p. 8 ff.; J. Hall, *General Principles...*, op. cit., pp. 36–48; G. Williams, *Criminal Law*, op. cit., pp. 576–579.

[50] Compare, for instance, G. Radbruch, H. Welzel, L. Schwartz, G. Williams, J. Hall. On the other hand A. Schönke and H. Schroeder hold that the prohibition of retroactivity follows logically from the prohibition of analogy. See: A. Schönke, H. Schroeder, *Strafgesetzbuch, Kommentar*, München–Berlin, 1957.

[51] Polish legislation furnishes an example: for instance, the decree of January 22, 1946 concerning the "responsibility for the September defeat and for implementation of fascist rules into the life of the state", (Dz. U. No. 5, Item 46) introduced retroactive penal sanctions in respect to entirely new fact situations, without the violation of the principle *nullum crimen sine lege*. On the other hand we know of legal systems which prohibit retroactive penal legislation but in which the principle of *nullum crimen sine lege* is not in force (for instance, a number of states in the United States of America).

law.[52] Both principles are so closely connected within the framework of the principle of legality that they are often drafted in one legal provision.[53] They are both rooted in the common tradition of the Enlightenment which inspired the fight for safety under the law and were introduced as an inseparable postulate. In other words, the principle *nullum crimen sine lege* guards the freedom of the individual against the abuse of official power other than legislative, while the prohibition of retroactive laws equips the individual with a safe conduct against the interference of the legislator himself.

The over-all prohibition of retroactivity as to both penalization and increase of existing penalties became a rule of international law through the adoption of Article 11(2) of the Universal Declaration of Human Rights, which was pronounced by the General Assembly of the United Nations in 1948, by Article 7 of the European Convention on Human Rights of 1950 and by Article 15, Sec. 1 of the U.N. International Covenant on Civil and Political Rights (1966) which states in part: "No one shall be held guilty of any criminal offence on account of any act or omission which did not constitute

---

[52] There is also an opinion expressed in legal literature (Finger, Binding) that the statute enacting punishment may operate retroactively provided that the act, at time of its commission, was illegal although not criminal. The above mentioned authors advocate also the admissibility of *ex post facto* laws increasing penalty. S. Glaser, *O mocy obowiązującej...*, op. cit., p. 24; L. Kubicki, *Zbrodnie wojenne w świetle prawa polskiego* (War Crimes in the Light of the Polish Law), Warszawa, 1963, pp. 72–73.

[53] For instance, Paragraph 2 of the German Penal Code and Article I of the Polish Penal Code of 1969; compare also Article 8 of the Declaration of the Rights of Man of August 26, 1789. A further element which both principles have in common is that the violation of the first principle (*nullum crimen*) usually leads to the violation of the second by way of an *ex post facto* punishment. This is a frequent occurrence when new crimes are made by judges.

an offence, under national or international law, at the time when it was committed".[54]

The principle *nulla poena sine lege*—"no punishment without law"—is also closely connected with the principle *nullum crimen.*[55] The form in which this principle is applied in contemporary legal systems differs widely from its original form. The wave of mistrust toward the judges which swept Continental Europe at the end of the 18th and the beginning of the 19th century was reflected in the precise definition of the legal sanctions so as to leave no room for the judge to differentiate the kinds of punishment. With passage of time the fear of the court's arbitrariness diminished; at the same time it became obvious that strictly fixed sanctions conflicted with the concept of individualizing the punishment.[56] Consequently, at present the function of the principle of legality under *nulla poena sine lege* is reduced so as to define the kind of punishment and its upper limit.[57]

The ban on the retroactive infliction of a heavier penalty bears the same relation to *nulla poena sine lege* as the ban on retroactive laws punishing newly defined crimes has to *nullum crimen sine lege*. These rules are analytically independent although they complement each other.[58]

---

[54] See: G. Williams, *Criminal Law*, op. cit., p. 577, and *Basic Documents on, International Protection of Human Rights* (L.B. Sohn and T. Buergenthal, eds.), The Bobbs Merril, 1973.

[55] The two principles are nonetheless independent and may be enacted separately. Compare examples quoted in: *Encyklopedia podręczna*, Issue XVIII, op. cit., p. 1145.

[56] The provisions of the French Penal Code of 1791 are characteristic in this respect. Mistrust toward judicial discretion in defining crimes and in determining sentences was not unknown in American legal history. See for an interesting discussion M. J. Horwitz, op. cit. A contemporary manifestation of such a mistrust one may find in a famous US Supreme Court decision Furman, Georgia 408 US 238 (1972).

[57] G. Williams, *Criminal Law*, op. cit., p. 606.

[58] The Polish legislation may serve again as an example. The so-called August Decree, 1944, with no violation of the principle of *nulla poena sine*

When confronting the American common law with the principle *nullum crimen sine lege* we will take into consideration more than the mere breach of the rule that the statute is the sole basis of criminal responsibility. This rule is violated by the mere fact that the common law of crimes is in existence. Analyzing the whole set of problems we will try to discover to what degree the common law violates the principle of legality and, above all, to what extent it leaves room for the court to create new offenses. Also, we will often delve into the problem of retroaction in judge-made law since this issue raises most objections among American lawyers. Occasionally we will have to consider the problem of punishment.

---

lege introduced much more severe sanctions (as compared with the provisions of the Penal Code 1932) for crimes committed during World War II, thus breaking the principle of the primacy of the law which is more advantageous for the accused, as stipulated under Article 2 of the 1932 Penal Code (this principle in the Polish law is equivalent to the prohibition of *ex post facto* heavier penalty). See: L. Kubicki, *Zbrodnie wojenne...*, op. cit., pp. 69–74.

Chapter 1

THE GIST AND THE DEVELOPMENT OF THE COMMON LAW IN THE UNITED STATES

THE RECEPTION OF THE ENGLISH LAW IN THE UNITED STATES

English law through its reception in the United States became the foundation of present American legal systems. The reception constituted a point of departure for the systems and still remains a vital source for them. A knowledge of the process, of the scope and the methods of the reception is therefore very helpful to a proper understanding of the genesis and of the present shape of the American legal systems. The limited scope of the present work precludes an extensive discussion of the subject; the reader who wishes to study it more extensively is advised to consult more specific works.[1]

[1] In American literature probably the best relevant study is by F. W. Hall, "The Common Law: An Account of its Reception in the United States", *Vanderbilt Law Review*, 1951, Vol. 4. More detailed information about the reception of the English law in the particular American states is contained in R.P. Powell, *The Law of Real Property*, New York, 1949, Vol. I. See also: R. Pound, "The Development of American Law and its Deviation from English Law", *Law Quarterly Review*, 1951, Vol. 67; H. Pope, "The English Common Law in the United States", *Harvard Law Review*, 1910, Vol. 24; E. G. Brown, *British Statutes in American Law 1776–1836*, Ann Arbor, 1964; J. H. Smith, "New Light on the Doctrine of Precedent in Early America: 1606–1776", in: *Legal Thought in the United States of America under Contemporary Pressures*, Brussels, 1970; F.F. Stone, "The Reception of Law in Louisiana", ibidem. For a brief textbook discussion see: L. M. Friedman, *A History of American Law*, New York, 1973, pp. 15ff., 29ff., 96–98.

Compare also: S. Pomorski, "Recepcja prawa angielskiego w USA" (The Reception of the English Law in the United States), *Studia Prawnicze*, 1969, No. 21.

A supposition that the reception of the English law in the United States occurred on a fixed date and is completed would be erroneous. On the contrary, the reception is a complicated process of long duration, which involves the gradual verification and adaptation of the elements of the English law, a process whose inadequately explored origins can be traced back to the seventeenth century, which is not completed and still goes on in the American jurisdictions. The actual scope of the reception of the English law in the American colonies is not widely explored either. The opinion seems to prevail in the literature on the subject that the reception first gathered impetus in the eighteenth century.[2] Accordingly it would be safe to include the American law among the common law systems from about the middle of the eighteenth century.

Shortly after gaining independence each of the thirteen states found itself confronted with the task of building its own legal system and consequently with defining its attitude toward the legal heritage of the then hostile power—Great Britain. As we know, none of the thirteen states rejected this heritage. This fact may seem a peculiar or even paradoxical phenomenon: the revolutionary generation of Americans freed from the British yoke borrows from the English the essential parts of their legal system.

However, a closer look at the political and social structure of the newly-born country provides an explanation of this paradox. It was a country dedicated to the protection of personal freedom, a country based on the principle of private ownership free from feudal restrictions and set to defend property rights as among the fundamental civil liberties. Both for the state and its inhabitants there was no better model than the English system with its protection of rights and of personal freedom, its administration of justice executed by independent courts and the jury, with its developed property rights. It should be borne in mind that at that time other European

[2] F. W. Hall, op. cit., p. 794; L. M. Friedman, op. cit., p. 15f.

countries still endured the feudal system of law and government.[2a] Furthermore, the British model, basically the most satisfactory one, was the easiest to adopt in terms of legal technicalities because it was not only known but also at least partially used in the colonies.

The scope of the reception was broad: beside the English common law it also included the statute law, equity and the law of merchants. In this way all the elements of the English legal system became components of the American common law.[3] However, taking into consideration the distinct political, social and economic features of the new country and the fact that it was born and consolidated in the fight against the old imperium, we must acknowledge that the process of reception could not have been limited to a mechanical assimilation of the elements of the British system nor was the very *idea* of reception uncontroversial. Indeed the manifestations of hostility toward English law were quite strong and numerous.[3a] From its inception American courts exercised the right to select and verify the rules of the English legal institutions, hence their adaptation and application depended in every case on the decision of the court. Thus in American conditions the English law is only relatively binding.

This peculiar, relatively binding status of the English law in the United States has been usually explained by one of the two following doctrines:

According to a rather popular theory in judicature called the declaratory theory of precedent, the common law consists of "eternal usages and customary rules". The precedents are

[2a] T. Parsons, "Evolutionary Universals" in: *Sociological Theory and Modern Society* (1967), pp. 513–514, Horwitz, op. cit., p. 292f.

[3] F. W. Hall, pp. 791–792.

[3a] Compare: L. M. Friedman, op. cit., p. 94ff.; M. J. Horwitz, op. cit.; F. W. Hall, op. cit., p. 820; R. Pound, "The Place of Judge Story in the Making of American Law", *American Law Review*, 1914, Vol. 48, p. 686; B. Schwartz, *The Law in America. A. History.* McGraw-Hill Book Company, 1974, pp. 8–15.

simply illustrations of these usages and rules. Hence the reception of the English common law is not tantamount to the reception of the English precedents. Consequently the English precedents are not binding and are applied at the discretion of the American courts.[4]

The second, more widely accepted, doctrine leads to a similar end though in a much more complicated way. It asserts that the reception does not include the total English law but only those parts which are useful and applicable in the local conditions of the given state.[5] Tacitly acknowledging the binding character of the English law, the doctrine nevertheless creates vast possibilities to eliminate those parts of the English law which fail to find the approval of the court. Both doctrines make the reception flexible and grant the judiciary the right to determine its actual scope.

The reception did not take place in a uniform fashion all over the country but came to pass separately in each state. Following the example of the original thirteen states, which had already gone through the process, the new states also received the English law. At present Louisiana is the only state which has not formally received the English law.[6] In the majority of the states the reception included the English common law, the statute law and the principles of equity prior to

---

[4] See, inter alia, the decision in *Williams* v. *Milles*, 58 Neb. 463 (1903); *Forbes* v. *Scannel*, 13 Cal. 242 (1859). For the critical assessment of the theory see H. Pope, op. cit., p. 14.

[5] See the opinion of the famous Justice Story in *Van Ness* v. *Packard*, 7 L.Ed. 374 (1829) who said as follows: "The common law of England is not to be taken in all respects to be that of America. Our ancestors brought with them its general principles, and claimed it as their birthright; but they brought with them and adopted only that portion which was applicable to their situation." See also J. H. Smith, op. cit., supra, ft. 1.

[6] The Constitution of the State of Louisiana (1812) Article IV, Sec. II. Compare also F. F. Stone, op. cit., pp. 135–147. See however an act for the punishment of crimes and misdemeanors, May 4, 1805.

1776. Other, earlier dates defining the limits of reception were accepted in only a few states.[7]

The reception was accomplished in two ways: by legislation and by adjudication.

The legislature played a rather secondary role in the process. This is evident from the mere fact that in some states the reception took place without any act on the part of the legislature,[8] while in others the statutes effecting the reception were no more than the starting point in the process. In the majority of the jurisdictions the reception statutes constituted a framework for the judiciary. The courts, however, played and still play a decisive part in the process of reception. The basic criterion of the selection of the principles of the English law, namely the criterion of applicability to the local conditions of the particular state, was laid down by the courts usually quite independently from the legislature.[9] This criterion, although accepted by the courts throughout the country, is nevertheless applied in different ways. This is perfectly clear for the "applicability to the local conditions of the particular state" has a different meaning in New England or in Florida or in California.

Thus the reception of the English law in the particular states shows substantial discrepancies both in terms of its general

---

[7] And so, for instance, the Virginia reception statute of 1776 held that included in the reception are only English statutes enacted before 1606. Virginia (which a few years later amended the reception statute) was followed by some other states, such as Illinois, Indiana, Ohio and Kentucky. For further discussion of the reception of British statutes see E. G. Brown, supra note 1.

[8] In Connecticut and in Utah.

[9] Only in fourteen states "applicability clause" was introduced by the legislation. As to the origin of the "applicability test" see: R. S. O'Regan, "The Common Law Overseas—A Problem in Applying of the Test of Applicability", *International and Comparative Law Quarterly*, 1971, Vol. 20.

outlines (contained usually in legislative acts) and the practical form imposed by the courts.

Despite its flexibility and non-uniformity, the process of the reception constitutes one of the most important elements of the integration of the American legal systems. If the existence of about fifty-five legal systems in the United States[10] does not prevent us from speaking about the American law rather than about California or New York law, we owe this largely to the unifying impact of the reception. The overwhelming majority of the American systems, notwithstanding the differences setting them apart, established a connection with the same common law tradition through the process of reception. Although many institutions and principles of the English law had been discarded, although others had been transformed, not only some basic ideas of the common law (such as the law-making function of the courts) prevailed in all American systems but also the approach to legal matters characteristic of the common law and of the English legal mind transfused the American law.

THE CONCEPT OF PRECEDENT IN THE COMMON LAW SYSTEMS

As we mentioned earlier the common law was born and developed in England. A product of the central Royal Courts, it was created during the twelfth and thirteenth century. These courts gradually ousted the local laws and imposed throughout the country the law made by themselves. Thus, right from the beginning, judicial decisions were the main substance of the common law.[11] In the initial stage precedent played an

[10] Fifty state jurisdictions, the federal jurisdiction and four more: the District of Columbia, the Commonwealth of Puerto Rico and two Territories: Virgin Islands and Guam. Comp.: E. Griswald, *Law and Lawyers in the United States*, Cambridge, Mass., 1964, p. 2.

[11] C. K. Allen, *Law in the Making*, 7th ed., Oxford, 1964, pp. 187–190; T. F. T. Plucknett, *A Concise History of the Common Law*, 5th ed., Boston, 1956, pp. 343–346.

important role as the proof of the existence of an established practice, as an illustration of the judicial custom according to which cases were solved in a certain manner. A single precedential decision did not however have the force of law. So, for several centuries the common law was the customary law of the courts rather than a judicially enacted law. The binding character of single precedents was established in the course of a long evolutionary process and first crystallized as a binding principle in the English and American legal systems in the nineteenth century.[12] Henceforth the common law ceased to be the customary law of the court and became a law enacted by the court. The common law rule attains its present force not because the courts used to apply it but because it was established by a binding decision.

The classics of the English legal literature such as Hale and Blackstone answered in the negative the question whether precedents are the source of the common law. Beginning with the premise of natural law they saw the source of the common law in the preexisting "eternal usages and customary rules". In their opinion judicial precedents merely constitute evidence of the existence of a law based on a custom; the judges never make law, they are, in a manner of speaking depositaries of the common law. It is not the role of the judge to make law; he has only to authenticate legal principles and rules which lead an entirely independent existence. In other words, the authority of a judicial precedent is of a declaratory, not of

---

[12] T. F. T. Plucknett, op. cit., pp. 347–350; C. K. Allen, op. cit., pp. 124–126, 233–235; R. Cross, *Precedent in English Law*, 2nd ed., Oxford, 1968, p. 20; J. Dawson, *The Oracles of the Law*, Ann Arbor, 1968, pp. 59, 64, 78; F. G. Kampin, "Precedent and Stare Decisis: The Critical Years 1800–1850", *American Journal of Legal History*, 1959, Vol. 3, pp. 30–31. Compare also: W. Holdsworth, *History of the English Law*, Boston, 1938, Vol. XII, p. 146; T. Lewis, "History of Judicial Precedent", Part III, *The Law Quarterly Review*, 1932, Vol. 48, p. 246.

a constitutive, order (the so-called declaratory theory of precedent).[13]

The declaratory theory was fiercely criticized as early as the first half of the nineteenth century. Bentham[14] and Austin,[15] and more recently the well-known American writer, the forerunner of legal realism, J. Gray,[16] have been among its chief critics. The critics maintained that the declaratory theory tries to negate obvious facts by looking for the source of law in the allegedly ancient customs and denying the law-making role of the court. In actual fact it was the judicial decisions which for centuries made the binding rules of law. The representatives of what is known as analytical jurisprudence (Austin) called this theory a childish fiction, and advanced their own theory about the law-making, constitutive character of judicial precedents (the so-called originative theory).[17]

In spite of the substantiated and crushing criticism the declaratory theory continues to have its advocates until the present day especially among the English and American judges.[18] There are several reasons which account for this fact.

---

[13] M. Hale, *The History and Analysis of the Common Law of England*, Stafford, 1713, pp. 23–24; W. Blackstone, *Commentaries on the Laws of England*, Philadelphia, 1898, Vol. I, Book I, pp. 67–68. Declaratory theory as represented by classic writers of American law, compare: J. Kent, *Commentaries on American Law*, 12th ed., Boston, 1896, Vol. I, pp. 473–474. Compare also: R. Cross, op. cit., pp. 23–29; C. K. Allen, op. cit., p. 229.

[14] J. Bentham, *The Works of Jeremy Bentham*, Edinburgh, 1843, Vol. V, p. 546 and Vol. VI, p. 552.

[15] J. Austin, *Lectures on Jurisprudence or The Philosophy of Positive Law*, 3rd ed., London, 1869, Vol. II, Lecture XXX, pp. 550–567.

[16] J. Gray, *The Nature and Sources of the Law*, Boston, 1963, p. 218 passim.

[17] E. W. Patterson, *Jurisprudence, Men and Ideas of the Law*, Brooklyn, 1953, p. 302.

[18] E. W. Patterson, op. cit., p. 302; *Callet* v. *Alioto*, 210 Cal. 65 (1930); *Legg's Estate* v. *Commissioner*, 114 F. 2d 760 (1940); *Fleming* v. *Fleming*, 264 US 29 (1924).

One of them is that the declaratory theory, referring to the mythical "eternally existing" common law makes it easier for the only real makers of the common law, i.e. the judges, to evade the responsibility for the content of the law they make. It is also easy to invoke the declaratory theory in order to justify the departure from precedents while continuing to proclaim the stability of the law. In this way this theory masks the retroactive function of precedent law. A new precedent, according to the declaratory theory, does not really make a new law but only "discovers", "declares", and "authenticates" the existing law, hence the question of retroactivity of the new laws made by the courts does not arise. This is a matter of considerable significance, in particular in the American jurisdictions, where the precedent law is in constant flux.

It is worthwhile to mention that the declaratory character of precedents is in accord with the theory of the separation of powers while the constitutive theory countervails or, at least, blurs the division between the legislature and the judiciary. Finally, the attachment to the natural law concepts carries some weight as well.

The qualities discussed above account for the popularity which the declaratory theory of precedent enjoys among the judges. At present only a handful of legal scholars advocate this theory.[19]

Some significant practical consequences of what appears to be only an abstract theory will be discussed in detail in the subsequent chapters.

Now we will discuss the concept of precedent as the general and abstract normative element of judicial decisions.

Certain categories of judicial decisions in the common law systems are the bearers of normative content which have precedential character. This content is not given in a "ready form".

---

[19] See: P. J. Mishkin, "The High Court, the Great Writ and the Due Process of Time and Law", *Harvard Law Review*, 1965, Vol. 79, p. 62 passim.

A judicial decision naturally tends to solve a concrete case within the context of a given fact situation, rather than to stage general, abstract norms. Hence the normative content must, in effect, be extracted by means of a conceptual analysis.

The precedent (*ratio decidendi*) is, according to the "classical theory", only that portion of the decision which formulates a general proposition of law, if this was the proposition employed by the court in deciding a concrete case and if the formation of it was necessary for the decision.[20]

In order to isolate the normative element of the decision it is therefore necessary to separate the "legal" part of the decision from the "factual" part—because only the first one has the force of precedent.[21]

The legal part of a judicial decision may split into two further parts. The principal part is the legal rationale of the decision, or to be more precise, that part of the rationale which is indispensable to decide the actual case. This is what is called *ratio decidendi* or, in American terminology, the holding. Only this part of the decision carries the force of precedent. The connection between *ratio decidendi* and its factual context is, as we see, very close. In order to ascertain what the *ratio decidendi* is in a particular opinion it must be established what the point in question in the given case was. A general proposition of law, even delivered by a court of the highest order,

---

[20] *Barnet* v. *Coronado Oil Co.*, 285 US 393 (1932); *Humphrey* v. *United States*, 295 US 602 (1935); *Pape Television Co.* v. *Ass. Artists Production Corp.*, 279 F. 2d 217 (1960); *Hill and MacMillan* v. *Taylor*, 304 Pa. 18, 155 A. 103 (1931). Compare also: J. Gray, op. cit., p. 261; H. C. Black, *Handbook on the Law of Judicial Precedents*, St. Paul, Minn., 1912; R. Cross, op. cit., p. 77; J. Salmond, "The Theory of Judicial Precedents", *The Law Quarterly Review*, 1900, Vol. 16, pp. 387–388.

[21] *Barnet* v. *Coronado Oil Co.*, op. cit.; *Swilley* v. *McCain*, 374 SW 2d 871 (1964). See also: *American Jurisprudence*, 2nd ed., S. Francisco, 1965, Vol. 20, pp. 521, 525.

constitutes a precedent only if applied to the facts in the specific case in which it was stated.[22]

Those portions of the opinion which were unnecessary in deciding the case are *obiter dicta*. They do not have the authority of precedent and do not constitute law.[23]

The separation of *ratio decidendi* from *dictum* is not always easy, in particular when we deal with decisions of appellate courts in which different judges have delivered separate opinions.[24]

There is already a vast literature about the methods of extracting *ratio decidendi*. Various methods of performing this operation are suggested. For example, E. Wambaugh suggests consideration of the *ratio decidendi* as the major premise of a syllogism whose minor premise is the fact situation of the case, and whose conclusion is the decision. If a change of the supposed content of *ratio* entails a change in the decision, it means that the supposed *ratio* is the real *ratio*. If, however, the changed content of the supposed *ratio* leaves the decision unchanged, it means that the supposed *ratio* is mere *dictum*.[25] E. W. Patterson[26] expressed a similar opinion.

It is worthwhile to examine the method of Professor A. Goodhart. Goodhart is mistrustful of judicial opinions. "There may be", he argues, "no rule of law set forth in the opinion, or the rule when stated may be too wide or too narrow. In appellate courts, the rules of law set forth by the different judges may have no relation to each other. Nevertheless

---

[22] *Humphrey* v. *United States*, op. cit.; *Pape Television Co.* v. *Ass. Artists Production Corp.*, op. cit.; *Rush* v. *Chattanooga Du Pont Empl. Credit Union*, 358 SW 2d 333 (1962).

[23] *Cohens* v. *Virginia*, 6 Wheat. 264 (1821); *Union P.R. Co.* v. *Mason City and Ft. D.R. Co.*, 199 US 160 (1905); *Humphrey* v. *United States*, op. cit.; *Green* v. *United States*, 355 US 184 (1957).

[24] C. K. Allen, op. cit., pp. 266–268.

[25] E. Wambaugh, *The Study of Cases*, 2nd ed., Boston, 1894, pp. 11–18.

[26] E. W. Patterson, op. cit., p. 313.

each of these cases contains a principle which can be discovered on proper analysis".[27]

Goodhart divides the analysis into several stages. The most important stage, and at the same time the most complicated one, is to determine which facts of the case are seen by the court as material and included as the basis of the decision, and which are considered immaterial and excluded. Material facts and the conclusion reached by the judges constitute the normative element of the decision. "In a certain case", says Goodhart, "the court finds that facts A, B and C exist. It then excludes fact A as immaterial, and on facts B and C it reaches conclusion X. What is the *ratio decidendi* in this case? There are two principles: (a) in any future case in which the facts are A, B and C, the court must reach conclusion X, and (b) in any future case in which the facts are B and C, the court must reach conclusion X".[28]

According to Goodhart, while *ratio* is a conclusion based on facts whose existence has been established by the court, *dictum* is a conclusion based on hypothetical facts.[29]

Goodhart's model of *ratio decidendi* is very similar to the model of a legislative norm suggested by many writers. The so-called hypothesis is replaced in it by facts accepted as material, while the place of the so-called disposition is taken by the conclusion, i.e., the actual decision of the court. The difference is that the facts upon which the precedent is based must be recognized by the court as existent in the actual case, while the fact situation contained in a legislative norm is abstract and hypothetical.

H. Oliphant presented an entirely different, behavioristic concept of *ratio decidendi*. He represents the extreme trend in

---

[27] A. L. Goodhart, "Determining the *Ratio Decidendi* of a Case", in the collection: *Essays in Jurisprudence and the Common Law*, Cambridge 1931, pp. 5–6.

[28] Ibid., p. 22.

[29] Ibid., p. 26.

the functionalist school of thought in American jurisprudence known as legal realism. Oliphant recommends that the legal reasoning of the decision as vocal behavior be ignored entirely, and that all facts on the court's record be viewed as a stimulus, with the actual decision as a response to this stimulus. The combination of stimulus and response is, according to him, *ratio decidendi.*[30]

This theory wholly negating the significance of precedent as a general and abstract norm, is characteristic of the legal nihilism of the realists.

The difficulty of establishing a universal method of separating *ratio* and *dictum* is shown in an excellent monograph on precedent in English law (1st edition published in 1961, 2nd edition in 1968) whose author, after having critically analyzed the existing methods, concludes that it is impossible to devise any satisfactory general formula.[31]

To conclude the general remarks concerning *ratio decidendi* let us add a few words about some specific situations.

There are cases with more than one *ratio*—in this event each *ratio* is a precedent.[32]

When an appellate court is divided and the majority wants to base the decision on proposition A, while the minority wants to base it on proposition B, the opinion of the majority is considered as *ratio decidendi* (these rules are applicable both in English and in American law). When in an evenly divided appellate court half of the judges declare themselves for overruling

[30] H. Oliphant, "A Return to *Stare Decisis*", *American Bar Association Journal,* 1928.

[31] R. Cross, op. cit., pp. 76–77. A very interesting concept of ratio decidendi has been presented by Professor Julius Stone. See: J. Stone, *The Province and Function of Law. Law as Logic and Social Control. A Study in Jurisprudence,* London, 1947, pp. 186ff.; J. Stone, "Ratio of the *Ratio Decidendi*", *The Modern Law Review,* 1959, Vol. 22.

[32] *Woods* v. *Interstate Realty Co.*, 337 US 535 (1948); *Joyce* v. *Wyant,* 202 F. 2d 863 (1954).

a decision of the court of first instance and the other half dissent, then according to the American common law the decision in question does not have the authority of a precedent, although the appealed decision in the specific case is upheld.[33] The House of Lords follows a different principle. In other English appellate courts the situation is unsettled.[34]

The concept of *dictum* is closely connected with the concept of *ratio*. Starting from a negative assumption it may be said that any general proposition of law contained in the decision of the court which is not *ratio* is *dictum*. The definitions of *dictum* suggested by Goodhart and Patterson have already been mentioned. The characteristic feature of *dictum* is that *dictum* is not law and is not binding in future cases. The real significance of *dicta*, however, and the influence they exert on the courts vary depending on their authority and on the situation in which the given *dictum* was declared. For the sake of argument, let us imagine a situation in which the United States Supreme Court pronounced unanimously a general proposition of law which did not achieve the rank or *ratio* because an actual decision was founded on an entirely different legal principle. In this event the authority of *dictum* carries so much weight that it is hard to imagine a lower court which would refuse to follow the Supreme Court's decision.

The court ought to follow precedents. This means that future similar cases ought to be decided in the same way as the precedential cases (the doctrine *stare decisis*).[35] There are two degrees contained in this obligation and consequently two degrees of authority of precedents: (a) persuasive precedents, and (b) binding precedents. The binding or persuasive value of a precedent is not inherent in it; the degree of authority is relative and depends on the addressee. For example, a precedent

[33] *Hertz* v. *Woodman*, 218 US 205 (1910).

[34] R. Cross, op. cit., pp. 92–96.

[35] Ibid., p. 4.

established by a state supreme court is binding for the lower courts in the same state but in the neighboring state it is treated barely as a persuasive precedent.[36] Persuasive precedents are followed depending on whether or not the court considering a case regards them as convincing.

Although courts are under an obligation to apply binding precedents this duty is subject to the decision of the court hearing the case. "When it is said that a court is bound to follow a case, or bound by a decision", writes Cross, "what it means is that a judge is under an obligation to apply a particular *ratio decidendi* to the facts before him in the absence of a reasonable legal distinction between those facts and the facts to which it was applied in the previous case".[37] As we see this obligation is by no means mechanical. For aside from the whole, sometimes complicated technique of interpretation followed by the court in order to define *ratio*, the second stage involves a comparison of the material facts of the precedent and the facts of the case before the court. The court is bound to follow a precedent in this case only if it is satisfied that there is no reasonable legal distinction between the two groups of facts.[38]

Applying Goodhart's method this operation can be also described as follows: the material facts forming the basis of the earlier decision must be defined and then the material facts of the case at bar must be established. If both groups of facts are of

---

[36] H. C. Black, *Handbook...*, op. cit., p. 9. See also: C. S. Lobingier, "Precedent in Past and Present Legal Systems", *Michigan Law Review*, 1946, Vol. 44, p. 966.

[37] R. Cross, op. cit., pp. 102–103.

[38] J. L. Montrose, "Distinguishing Cases and the Limits of *Ratio Decidendi*", *Modern Law Review*, 1956, Vol. 19, p. 525; H. C. Black, *Handbook...*, op. cit., p. 39. Under the Continental legal systems it is, in principle, the legislator, not the judge who decides what categories of facts are legally relevant. Hence the wide usage of *lege non distinguente* argument in statutory interpretation.

identical categories then the earlier decision constitutes a binding precedent for the case before the court; the court's decision in the actual case will be the same as in the precedent. If a material fact which occurs in the actual case is missing in the earlier decision or if the earlier decision contains additional material facts absent in the actual case, then the earlier decision does not constitute a precedent. In the latter situation, however, the earlier case might be useful as a basis for applying analogy.[39]

The process of differentiating relevant facts, known as "distinguishing cases", may be turned into a method for the disguised abolition of precedents. This practice has been followed with those precedents in particular which do not find approval among the judges.[40] Mr. Justice Holmes pointed out in his usual laconic manner the unlimited possibilities of the distinguishing technique. He wrote: "... I will admit any general proposition that anyone wants to lay down and decide the case either way."[41] The hazards are obvious. The courts often abuse the distinguishing method in order to avoid following a precedent, hunting factual differences in cases where such differences simply do not exist.[42]

THE FUNCTION OF THE PRECEDENT. THE AMERICAN DOCTRINE *STARE DECISIS*

There is a general rule in contemporary American law that a lower court is bound to follow a precedent decided by a court

[39] A. L. Goodhart, op. cit., pp. 3–24.

[40] J. L. Montrose, op. cit., p. 525 passim; C. K. Allen, op. cit., pp. 191, 244, 296ff.

[41] O. W. Holmes, H. J. Laski, *Holmes–Laski Letters; The Correspondence of Mr. Justice Holmes and Harold J. Laski, 1916–1935*, Cambridge, Mass., 1953, p. 390.

[42] C. S. Lobingier, op. cit., p. 975.

above it. Such precedents are binding.[43] There is no difference in this respect between the English and the American law.

There are at least two exceptions to this rule. As we indicated earlier, a decision of an evenly divided appellate court is not binding. Also, a decision tacitly (*sub silentio*) approving a general proposition but containing neither legal considerations nor an explanation does not constitute a precedent.[44]

The most important difference between the American and the English concepts of *stare decisis* rests on the attitude of the appellate courts to their own precedents. American appellate courts, both federal and state, as distinct from the English courts, neither were or are bound to follow their own earlier decisions.[45] Every American court is free to depart from its earlier decision should this be considered desirable for any reason.

---

[43] H. C. Black, op. cit., p. 10; J. Gray, op. cit., p. 242; *Stell* v. *Savannah Chatham County*, 333 F. 2d 55 (1964). Nevertheless such precedents may not be followed by lower courts when strong enough indications exist (e.g., judicial dicta) that the court above is inclined to overrule them. Compare: *James* v. *United States*, 366 US 213 (1961). Compare also a dissenting opinion of Mr. Justice Harlan in *Desist* v. *United States*, 394 US 244, 265 (1969): "It is hard to believe that any lawyer worthy of the name could, after reading Silverman, rely with confidence on the continuing vitality of the Goldman rule. Nor is it by any means clear to me that it would have been improper for a lower court to have declined to follow Goldman in the light of Silverman" (emphasis added—S.P.). Justice Harlan refers in the passage quoted to the U.S. Supreme Court decisions in *Goldman* v. *United States*, 316 US 129 (1942) and *Silverman* v. *United States*, 365 US 505 (1961).

[44] *Webster* v. *Fall*, 266 US 507 (1924); *United States* v. *Tucker Truck Lines*, 344 US 33 (1952).

[45] A. L. Goodhard, "Case Law in England and America", in the collected: *Essays in Jurisprudence and the Common Law*, Cambridge, 1931, p. 58; J. C. Gray, op. cit., p. 242. Furthermore, it should be noted that as of July 1966 the English House of Lords declared itself free not to follow its own precedents. See: Note, *The Law Quarterly Review*, 1966, Vol. 82, pp. 441ff.; R. Cross, op. cit., p. 107.

The formulation of the American doctrine of precedent by the U.S. Supreme Court in *Hertz* v. *Woodman*[46] is considered a classic. "The rule of *stare decisis,* though one tending to consistency and uniformity of decision, is not inflexible. Whether it shall be followed or departed from is a question entirely within the discretion of the court, which is again called upon to consider a question once decided."[47] It does not follow here that in this most essential aspect of the functioning of the legal system there is complete freedom of action. There are certain rules to be followed, rules based on the premises of utility and rooted in the pragmatic philosophy of law. They can be summarized as follows:

— As a rule precedents ought to be followed because it is in the interest of the society that law shall be stable and uniform.[48]

— The court is free or even bound to depart from a precedent if, because of a change in circumstances or in social needs, adherence to precedents will be injurious to a public interest which in a given case might be more important than the stability of law itself.[49]

— The evaluation whether a precedent should or should not be followed ought to be based on the criteria of social utility. The desire to make a just decision in a given, concrete

---

[46] 218 US 205 (1910).

[47] *Hertz* v. *Woodman,* op. cit., p. 212. See also the decision in *Helvering* v. *Hallock,* 309 US 106 (1940): "This Court unlike the House of Lords has from the beginning rejected a doctrine of disability of self-correction".

[48] B. Cardozo, *The Nature of the Judicial Process,* New Haven and London, 1964, pp. 112–113. Justice Frankfurter in *Helvering* v. *Hallock,* op. cit.: "We recognize that *stare decisis* embodies an important social policy. It represents an element of continuity in law and is rooted in the psychologic needs to satisfy reasonable expectations". See also Justice Brandeis in *Barnet* v. *Coronado Oil and Gas Co.,* op. cit., p. 406: "*Stare decisis* is usually the wise policy, because in most matters it is more important that the applicable rule of law be settled than it be settled right".

[49] B. Cardozo, op. cit., p. 113.

case ought not to be considered a sufficient justification for overruling.[50]

Why does the American doctrine of precedent differ so substantially from its English counterpart? There are many reasons. First of all, Goodhart rightly observes, the social and economic conditions in the United States change so rapidly that methods accepted in the more stable English context would have proved unsuitable.[51] It should be remembered that the second half of the nineteenth century witnessed both the crystallization of the English *stare decisis* and a particularly tempestuous period in American economics.

The unprecedented dynamism of American development coupled both with some traditional features of the English mercantile mind and attitudes developed on the American frontier account for the enormous success and popularity of the pragmatic philosophy. This philosophy quickly penetrated the law and occupied a dominant place.[52] An instrumental conception of law as a means to achieve some end, as a tool of policy, as explicitly expressed on the Continent by Ihering, was well received in the thoroughly practical, industrially oriented society.[53] "The sociological movement in jurisprudence", wrote Roscoe Pound in 1908, "is a movement for pragmatism as a philosophy of law; for the adjustment of principles and doctrines to the human condition..."[54]

---

[50] *Silliman* v. *United States*, 101 US 465 (1879).

[51] A. L. Goodhart, "Case Law...", op. cit., pp. 68–69.

[52] Compare: the collection of articles *American Pragmatists*, New York, 1960; J. Hall, "Methods of Sociological Research in Comparative Law", in: *Legal Thought...*, op. cit. Compare also: K. Opałek i J. Wróblewski, *Współczesna teoria i socjologia prawa w Stanach Zjednoczonych* (Contemporary Jurisprudence and Sociology of Law in the United States of North America), Warszawa, 1963, pp. 106ff.

[53] O. W. Holmes, "The Path of the Law", *Harvard Law Review*, 1897, Vol. 10, p. 474.

[54] R. Pound, "Mechanical Jurisprudence", *Columbia Law Review*, 1908, Vol. 8, p. 609.

The American variation of *stare decisis* should be evaluated in this context, i.e., as an expression of, and at the same time as a means to implement, the pragmatic concept of law. This is the source of its flexibility, this is why it is persuasive rather than binding, why it is dominated by the criterion of utility.

Analyzing the reasons for the flexibility of the American doctrine of precedent, one should bear in mind that the reception of the English law was the starting point of the development of American law. As mentioned above only so much of the English law was received as was found to meet the test of applicability to the local conditions. Thus from the very outset the American courts enjoyed, and still do, a great deal of freedom with which to decide whether an English precedent shall be adhered to or departed from. This could hardly fail to exert an influence upon the attitude toward precedent in general.

Another important factor which should be mentioned in this connection, is the dominant role of constitutional questions in American law. Application of precedents in constitutional adjudication requires the utmost elasticity from the courts. Essentially these decisions are more political than legal in nature. The departure from precedent in this area occurs frequently and this practice naturally exerts an influence on the judicial practice in other areas.[55] The legal literature also mentions some other reasons underlying the specific development of *stare decisis* in the United States.[56]

---

[55] A. L. Goodhart, "Case Law...", op. cit., p. 68.

[56] Professor Goodhart ("Case Law...", op. cit.) points to some other reasons which account for the specific and different character of the American doctrine of precedent: 1. the huge bulk of law reports published in the United States, containing decisions which are often contradictory and conflicting, causes confusion and undermines the significance of the precedent; 2. the method of teaching in the American law schools is the method of comparative law in which various principles, rules and doctrines laid down by several American state courts are analyzed and compared; in dealing with the comparative law method of instruction the

It is obvious that in the light of the American doctrine precedent constitutes a source of law marked with some peculiar features. It is a law which the court is under no obligation to follow should it decide that a departure from it is justified by the public interest. What follows is a considerable fluidity in the case law. Theorists find this problem rather embarrassing and explain it in a variety of ways.

In order to save at least the fictional stability of law the traditionalists (mainly the judges) invoke the declaratory theory of precedent. This theory, which one would think had long since been discredited, has been revived in recent literature in a slightly modified form.[57]

The fluidity of the case law led the representatives of legal realism (the extreme wing of functionalisms in the American

---

American law student is less inclined to respect the binding precedents within a particular law system than is his English colleague; 3. the publication of model codes of law by the American Law Institute facilitates the departure from the precedent since these codes offer ready alternative solutions.

The conditions particular to England, Goodhart emphasizes, which are indispensable for the case-law to function successfully are absent in the United States. These are in particular: a) a centralized judiciary; b) a learned bar tied by the common professional tradition; c) an independent, adequately salaried bench consisting in general of better minds than the bar has.

E. W. Patterson indicates that there is an additional factor undermining the American doctrine of precedent, and this is the practice of using precedents of other jurisdictions. E. W. Patterson, op. cit., p. 304.

[57] J. A. Spruil, "The Effect of an Overruling Decision", *North Carolina Law Review*, 1949, Vol. 199, pp. 204–205; P. J. Mishkin, "The High Court, the Great Writ, and the Due Process of Time and Law", *Harvard Law Review*, 1965, Vol. 79, pp. 62–70. These authors admit that the declaratory theory is based on fiction. Still, in their opinion, it is a useful fiction. Using the symbolism of the pre-existent law, which the judge only "discovers", it depersonalizes the commands of the law thus elevating its authority. The formulae of "law discovering" are more appealing to the addressee of the legal norm who yields easier to the commands of the preexisting law than to those of the judge.

philosophy of law) to the conclusion that the law does not exist at all as a source of general and abstract norms; the only law that exists in reality is the valid final judicial decision which makes law in a given case, and which is binding upon the parties in the given case.[58] As a general norm precedent is a fiction since the courts are under no obligation to follow this norm.

The advocates of "policy oriented jurisprudence" would discard what they consider the false assumption that judicial decisions are non-political in character. They carry the assumptions of the functionalists to their logical extreme by suggesting that the courts are political bodies and that their decisions are political decisions. Therefore precedents must be as flexible and as stable as is politically expedient. Instead of slavishly following the old formula and preaching that adherence to precedent is a rule and the departure from it is an exception (although no one seems to know where the rule ends and the exception starts), they recommend the following guides for making judicial decisions seem as political decisions:

— The *status quo* is to be maintained as long as it does not prevent the achievement of an accepted goal.

— The impossibility of achieving the goal under the *status quo* stimulates the search for a new alternative. In terms of a judicial decision this means that the existing law no longer satisfies the needs of society and a need arises to make a new law.

— The choice of a new alternative is not arbitrary. The solution which should be chosen is the one which is closest to the *status quo* and which also fulfills the actual social need. This is in keeping with the tradition of a slow and gradual development of the case law because the new law is not made

[58] J. Frank, *Law and Modern Mind,* New York, 1936, p. 47; J. Brown, "Law and Evolution", *Yale Law Journal,* 1919, Vol. 29, pp. 394–395.

in abstracto but is closely related to the facts of the cases decided by the court.[59]

Usually the departure from precedent takes the form of the overruling of a decision and its replacement with a new precedent. A higher court has the power to overrule a precedent of a lower court; also, a court which made the given precedent has the authority to overrule it. A precedent may also be overruled silently or by implication, as when a proposition is pronounced which is incompatible with the earlier precedent.[60] In theory a precedent is binding until overruled by the proper court.[61] Under certain circumstances the court has not only the right but the duty to overrule a precedent.[62]

Overruling is rather popular in American judicial practice. Ample proof is furnished by the United States Supreme Court, which perhaps more frequently than other courts overrules its own precedents.[63] The figures quoted by American authors seem to indicate that the frequency of such a practice is increasing.[64]

The Supreme Court overrules its precedents more frequently than other courts because constitutional law is its principle domain[65] and in this sphere the stability of the precedent is

---

[59] M. Shapiro, "Stability and Change in Judicial Decision Making: Incrementalism or *Stare Decisis*", *Law in Transition Quarterly*, 1965, Vol. 2, p. 134 and pp. 156–157. For a general discussion of "the policy oriented jurisprudence" see for example: M. McDougal, "Some Basic Theoretical Concepts about International Law: A Policy Oriented Framework of Inquiry", *The Journal of Conflict Resolution*, Vol. IV, 1960; K. Opałek i J. Wróblewski, *Współczesna teoria...*, op. cit., p. 267ff.

[60] This way of overruling precedents was criticized in literature. Comp.: C. S. Lobingier, op. cit., p. 984.

[61] Ibid., p. 973; compare also *Capers* v. *Ball*, 87 SE 2d 85 (1955).

[62] *Douglas* v. *Pike County*, op. cit.

[63] C. S. Lobingier, op. cit., pp. 977–978.

[64] W. Douglas, "*Stare Decisis*", *Columbia Law Review*, 1949, Vol. 49, p. 735 passim.

[65] P. A. Freund, *The Supreme Court of the United States*, Cleveland and New York, 1964, p. 18.

most vulnerable.[66] The importance of making the right decision in constitutional questions is so enormous that it always outweighs considerations of the stability of the legal system.[67] Moreover, overruling is the only readily available way to change the law because it is very hard indeed to amend the Federal Constitution.[68] However, precedents concerning property laws are stable. This is because social interest demands particular certainty and predictability in this realm.[69]

The existence of the federal judicial system parallel to individual state judicial systems and the fact that each of these systems consists of a hierarchy of courts presents specific problems: 1) the significance of a federal court precedent for other federal courts; 2) the significance of a federal court precedent for state courts; 3) the significance of a state court precedent within that state's system; 4) the significance of a state court precedent for federal courts; 5) the significance of a precedent established by the courts of one state for the courts of other states.

The federal judicial system consists of the Supreme Court of the United States, eleven United States Circuit Courts of Appeals, about ninety United States District Courts and the special courts.[70] Military courts are also federal courts in a separate system.

The precedents of the U.S. Supreme Court are binding for all federal courts by virtue of the general principle which makes

---

[66] *Glidden Co.* v. *Zdanok*, 370 US 530 (1962).

[67] *Graves* v. *Schmidlapp*, 315 US 657 (1942).

[68] *Barnet* v. *Coronado Oil and Gas Co.*, op. cit.; P. A. Freund, op. cit., pp. 26–27 and 53–55.

[69] *National Bank* v. *Whitney*, 103 US 99 (1880); *Dun* v. *Mieco*, 106 F. 2d 356 (1939).

[70] *Corpus Juris Secundum*, Brooklyn, New York, 1960, with *1972 Cumulative Annual Pocket Part*, Vol. 36, p. 779; A. B. Morris, "The Federal Judicial System", in: *Modern Federal Practice Digest*, St. Paul, Minn., 1960 with *1971 Cumulative Pocket Part*, Vol. 12, pp. 820–821.

the precedents of a higher court authoritatively binding on lower courts.[71] If some inconsistency occurs between Supreme Court decisions a lower federal court must follow the later precedent.[72]

The decision of a U.S. Circuit Court of Appeals is a binding precedent for all federal district courts within the same circuit.[73] Other appellate courts and district courts in other circuits are not bound by it.[74] But all Courts of Appeals must follow the precedent of a Court of Appeals which has been explicitly approved by the U.S. Supreme Court.[75] Precedents of a Court of Appeals although not having the force of law outside that Court's circuit, should still be considered precedents of a persuasive authority.[76]

The Supreme Court of the United States is the only federal court whose precedents may be binding on state courts. Although there are many extensive formulations to be found in the decisions of various American courts concerning the authority of the precedents of the U.S. Supreme Court,[77] in actual fact its binding authority is limited to precedents pertaining to federal questions.[78] If a controversy arises between precedents of a state court and the U.S. Supreme Court in regard to a federal question, the precedent of the U.S. Supreme

---

[71] Compare, however, footnotes 43, 44 and accompanying text in this chapter indicating possible exceptions to this general rule. Compare also footnote 17 in Chapter VII.

[72] *Tilton* v. *Missouri Pac. R. Co.*, 306 F. 2d 870 (1962), *R. J. Reynolds Tobacco Co.* v. *Robertson*, 80F. 2d 966 (1936).

[73] *Powell* v. *United States*, 338 F. 2d 556 (1964).

[74] *Poole* v. *Stevens*, 190 F. Supp. 938 (1960); *Allstate Insurance Co.* v. *Stevens*, 445 F. 2d 845 (1971).

[75] *Norton* v. *McShane*, 332 F. 2d 855 (1964).

[76] *Homont* v. *United States*, 279 F. 2d 767 (1960).

[77] See for example: *State* v. *Weinstein*, 108 A. 2d 362 (1964).

[78] *Chesapeake and O.R. Co.* v. *Martin*, 283 US 209 (1931); H. C. Black, *Handbook...*, op. cit., p. 336.

Court is binding.[79] The federal questions are: the interpretation of the Federal Constitution, the interpretation of federal laws and of international treaties.[80] This is why a decision of the U.S. Supreme Court concerning the conformity of state law with the Federal Constitution is authoritatively binding on state courts.[81]

Until 1938 American law accepted the concept of a general federal common law, sanctioned by the decision of the U.S. Supreme Court in *Swift* v. *Tyson*.[82] This general law developed by federal courts (mainly by the Supreme Court) was meant to provide the link connecting the common law systems of the various states and a means by which the Supreme Court could exert an influence on shaping the systems.

Under the doctrine of *Swift* v. *Tyson*, decisions involving the general law presented federal questions, and were applied in diversity of citizenship cases by federal courts to the exclusion of state law.

The year 1938 brought a complete reversal with the Supreme Court decision in the famous case of *Erie* v. *Tompkins*[83] which overruled *Swift* v. *Tyson*. The Supreme Court declared that there is no general federal common law and that the only existing common law is the common law of the states;[84] *Erie* v.

---

[79] Ibid., pp. 298ff.; *S. Carolina* v. *Bailey*, 289 US 412 (1933); *Henry* v. *City of Rock Hill*, 376 US 776 (1964).

[80] Article VI, Section 2 of the Constitution of the United States; 28 USC 1331 "a".

[81] *Cook* v. *Moffat*, 46 US 295 (1847).

[82] *Swift* v. *Tyson*, 16 Pet. I (1842).

[83] *Erie* v. *Tompkins*, 304 US 64 (1938).

[84] "There is no federal common law", Ibidem. Compare later decisions for instance: *Barholome Corp.* v. *United States*, 253 F. 2d 716 (1957); *Celebrezze* v. *Kilborn*, 322 F. 2d 166 (1963). This general principle is qualified by several exceptions. First of all the Erie doctrine has not excluded federal common law concerning procedural matters. For further discussion of limitations and qualifications imposed on the Erie doctrine see: P. Hay, "Unification of Law in the United States: Uniform State Laws, Treaties and Judicially Declared Federal Common Law", in: *Legal Thought in the United States...*, op. cit.

Tompkins defined in general the boundary between state and federal law.[85]

Opinions are divided as to the binding force of a precedent of a lower federal court (i.e., appellate and district) for a state court in connection with a federal question. The majority of the state courts holds that the decisions of a U.S. Circuit Court of Appeals (particularly the one in whose circuit the state is located) dealing, for example, with the interpretation of the Federal Constitution, are not binding on them.[86]

Within the state, decision of the highest state court are naturally binding on all lower courts, following the principle of hierarchy. In this sense *stare decisis* is applied to the full extent within a given jurisdiction.[87]

The role of the decisions of intermediate appellate courts is to a certain degree vague. Usually there is a number of such courts in the state, one for each district.[88] There is no question that these decisions are binding on courts of first instance within the given appellate district; it is controversial however whether they are binding on courts of first instance outside the given appellate district. There are two conflicting trends with regard to this question: according to the first one a decision of a lower appellate court is mandatory in

---

[85] Except in matters governed by the Federal Constitution, by acts of Congress or international treaties, the law to be applied in any case is the law of the state. *Erie* v. *Tompkins*, op. cit.

[86] *People* v. *Stansberry*, 268 NE. 2d 431 (1971, Supreme Court of Illinois). Compare *Commonwealth ex rel. Goodfellow* v. *Rundle*, 201 A. 2d 615 (1964) in which one of the courts of the first instance of the State of Pennsylvania pronounced the following principle: "Decisions of lower federal courts are not binding on state courts even though federal question is involved".

[87] T. M. Cooley, *A Treatise on the Constitutional Limitations*, Boston, 1927, p. 118. Compare, however, footnote 43 in this chapter and footnote 17 in Chapter VII.

[88] P. J. Mishkin, C. Morris, *On Law in the Courts*, Brooklyn, 1965, pp. 3–4. Intermediate appellate courts do not exist in all states.

the whole state until overruled; according to the second, represented by the Ohio courts, a decision of a lower appellate court is binding on one district only.[89] This would mean that in other districts it is treated as a persuasive precedent.

As we mentioned earlier, according to the *Erie* v. *Tompkins* doctrine the only substantive common law in existence is the common law of the states. Accordingly, state courts are the sole bodies possessing the power to make the common law in a given state and to interpret the state constitution and state statutes. The state supreme court resolves finally and authoritatively the state's legal questions.

Federal courts handle civil cases which involve citizens from different states; they then apply the state law according to the principles laid down in conflicts of law rules.[90]

In such cases all federal courts, including the U.S. Supreme Court, are bound by decisions of the state courts of last resort.[91]

As to the binding force of a precedent of an intermediate state appellate court, for a federal court there are two different trends in the federal decisions similar to the two trends among state courts as discussed above.

Similarly, if a court in one state is required to apply the law of another state, the decision of the highest court of the state whose law was applied is binding.[92]

Decisions of courts of other states are usually accepted only in their persuasive capacity. Whether or not they are applied at all depends mainly on the court which may or may not find the precedent convincing.

---

[89] *Murphy* v. *Porter*, 114 NE 2d 89, 97 (1953); *Frecker* v. *City of Zanesille*, 72 NE 2d 477 (1946).

[90] P. J. Mishkin, C. Morris, op. cit., p. 5.

[91] "A federal Court exercising jurisdiction over such a case on the ground of diversity citizenship, is not free to treat this question as one of so-called 'general law' but must apply the state law as declared by the highest state court". *Erie* v. *Tompkins*, op. cit.

[92] H. C. Black, *Handbook...*, op. cit., p. 380.

Blackstone's declaratory theory accepted the retroactivity of precedential law as a logical necessity and at the same time masked the retroactive quality of this law.[93] To some degree this theory was instrumental in creating one of the paradoxes in American law, namely that the constitutional prohibition of *ex post facto* laws[94] was conceived as referring to statutory law but not to precedential law.[95] In spite of this, by the middle of the nineteenth century decisions had been made which gave some precedents only a prospective effect where a retroactive effect could have produced socially disadvantageous results. This technique is called prospective overruling: an old decision is overruled and in its place a new one, effective only for the future, is established.[96]

First George F. Canfield in 1917,[97] then other authors who

[93] Note, "Prospective Overruling and Retroactive Application in the Federal Courts", *Yale Law Journal*, 1962, Vol. 71, p. 907 and p. 916.

[94] Article I, Sections 9 and 10 of the Constitution of the United States provide in relevant parts: "No bill of attainder or *ex post facto* law shall be passed"; "No state shall... pass any bill of attainder, *ex post facto* law, or law impairing the obligation of contracts..."

[95] Compare the decisions of the United States Supreme Court in *Ross* v. *Oregon*, 227 US 150, 161 (1913) and *Frank* v. *Mangum*, 237 US 309 (1915).

[96] And so, for instance, in the 19th century divorces were granted in a number of states (for example in Ohio) by the passage of special legislative acts. When finally such acts had been declared void by the courts on grounds of unconstitutionality the decisions declaring them void were given prospective effect. Their retroactive operation, the courts believed, would upset the basis of fundamental social arrangements. Compare a typical decision in *Bingham* v. *Miller*, 17 Ohio 445 (1848). At the beginning of this century some decisions were announced which restricted the retroactive operation of precedent also in criminal cases; we will discuss them at greater length in Chapter 7.

[97] G. F. Canfield, "An Address Annual Meeting South Carolina Bar Association", *South Carolina Bar Ass. Report*, 1917, pp. 17–19.

advocated this idea,[98] proposed that the technique of prospective overruling[99] be applied on more conceptualized and general grounds. Benjamin Cardozo's statement in this matter deserves special attention. A typical pragmatist, he contributed some extremely interesting comments.[100] Prospective overruling, he maintained, will encourage the courts to change outdated rules and will allow revisions without disadvantageous effects for the parties who acted in reliance on the old decision. The case which has occasioned the overruling must be decided by following the old decision; the new principle is conceived as a *dictum*. The announcement of the new principle is not yet law but a declaration that such a law will be laid down in the future.[101] Thus the problem of prospective overruling was well known both in court decisions[102] and in American legal literature when in 1932 the U.S. Supreme Court

---

[98] See C. E. Carpenter, "Court Decisions and the Common Law", *Columbia Law Review*, 1917, Vol. 17; R. H. Freeman, "The Protection Afforded Against Retroactive Operation of an Overruling Decision", *Columbia Law Review*, 1918, Vol. 18; J. H. Wigmore, *Problems of the Law: Its Past, Present and Future*, New York, 1920, pp. 79–82. Some earlier remarks by J. H. Wigmore, commenting on the technique of prospective overruling may be found in his "Preface to Science of Legal Method" in: *The Modern Legal Philosophy Series*, Vol. 9, 1917.

Some more recent opinions advocating the prospective overruling: A. Kocourek, "Retroactive Decisions and *Stare Decisis* and Proposal", *American Bar Association Journal*, 1931, Vol. 17, and B. Cardozo, "An Address to New York Bar Association", *New York Bar Ass. Report*, 1932. For much earlier comments upon the subject matter by B. Cardozo see W. V. Schaefer, "The Control of Sunburst: Techniques of Prospective Overruling", *New York University Law Review*, 1967, Vol. 42, p. 633.

[99] Compare Note, "Prospective Overruling...", op. cit.

[100] B. Cardozo, "An Address...", op. cit., p. 263.

[101] Ibid., pp. 294–296.

[102] For the decisions prior to 1932 see Note, "Right of Court in Overruling Earlier Precedent to Apply New Rule Prospectively and Adhere to Old One as Regards Past Transactions", A.L.R., 1933, Vol. 85.

in *Great No. Ry.* v. *Sunburst Oil and Ref. Co.*[103] faced the question whether or not prospective overruling is constitutional.

The Supreme Court in the case mentioned ruled that prospective overruling is not unconstitutional. The due process of law clause (Fourteenth Amendment) contains no restrictions with regard to state courts so that they are free to choose at their discretion between prospective and retroactive overruling. The choice is determined by the state judge's philosophy of law and his concept of its origins and essence.[104] The Sunburst decision was almost unanimously acclaimed in the legal literature.[105] Although its principles are still binding[106] it left many questions open. For one thing the question of when the new decision should be applied retrospectively and when prospectively? What criteria are to be followed by the courts? Is prospective overruling applicable only in state courts or in federal courts as well? How are the courts to apply precedents which decide the constitutional validity of legislative acts? Can such precedents also be prospectively limited? To answer these questions we must look into the court decisions and the literature published after the *Sunburst* decision, i.e., after 1932.

When a new precedent is made and the old one overruled at least three ways present themselves in which the court may apply the new precedent:

1. The court may apply the new precedent only to facts which occurred after the new rule was announced, so that the new rule would not apply even to the case which occasioned

---

[103] 287 US 358 (1932).

[104] Ibid., p. 364. The decision for the unanimous Court was written by Justice Cardozo.

[105] B. H. Levy, "Realist Jurisprudence and Prospective Overruling", *University of Pennsylvania Law Review*, 1960, Vol. 15, pp. 16–17.

[106] Compare the Dissenting opinion of Justice Black in *Moser* v. *Dorrow*, 341 US 267, 275 (1951) and the opinion of Justice Frankfurter in *Griffin* v. *Illinois*, 351 US 12, 20 (1956).

the overruling. Following the Supreme Court let us call this method a purely prospective application.[107]

2. The court may apply the new precedent to facts which occurred after the new rule was announced and to the facts of the case before the court. This method can be called regular prospective application.[108]

3. The court may apply the new rule to facts which occurred both prior to and after the new ruling. Let us call this a retroactive method.[109] Unlike methods (1) and (2) retroactive application is not an unambiguous notion: we distinguish full retroaction, whereby the new rule is applicable to all facts which occurred before it was created, and limited retroaction, whereby the new rule applies to facts which existed before it was created but only in cases in which a final judgment had not been entered at the time the new precedent was announced. A specific type of limited retroactivity was introduced by the United States Supreme Court decision in *Johnson* v. *State of New Jersey* (1966). There the Court limited the application of the new precedent to cases in which trials did not commence before the rule was announced.[110]

---

[107] *Linkletter* v. *Walker*, 381 US 618, 620 (1965): "A ruling which is purely prospective does not apply even to the parties before the court". For the purely prospective application see *England* v. *Louisiana State Board of Medical Examiners*, 375 US 411 (1964).

[108] Note, "Prospective Overruling...", op. cit., p. 933. Compare also *Molitor* v. *Kaneland Community Unit Dist.* No. 302, 18 Ill. 2d 11 (1959); *Gilbert* v. *California*, 388 US 263 (1967) and *Stovall* v. *Denno*, 388 US 293 (1967)—in the latter case it was held that Gilbert is applicable prospectively; *Katz* v. *United States*, 389 US 347 (1967) and *Desist* v. *United States*, 394 US 244 (1969)—in the latter case the holding of Katz was made applicable prospectively. Nevertheless litigants Gilbert and Katz benefited from the new rulings announced in their cases.

[109] Note, "Prospective Overruling...", op. cit., 933.

[110] 389 US 719 (1966). This decision dealt with the application of two extremely important constitutional precedents: *Escobedo* v. *Illinois*, 378 US 478 (1964) and *Miranda* v. *Arizona*, 384 US 436 (1966). The

If we can speak at all about some general rules in this complicated sphere (which, as we will soon see, is ruled by unsteady criteria), then limited retroaction constitutes such a rule.

The principle of limited retroaction has been known in American law since the beginning of the nineteenth century and was first laid down in *United States* v. *Schooner Peggy*.[111] For this reason it is sometimes called "Schooner Peggy Doctrine". According to this doctrine the appellate court is obliged to follow the law in force at the time when the decision is made even if, because of a statutory modification or a change in precedent, the law was changed after the decision of the court of first instance.

The Schooner Peggy precedent, although based on a very specific factual and legal situation,[112] initiated a practice which is widely applied in the case of both legislative[113] and constitutional[114] amendments and when precedential law is changed.[115]

---

justification given in Johnson for the designated cut-off point seems to be hardly convincing. It is also entirely inconsistent with the general criteria drawn in *Linkletter* v. *Walker*, op. cit. For the well founded criticism of Johnson see W. V. Schaefer, op. cit., p. 646. It should also be noted that according to the Supreme Court decision in *Jenkins* v. *Delaware*, 89 S. Ct. 1677 (1969) Escobedo and Miranda holdings are not applicable to retrials of cases tried prior to those decisions but retried after following the reversal.

[111] 5 US (I Cranch) 102 (1801).

[112] The French schooner "Peggy" has been seized under an order of the President of the United States which commanded that any armed French vessel found on the high seas be captured. An order of condemnation was entered on September 23, 1800. While the case was pending before the Supreme Court the United States signed the agreement with France providing that any property captured and not yet definitely condemned must bė mutually restored. *Linkletter* v. *Walker*, op. cit., p. 625.

[113] *Carpenter* v. *Wabash R. Co.*, 309 US 23 (1940); *Hamm* v. *City of Rock Hill*, 378 US 306 (1964).

[114] *United States* v. *Chambers*, 291 US 217 (1934).

[115] *Vandenbark* v. *Owens-Illinois Gas Co.*, 311 US 538 (1941).

Hence limited retroaction, in the sense here discussed, can be called regular retroaction because it is used as long as special circumstances do not occur which demand the application of full retroaction or of the methods discussed under (1) and (2) or of special limited retroaction i.e. retroaction with cut-off points different than the time of regular appellate review.

One of these methods is the prospective limitation on the operation of the new precedent.

The limitation arises from the assumption that parties acting in reliance on the judge-made law in force must not be injured by a later change of this law. The Supreme Court long ago decided that constitutional provisions prohibiting the retroactive application of criminal law and the enactment of laws impairing the obligation of contract do not apply to changes in judge-made law.[116] Therefore the technique of prospective application of precedent has in fact a very important safeguarding function. The prospective overruling plays an especially significant role in the following categories of cases:

a) in criminal cases, when the judge-made law extends the criminal sanction to acts which were not punishable under prior law;[117]

b) in civil proceedings against officials who acted in accordance with a statute later declared unconstitutional;[118]

c) in civil cases against parties who entered into a contract or acquired property in reliance on a decision subsequently overruled or on a statute subsequently held unconstitutional; and

---

[116] *Frank* v. *Mangum*, 237 US 309, 343–344 (1915); *Ross* v. *Oregon*, 227 US 150 (1913).

[117] The principles of the temporal operation of the precedent in criminal cases are presented more fully in Chapter 7.

[118] Note, "Prospective Operation of Decision Holding Statutes Unconstitutional or Overruling Prior Decisions", *Harvard Law Review*, 1947, Vol. 60, p. 444.

d) to protect persons whose acts would not have exposed them to civil liability prior to the change in the case law.[119]

The prospective limitation in civil cases is rare in the case of a decision changing the common law; it is much more frequent with changes in the interpretation of the statute law.[120] Both the judicial decisions and the legal literature emphasize that the application of prospective overruling is justified only if a party has to be protected who acted in justifiable reliance[121] on the law prior to the change of the precedent.[122]

The requirement of justifiable reliance means something more than an action objectively consistent with the law then in force. There is no justifiable reliance when: 1. the parties acted in ignorance of the existence and contents of laws governing the area in question; 2. the overruled law was founded on an isolated precedent while at the same time there were

---

[119] Note, "Prospective Operation...", op. cit., pp. 441–443.

[120] H. M. Hart, A. M. Sacks, *The Legal Process: Basic Problems in the Making and Application of Law.* Tentative edition, Cambridge, Mass., 1958, p. 625. The same difference can be detected in criminal cases. This difference is unclear and illogical, at first sight, for a European lawyer; in his opinion, since the common law consists of precedents, a change of the precedent involves a change in the common law *sensu stricto.* The change of the interpretation of the statute is nothing else but a correction of an error in the construction. If the wording of the statute itself remained unchanged, it should be assumed that the law too remained unchanged. To the mind of a Continental lawyer a change of the common law rather than change of the construction of a statute justifies the prospective application of a new precedent. It is again declaratory theory where the explanation lies. This theory says that the change of a common-law precedent is not a change of law, that is, no new law is made but the old one is vindicated from misrepresentation; furthermore the judicial interpretation of the statute constitutes its integral part. Following the American way of thought, the change in the construction is almost equal to the amendment of the statute.

[121] R. J. Traynor, "Injustifiable Reliance", *Minnesota Law Review,* 1957, Vol. 42.

[122] For general information see R. J. Traynor, op. cit.; Note, "Prospective Overruling...", op. cit., pp. 946–947.

other precedents contradicting it; 3. the authority of the abrogated law had already been weakened by criticism, and by the process of "distinguishing", although the law itself was not explicitly overruled; 4. the law was based only on precedents of inferior courts without the authority of a court of the highest order within the given jurisdiction; 5. the party relied on a decision laid down long before the occurrence of substantial social, economic or other relevant changes in the given area.

According to another opinion, when prospective overruling is being considered, the general differentiation of two categories of rights and duties can be helpful, viz. primary rights and duties, and remedial rights and duties, corresponding, more or less, with substantive and procedural rights and duties. Only changes falling in the first category should be relevant to prospective overruling. For those authors who believe that prospective overruling depends on the existence of justifiable reliance, the question of proof of reliance becomes significant. Opinions are divided: some authors hold that the party who demands that the new law be only prospectively applied should bear the burden of proving justifiable reliance on the existing law;[123] others insist on applying a presumption of reliance which can be rebutted by evidence to be furnished by the other party.[124]

The criteria governing the application of full retroaction are even less definite than those governing prospective overruling. The U.S. Supreme Court has stressed in many instances the absence of general principles which would solve this problem.[125] In recent years the question has grown especially acute in connection with some fundamental (favorable for

[123] Note, "Prospective Overruling...", op. cit.

[124] O. O. Snyder, "Retrospective Operation of Overruling Decision", *Illinois Law Review*, 1940, Vol. 35, p. 147; *Nickol* v. *Racine Coat and Suit Co.*, 194 Wis. 298 (1927).

[125] *Chicot County Drainage Dist.* v. *Baxter*, op. cit., p. 374; *Linkletter* v. *Walker*, op. cit., p. 627.

the defendants) innovations introduced by the US Supreme Court in the interpretation of the constitutional principles governing criminal proceedings. To understand fully the practical significance and scope of this problem it suffices to mention that thousands of criminal cases have been finally decided according to rules declared unconstitutional by the recent rulings of the Supreme Court.[126] So, the freedom of thousands of people depends solely on whether or not the new constitutional decisions are declared fully retroactive.

The depth of the confusion is reflected in the story of the extremely important case of *Mapp* v. *Ohio*.[127] The Supreme Court held in this case that according to the Fourteenth Amendment evidence illegally seized is inadmissible in a state criminal trial. Ruling in *Mapp* v. *Ohio* the Supreme Court simultaneously overruled its earlier decision in *Wolf* v. *Colorado*.[128] Within a short time the courts were flooded with thousands of habeas corpus petitions from convicted and imprisoned people, demanding that the Mapp precedent be applied in their cases and asking for immediate release.[129] The opinions of the intermediate federal appellate courts were divided: the Fourth and Ninth Circuits proclaimed the Mapp precedent fully retroactive, i.e. applicable in the cases finally adjudicated; the Second, Fifth, Seventh and Tenth Circuits refused this application.[130] In this situation the US Supreme Court agreed to review *Linkletter* v. *Walker*[131] in order to determine

[126] We cite here only some selected cases: 1. *Griffin* v. *Illinois*, 351 US 12 (1956); 2. *Mapp* v. *Ohio*, 367 US 643 (1961); 3. *Gideon.* v. *Wainwright*, 372 US 333 (1962); 4. *Jackson* v. Denno, 378 US 368 (1964); 5. *Miranda* v. *Arizona*, op. cit.; 6. *Katz* v. *United States*, op. cit.

[127] Supra note 126.

[128] 338 US 25 (1949).

[129] A writ or order requiring that a prisoner be brought before a court at a stated time and place to decide the legality of his detention or imprisonment regardless of the stage of the proceedings.

[130] *Linkletter* v. *Walker*, op. cit., p. 620, ft. 2.

[131] Ibidem.

whether M a p p should be given fully retroactive effect. The answer was negative.

Let us look more closely at the argument underlying the decision, "Once the premise is accepted", said Justice Clark in his opinion, "that we are neither required to apply, nor prohibited from applying, a decision retrospectively, we must then weigh the merits and demerits in each case by looking to the prior history of the rule in question, i t s p u r p o s e a n d e f f e c t, a n d w h e t h e r r e t r o a c t i v e o p e r a t i o n w i l l f u r t h e r o r r e t a r d i t s o p e r a t i o n"[132] (emphasis added).

This statement makes clear that the chief criterion in this area is the ultimate purpose of the new law and the effect retroactivity has on the achievement of this purpose. Analyzing more closely the question of applying M a p p as fully retroactive, Justice Clark again stressed that the main criterion is t h e p u r p o s e o f t h e n e w r u l e but he also referred to two other criteria. "In short, we must look for the purpose of the M a p p rule"; we read in his opinion, "the reliance placed upon the Wolf doctrine; and the effect on the administration of justice of a retrospective application of M a p p".[133]

According to Justice Clark the purposes of the M a p p rule were as follows: to deter the lawless action of the police; to protect the privacy of the victims' homes and to have the federal and state organs follow the same legal standards. To make the M a p p rule fully retrospective will not serve these purposes.[134]

In the opinion of the Court there were two other factors speaking against retroaction: first—the reliance the state organs placed upon *Wolf* v. *Colorado*; second—the heavy tax put upon the administration of justice were the M a p p

[132] Ibid., p. 629.
[133] Ibid., p. 636.
[134] Ibid., p. 637.

precedent made retroactive. Hearings would have to be held in thousands of closed cases and enormous hardships encountered in securing evidence.[135]

Refuting the argument that a number of precedents were applied retroactively despite administrative difficulties Justice Clark pointed out the substantial difference between Mapp and the other precedents: the fact that some real evidence had been admitted which had been illegally obtained had no effect on the validity of the convictions because the reliability of such evidence had not been questioned, while in cases such as those involving the admission of coerced confessions, the denial of a right of appeal, or of a defense lawyer, the very integrity of the fact-finding process of proving the defendant's guilt was impaired.[136]

Currier's unique theory[137] concerning the operation of precedent in time deserves special attention. His reasoning is based on the advantages inherent in the observance of the precedent: the stability of social institutions,[138] encouraging reliance on law,[139] efficiency in the administration of justice, equality,[140] and the social image of justice.[141]

---

[135] Ibid., p. 637; see also *Stovall* v. *Denno*, 388 US 293, 297 (1967); *Desist* v. *United States*, 394 US 244, 248f. (1969). For a very interesting discussion of the Supreme Court practice see: dissenting opinion of Justice Harlan in Desist.

[136] Ibid., p. 637f.; the Linkletter doctrine was subject to sharp criticism. It was also pointed out in the recent American legal literature, that the actual practice of the U.S. Supreme Court is inconsistent with the general guidelines drawn in *Linkletter* v. *Walker*. Compare: J. B. Haddad, "Retroactivity Should be Rethought: A Call for the End of the Linkletter Doctrine", *Journal of Criminal Law, Criminology and Police Sciences*, 1969, Vol. 60, pp. 417ff.

[137] T. S. Currier, "Time and Change in Judge-Made Law: Prospective Overruling", *Virginia Law Review*, 1965, Vol. 51.

[138] Ibid., p. 236.

[139] Ibid.

[140] Ibid., p. 237.

[141] Ibid., p. 237f.

Currier draws the following general conclusions: "...prospective limitation normally minimizes or eliminates impairment of the values of stability and reliance, has a varying impact on the impairment of the value of efficiency in judicial administration, and (in many cases at least) significantly increases impairment of the values of equality and the image of justice... Prospective limitation has generally recommended itself to the courts in situations where the value of stability and reliance or both of them have been dominant and those of equality and the image of justice either not seriously impaired or relatively less important."[142]

It is interesting that he recommends the application of full retroactivity where a new rule has an ethical connotation: "...Equality of treatment is especially important to the image of justice where ethical or moral judgments are involved. For whatever reason, men do tend to 'universalize' these judgments, do claim for current notions of right and wrong a universal application."[143]

In general there are two ways in the American jurisdictions to determine the temporal effect of a precedent. Sometimes the court introducing a new rule simultaneously indicates how to apply it in other cases. This happened in the well-known case of *Durham* v. *United States*.[144] The District of Columbia Court of Appeals while laying down new criteria defining insanity and applying them to the case before the court pronounced the new law to be applicable in other cases only with future effect.

Usually the temporal effect of a new rule is determined by the court which made it only when this very point is in issue. If, however, the given decision does not directly involve the question of prospective or retrospective application of the new

---

142 Ibid., pp. 240 and 242.
143 Ibid., p. 238.
144 214 F. 2d 862 (1954).

law, the question is passed by, to be eventually decided by a court in a case in which this very point will be controversial between the parties.[145]

It is interesting to note that the first of the two methods under discussion was criticized in the American legal literature. The critics maintained that in accordance with the general principle of judge-made law, retroactive or prospective application ought to be decided only when it is the subject of a concrete controversy—just as any other question is. Otherwise the opinion is but a *dictum* uttered by a court *in abstracto*, without either the valuable controversial arguments of the parties or the compulsion to make a close examination of the practical effects of the decision.[146]

In conclusion let us state that there are two assumptions underlying the approach of the courts in determining the temporal effect of newly established precedent in contemporary American law: on the one hand it is based on teleological arguments weighing the social ends and functions of the new law; on the other, on the criteria of elemental rightness and justice, and on the notion of fairness toward people who trust the old laws. The protection of final judgments and the capacity of the courts to reopen closed cases which will have to be revised in the light of the new law if it were made fully retroactive are also taken into account.

[145] This method was applied by the U.S. Supreme Court in *Griffin* v. *Illinois*, op. cit.

[146] Note, "Prospective Overruling...", op. cit., p. 920.

Chapter 2

THE COMMON LAW AND STATUTORY LAW

Since the common law and legislation are the two main sources of law it is essential to investigate their mutual relationship. The interrelation of these two sources of law is reflected in a number of various ways; what we are interested in however are the ways in which they both compete with and complement each other. The common law will be discussed further from the vantage point of its significance for statutory construction.

THE COMPLEMENTARY RELATIONSHIP

The common law is acknowledged as a broader and historically older source of law than the legislation. Therefore in the absence of a legislative decision the common law is imperative.[1]

Although the role of legislation is rapidly increasing and, consequently that of the common law decreasing,[2] still the legislation is subject to serious fluctuations either because some regulations are repealed or declared unconstitutional. In such cases the repealed statutes are replaced by earlier common law rules.[3] Therefore it may be said that a common law rule even ousted by legislation, is not dead, rather (if this

[1] J. G. Sutherland, *Statutes and Statutory Constructions*, 3rd ed., Chicago, 1943, Vol. III, p. 1.

[2] Ibidem, p. 42.

[3] Ibidem, p. 4. Compare also *People* v. *Davis*, 1 Ill. 2d 597 (1954); *State ex rel. Rich* v. *Idaho Power Co.*, 81 Idaho 487, 346 P. 2d 596 (1959).

metaphor may be used) it falls into lethargy and, in some circumstances, may come back to active life.

THE COMPETITIVE RELATIONSHIP

The legislator can change or derogate the common law.[4] What happens if a statute coincides or collides with a common law rule? Is the statute decisive as a norm of a higher order? The conclusion seems obvious: since a legislative norm holds higher rank than a common law rule the former should be accepted in case of conflict. This sequence is recognized in theory: "In cases of conflict between legislation and the common law", writes Sutherland, "legislation is superior, and, being the latest expression of the law, it will govern".[5]

Is the derogation of the common law subject to some specific conditions or is a contradiction between the statute and the common law a sufficient cause for derogation?

This question is known in American jurisprudence as a dispute on the principle of the strict construction of statutes in derogation of the common law.[6]

The principle itself is a product of the common law but its origin is controversial. Some authors maintain that it is a product of the nineteenth century judicial decisions which

[4] J. G. Sutherland, op. cit., Vol. II, p. 164, Chapter 62, "Statutes in derogation of the common law". See also more recent decisions: *State* v. *Blacker*, 380 P. 2d 789, Oregon (1963); *Smith* v. *United Contr. Workers*, 122 So. 2d 153 (Alabama, 1960); *Gonzales* v. *Atchison Tel. and S.F. Ry. Co.*, 371 P. 2d 193 (Kansas, 1962). On the historical development of the common law vs. statute law in England see W. Zakrzewski, *Ustawa i delegacja ustawodawcza w Anglii* (The Statute and Statutory Delegation in England), Kraków, 1960, pp. 2–40.

[5] J. G. Sutherland, op. cit., Vol. III, pp. 2–3; see also the decisions cited in footnote 6 and in the Supplement 1964, p. 2.

[6] J. B. Fordham, J. R. Leach, "Interpretation of Statutes in Derogation of the Common Law", *Vanderbilt Law Review*, 1950, Vol. 3, p. 440.

erroneously interpreted the old English legal authorities.[7] Others suggest that it may be traced back to the fourteenth century.[8]

In any case the principle of strict construction of statutes in derogation of the common law made its appearance in American decisions at the end of the eighteenth century in *Brown* v. *Barry*[9] and has since been widely applied.

What is the gist of this principle?

Negatively it can be defined as a restriction on a liberal construction of statutes in derogation of the common law, and in particular as a ban on the application of analogy. Strict construction means however something more: it also means that all concepts of a statute in derogation of the common law ought to be interpreted within the strictest limits of its express language[10] whereby it is implied that the statute and the common law are accordant.[11] If the legislative intent for a change in the common law is expressed in a way leaving no room for doubt, then only is the derogation acceptable.[12] In other words: should the statute conflict with the common law decision, the statute can be applied only if the derogation of the common law was put down *expressis verbis*, or if the statute makes it a logical necessity.[13]

This principle, Roscoe Pound rightly observed,[14] reflects the typical reluctant attitude of the lawyers, and in particular

---

[7] This viewpoint is supported above all by Roscoe Pound in his well-known article: "Common Law and Legislation", *Harvard Law Review*, 1908, Vol. 21, p. 402.

[8] C. K. Allen, op. cit., p. 456f.

[9] 3 Dall. 365 (1797).

[10] R. Pound, "Common Law...", op. cit., p. 385.

[11] *Isbrandtson Co., Inc.* v. *Johnson*, 343 US 779 (1951).

[12] J. G. Sutherland, op. cit., Vol. III, p. 165; *State* v. *Western Union Telegraph Co.*, 97 A. 2d 480 (New Jersey, 1953).

[13] *State* v. *Western Union Telegraph Co.*, op. cit.

[14] R. Pound, "Common Law...", op. cit., p. 386. See also W. Zakrzewski, op. cit., p. 34.

of the judges in the common law systems, toward the legislature. This reluctance was justified on the grounds of the superiority of the judge-made law over the legislation.[15] The advocates of stronger influence of the legislation denounced the irrationality of such an approach pointing out, among other arguments, that the complicated legislative process which, almost as a rule, precedes a statute is an adequate guarantee of its proper legal quality.[16] It was also shown that in American conditions there is no rational justification for a narrower variance of this doctrine, viz. for the strict construction of statutes in derogation of natural and common rights, since these rights are sufficiently protected by the Federal Constitution. Consequently, it would be sufficient in the United States to have a rule that the courts ought to avoid a construction inconsistent with the Federal Constitution.[17]

The critics of the strict construction of statutes in derogation of the common law were promptly supported by the legislation itself. In 1950 as many as forty-one states and three federal territories enacted special statutes abolishing the strict construction principle either totally or partly.[18] A total abolition of the strict construction of statutes in derogation of the common law was provided for by twelve states, whereas in other jurisdictions the principle was abolished with respect to some spheres of legislation or even with respect to some specific statutes.[19] The code of the State of Kentucky provides an example of a complete abolition of the principle of interpretation.[20]

---

[15] Compare C. K. Allen, op. cit., p. 457ff.

[16] Compare R. Pound, "Common Law...", op. cit., p. 384; J. B. Fordham, J. R. Leach, op. cit., pp. 441–443.

[17] J. B. Fordham, J. R. Leach, op. cit., pp. 444–445.

[18] Ibid., p. 449.

[19] Ibid., p. 450.

[20] Kentucky Revised Statutes, 1971, Vol. 16, Title XLI, Sec. 446 080 (1).

In spite of the critical stand of the theorists and, what is still more significant, sometimes in defiance of explicit legislative rules the courts usually remained faithful to the old rule, either simply ignoring the statutory rules of interpretation[21] or avoiding them in various ways.[22] Parenthetically it should be added that in a similar fashion the courts disregarded the legislative measures which abolished the common law principle of strict construction of penal statutes and persistently clung to the traditional rule.[23]

The persistence of the courts is however not matched by a universal or even uniform application of the traditional rule. Sutherland observes that this rule is applied in particular when the statute tends to interfere with established property rights or the right to free contract as provided by the common law, or when it imposes new obligations unknown under the common law.[24]

On the other hand, Sutherland indicates, the whole area of what is known as social legislation is liberally interpreted by the courts, contrary to the canon in question.[25]

THE COMMON LAW AS THE GENERAL BACKGROUND AND AS THE SOURCE OF STATUTORY CONSTRUCTION

In the American system, just as in the English one, the statutory law bears such a relation to the common law as particular norms bear to the general norms of law. The common law is actually present when the new statute is made. A statute, in order to become a component of the legal system must be woven into the common law fabric and analyzed in the light

[21] See, for instance, *Armas* v. *City of Oakland*, 135 Cal. App. 411, 27 P. 2d 666 (1933): "Statute in derogation of settled rule of law requires strict construction".

[22] J. B. Fordham, J. R. Leach, op. cit., p. 452.

[23] L. Hall, "Strict or Liberal Construction...", op. cit., pp. 755–756.

[24] J. G. Sutherland, op. cit., Vol. III, pp. 268–269.

[25] Ibidem, pp. 171–172.

of the common law.[26] The first thing an interpreter does or should do is to assess the statute against the common law and furthermore analyze the status of the common law at the time directly preceding the statute.

The four interpretation directives laid down in *Heydon*'s case (known as mischief rule)[27] are considered by some American and English authors[28] as both classic and still valid. The directives are in the form of questions to be answered by the judge who is assessing the statute. The first two questions relate to the common law and they are as follows:

"1. What was the common law before the making of the Act?"

"2. What was the mischief and defect for which the common law did not provide?"

In case of doubt concerning the meaning of the statute it should be checked against the common law which provides the decisive clue. When used in connection with the same or similar subject matter the words and phrases of the statute are to be interpreted in the same sense as under common law.[29]

Federal statutes ought to be interpreted in the light of the common law existing before the Declaration of Independence. The *Erie* doctrine (compare Chapter 1) does not apply to procedural law, and so the federal procedural law should be interpreted in the light of the common law made by the federal courts.[30]

The rules of statutory construction, which although not binding[31] still profoundly influence the construction, are a part

---

[26] Ibid., p. 3; C. K. Allen, op. cit., p. 495f.

[27] *Heydon*'s case, 3 Co. Rep. 72, 76 Eng. Rep. 637 (1584).

[28] J. G. Sutherland, op. cit., Vol. III, p. 314; C. K. Allen, op. cit., p. 495.

[29] J. G. Sutherland, op. cit., Vol. III, p. 9.

[30] Ibid., pp. 11–12.

[31] *Boston Sand Co.* v. *United States*, 278 US 41, 48 (1928); *U.S.* v. *Universal C.I.T.* Credit Corp., 344 US 218, 221 (1952): "Generalities about statutory construction help us little. They are not rules of law but merely axioms of experience".

of the common law.[32] As a creation of the courts they display considerable vitality. This is clearly visible in the courts' reluctant attitude toward the legislators as the makers of the new rules of construction and in the courts' persistent usage of the traditional rules. Furthermore this is probably one of the few spheres of federal substantive common law which survived the general abolition introduced by *Erie* v. *Tompkins*.[33]

The approach of the courts and of the American theorists toward this problem doubtlessly remains under the considerable influence of the traditional common law concepts; on the other hand however it has its roots in the particular role of the courts within the American system as well as in the pragmatic philosophy of law. The full scope of the law-making role of the courts manifests itself in the law made exclusively by the courts, i.e., in the common law. This essential and inherent fact standing for all common law systems, namely that it is the courts that make the law, could not remain without influencing the methods employed by the courts in the sphere, at least theoretically, ruled by the legislation, viz., the sphere of statutory law. Within the framework of one legal system it would be impossible indeed to separate the function of the courts as interpreters of the statutory law from their function as the makers of the common law.

Therefore the common law courts do not have the sense of being restricted by the statute as do their Continental counterparts: this is easily understandable in view of the fact that the common law courts maintain their function of law-makers while interpreting statutes as well.

The sense of freedom to operate within the spheres ruled by the legislator and the awareness of being unrestricted by the statute is still more intense as far as the American courts are

[32] J. G. Sutherland, op. cit., Vol. III, pp. 3–4.
[33] Ibid., p. 329.

concerned. It is so for two reasons: first, the American courts exercise the role of supervisors of the constitutionality of statutes thus dominating the legislature; second, the intensely pragmatic approach to the law in the United States implies that the legal norm is treated as a means to achieve a definite purpose. Consequently, it is the purpose which comes to the forefront, not the legal norm which performs only an instrumental function in relation to this purpose. It seems that these are the factors which ascertained the supremacy of the teleological construction which left abundant freedom to the courts and which quite often is just a make-believe construction. Studying the American courts' decisions. one sometimes feels that the statute is considered not as much as a binding legal norm but rather as a starting point for a teleological argument whose outcome has often little in common with the contents of the statute. In such cases the statute is a springboard or simply an excuse to make a precedent, rather than "a source of law".

The American literature is exceptionally rich in works on the methods of statutory construction and this is not the place to go deeper into this vast and complicated field.[34]

We will dwell however a little longer on the methods of construction of penal statutes which are directly related to the principle of legality in the criminal law.

STRICT CONSTRUCTION AS A METHOD OF INTERPRETATION OF PENAL STATUTES. THE CONSTITUTIONAL DOCTRINE VOID FOR VAGUENESS

The doctrine of strict construction of penal statutes dates back to the XVIIth century, although isolated instances of its usage can be traced to an earlier time. The English common law courts introduced this doctrine in order to soften the Draco-

[34] For the general and extensive discussion of the methods of statutory construction in England and in the United States see: P. B. Maxwell, *Maxwell on the Interpretation of Statutes*, 12th ed., London, 1969; J. G. Sutherland, op. cit.; J. Wróblewski, *Teoria wykladni prawa ludowego* (The Theory of Interpretation of People's Law), Warszawa, 1959.

nian statutory law, and especially to restrict the death penalty inflicted even for petty breaches of law. The death penalty was liberally used in particular for crimes against property.[35] To counter this harsh measure juries often returned verdicts of not guilty contrary to the evidence and the judges carried

[35] The harshness of the English criminal law was mitigated until the XVI century by a special privilege called benefit of clergy. Originally it was indeed the clergy only who enjoyed the preferential treatment (death penalty for a clerk, for that instance, was commuted to banishment from the country); as time went on, however, laymen became included too, until finally the privilege was commonly used. The end of the XV century brought restrictions in the application of the privilege, most markedly in the reign of Henry VIII when, it is said, 72,000 people were executed. Throughout the XVII and the XVIII century the process of excluding specific crimes from the benefit-of-clergy treatment gradually gained ground, especially where crimes against property were involved. Vagrancy was punished with unusual cruelty. The doctrine of strict construction thus became a weapon used by the common-law courts against the bloody legislation of the Parliament. L. Hall, "Strict or Liberal Construction...", op. cit., pp. 750–751; G. Williams, *Criminal Law*, op. cit., p. 587.

The Parliament reacted with this kind of penal legislation to the unprecedented increase of crime which, in turn, was a product of the massive expropriation of the peasantry and of the disintegration of feudal courts; vast numbers of the population found themselves in a desperate situation. Karl Marx characterized this process as follows: "Die durch Auflösung der feudalen Gofolgschaften und durch stossweise, gewaltsame Expropriation von Grund und Boden Verjagten, dies Vogelfreie Proletariat konnte unmöglich ebenso rasch von der aufkommenden Manufaktur absorbiert werden, als es auf die Welt gesetzt wurd. Andrerseits konnten die plötzlich aus ihrer gewohnten Lebensbahn Herausgeschlenderten sich nicht ebenso plötzlich in die Disziplin des neuen Zustandes finden. Sie verwandelten sich massenhaft in Bettler, Räuber, Vagabunden, zum Teil aus Neigung in den meisten Fällen durch den Zwang der Umstände. Ende des 15 und wahrend des ganzen 16 Jahrhunderts daher in ganz Westeuropa eine Blutgesetzgebung wider Vagabondage. Die Vater der jetzigen Arbeiterklasse wurden zunächst gezüchtigt für die ihnen angetane Verwandlung in Vagabunden und Paupers. Die Gesetzgebung behandelte sie als 'freiwillige' Verbrecher und unterstellte, das es von ihrem guten Willen abhänge, in den nicht mehr existirende alten Verhältnissen forzuarbeiten." K. Marx, *Das Kapital*, op. cit., Vol. I, pp. 761–762.

the strict construction to its most absurd limits to save the defendant's head.[36] The rule of strict construction was brought to the American continent in a form shaped in the ancient days by the English courts and the common law writers.[37]

The progressive humanization of the criminal law deprived the classic rule of strict construction of its rationale. Therefore the middle of the nineteenth century witnessed veritable offensive state by legislatures against strict construction of penal statutes, however, as emphasized by American sources, without notable success.[38]

Nevertheless it would be wrong to presume that the humanization of the criminal law left the contents and the function of the rule of strict construction intact. Although, for quite a long time, some courts yielded to tradition, still as time went on the rule underwent some changes: the method of evading the employment of penal statutes and of distorting

---

[36] L. Radzinowicz, *A History of English Criminal Law and its Administration from 1750*, Vol. I, London, 1948, pp. 83ff., 660ff.; P. B. Maxwell, op. cit., p. 238ff.; L. Hall, "Strict or Liberal Construction...", op. cit., p. 751.

[37] L. Hall, "Strict or Liberal Construction...", op. cit., p. 751.

[38] Ibid., pp. 755–756; J. G. Sutherland, op. cit., Vol. III, pp. 58–63; J. Hall, *General Principles of Criminal Law*, op. cit., p. 48. This trend of the American penal legislation, although present in some criminal codes recently enacted, became to a considerable degree mildened. See: W. R. La Fave and A. W. Scott, *Handbook on Criminal Law*, St. Paul, Minn., 1972, p. 73; National Commission on Reform of Federal Criminal Law, *Working Papers*, Washington, D.C., 1970, Vol. I, p. 9. Another possible explanation of the legislative attack against the canon of strict construction is that the rule gave still more discretion to the judiciary.

As Professor L. M. Friedman suggests: "The canon of strict construction, in theory, expressed the humble role of judges, subordinate to the people and their elected representatives. But there was no short-run control over whether courts used the canon or avoided it. Hence its application was in fact if not in theory a matter of discretion. And what was or was not a strict or narrow construction was itself a difficult question, which gave still more discretion to the courts." L. M. Friedman, op. cit., p. 256.

their contents turned into the method of real strict construction.

This new form of the rule of strict construction of penal statutes was set forth by Chief Justice Marshall in *U.S.* v. *Wiltberger.*[39] Chief Justice Marshall emphatically stated that the old form of the doctrine had been modified. He dissociated himself from its distorting tendencies saying: "...though penal laws are to be construed strictly, they are not to be construed so strictly as to defeat the obvious intention of the legislature. The maxim is not to be applied as to narrow the words of the statute to the exclusion of cases which these words in their ordinary acceptation, or in that sense in which the legislature has obviously used them, would comprehend... Where there is no ambiguity in the words there is no room for construction."[40] In the opinion of Chief Justice Marshall the gist of strict construction is that it is inadmissible both to extend penal laws to embrace new crimes not enumerated in the statute and to apply analogy on grounds of the implied intent of the legislature.[41] This concept of strict construction would reduce it to a ban on analogy and would constitute an emanation of the principle of *nullum crimen sine lege.* Chief Justice Marshall's opinion justified this form of strict construction primarily on the grounds of the constitutional separation of powers and rather vaguely mentioned the protection of individual rights.[42]

Later relevant decisions bring to the forefront the protection of individual rights as the chief argument in favor of strict construction. Accordingly a penal statute must contain an explicit warning (known as fair warning) addressed to persons likely to violate its provisions. Criminal sanction

[39] 5 Wheat. 76; 5 L. Ed. 37 (1820).

[40] Ibid., p. 95.

[41] "To determine that a case is within the intention of a statute its language must authorize us to say so." Ibidem.

[42] Ibidem.

without an earlier explicit warning would violate the basic principle of fair play. Before the state metes out punishment it must give everybody a chance to avoid it by drawing a clear line between the prohibited and the permitted area.[43]

The ban on analogy which is the simplest consequence of the requirement of fair warning is at present a firmly rooted principle in the federal law, [44] and is generally accepted in state courts, although not without exceptions.[45]

---

[43] *McBoyle* v. *U.S.*, 283 US 25 (1931); *U.S.* v. *Harris*, 347 US 612, 617 (1953), *Bouie* v. *City of Columbia*, 378 US 347 (1964). This rationale of the modern rule of strict construction is well emphasized by Mr. Justice Holmes in *McBoyle* v. *U.S.*, op. cit., at p. 27: "Although it is not likely that a criminal will carefully consider the text of the law before he murders or steals it is reasonable that a fair warning should be given to the world in language that the common world will understand, of what the law intends to do if a certain line is passed. To make the warning fair, so far as possible the line should be clear."

[44] See *Pierce* v. *U.S.*, 314 US 306 (1941); it was declared in this case that § 332 of Title 18 of the U.S. Code (responsibility of a person who for fraudulent purposes identifies himself as a government official) does not apply to the defendant who identified himself as an official of a corporation owned by the government. See also *U.S.* v. *Evans*, 333 US 483 (1948) in which the U.S. Supreme Court refused to apply a penal sanction *per analogiam* to a factual situation described in the statute but not accompanied by a sanction.

[45] See *Lewis* v. *Commonwealth*, 184 Va. 69 (1945). The court refused to convict the defendant who was charged with obstructing order in a bus because the respective penal statute did not specify a bus among the means of public transportation where the crime could be committed. On the other hand even the state courts' decisions in the recent years contain cases of punishment *per analogiam*. And so, for instance, in *State* v. *Rinkes*, 306 P. 2d 205 (1957) the Supreme Court of the State of Washington upheld the conviction of a defendant who escaped from a county jail on the basis of a statute imposing punishment for escape from a state prison.

A drastic case of applying analogy is the decision of the South Carolina Supreme Court in *City of Columbia* v. *Bouie*, 239 S.C. 570, 124 SE 2d 332 (1962). In this case two Negro students who demonstratively refused to leave a restaurant "for whites only" were convicted by analogy on the

The inadmissibility of analogy constitutes only one of the elements of strict construction but does not exhaust its substance. Another significant rule is that the words of the statute are to be read in their ordinary sense and must be comprehensible to people of common intelligence. This rule, inherent in the requirement of fair warning, was strongly emphasized by Justice Holmes in the famous *McBoyle* v. *U.S.*[46] Another rule related to this one is *eiusdem generis* which requires that the "general words" used in penal statutes should receive a meaning close to the specific terms preceding them which define concrete categories of things, persons and events.[47]

---

ground of Paragraph 16-386 of the South Carolina Code. This was a criminal trespass statute proscribing entry upon the lands of another after notice prohibiting such entry. The defendants claimed they entered the restaurant with no objections on the part of the owner or his staff; they refused to leave only upon being asked to do so. Nonetheless they were convicted and the State Supreme Court upheld the conviction. The United States Supreme Court reversed the decisions of the South Carolina courts on the ground that it: "... in giving retroactive application to its new construction of the statute, has deprived petitioners of their right to fair warning of a criminal prohibition, and thus has violated the Due Process Clause of the Fourteenth Amendment". *Bouie* v. *City of Columbia*, 378 US 374 (1964).

[46] See ft. 43. In *McBoyle* v. *U.S.* the wording of the statute was discussed and specifically the meaning of: "any other self propelled vehicle not designed for running on rails". The question arose whether or not this formulation also includes an aircraft. Answering in the negative Justice Holmes referred to the commonly accepted usage of the term.

[47] The rule *eiusdem generis* was applied in *Alpers* v. *U.S.*, 175 F. 2d 137 (1949); a pornographic phonographic disc was declared to be "so radically different" from items listed under Paragraph 1462 Title 18 of the USC (books, pictures, printed matters, letters, newspapers) that the Court refused to include it under "other matter".

The application of *eiusdem generis* is however loose; compare, for instance, the decisions: *Cleveland* v. *United States*, 329 US 14 (1946); *Caminetti* v. *United States*, 242 US 470 (1917) in which the defendants were convicted despite the rule. See also: J. C. Quarles, "Some Statutory Construction Problems and Approaches in Criminal Law", *Vanderbilt Law Review*, 1950, Vol. 3, pp. 535–536; W. R. LaFave and A. W. Scott, op. cit., p. 78; C. K. Allen, op. cit., p. 490.

Strict construction is especially applicable when the court deals with a statute containing ambiguous terms and words. In such situations, with several possible interpretations at hand and no directive as to which one should be used, the court must give the words the narrow meaning, more advantageous for the defendant. This variance of strict construction is included in the decision of the U.S. Supreme Court in *Yates* v. *U.S.*[48]

We have reviewed the consequences of fair warning requirement in relation to the construction of penal statutes. The question arises, however, what line ought to be followed by the court when the statute is so vague that even the most rigorous construction fails to detect an indisputable pattern of prohibited behavior.

In the nineteenth century, when confronted with such problems, the federal courts submitted that a statute that vague was unenforcible.[49] At the beginning of the twentieth

[48] 354 US 298 (1957). In the case of the leadership of the Communist Party of California a controversy arose over the interpretation of the word "organize", which was used in Sec. 3 Para. 2385 Title 18 of the U.S.C. The defendants claimed that "organize" means to "establish", "found", "bring into existence", whereas the prosecution insisted that "organize" connotes a continuing process embracing diverse organizational activities. The meaning of the word "organize" was decisive for the solution of the case. The U.S. Supreme Court held that "organize" may be interpreted both ways and that there is no clue in the statute or in its history as to what the Congress meant by "organize". "In these circumstances we should follow the familiar rule that criminal statutes are to be strictly construed and give to 'organize' its narrow meaning, that is, that that word refers only to the creation of a new organization, and not to acts thereafter performed in carrying on its activities, even though such acts may loosely be termed 'organizational'...".

In effect of such an interpretation it was found that the three-year statute of limitations had run on the "organizing" charge and convictions were reversed.

[49] See: *United States* v. *Brewer*, 139 US 278 (1891); *Chicago N.W.Ry.* v. *Dey*, 35 Fed. 866 (1888). See also: R. N. Aigler, "Legislation in Vague or General Terms", *Michigan Law Review*, Vol. 21, 1923.

century this practice turned into a constitutional doctrine known as the void for vagueness doctrine.

Starting in 1914, the U.S. Supreme Court invariably has held that a statute, federal or state, vaguely defining a punishable offense, violates the Fifth and Fourteenth Amendment due process clauses[50] and therefore is unconstitutional.[51] Thus it is this doctrine which enables the federal courts to invalidate penal statutes for their vagueness and consequently to dismiss or to bar a prosecution.[52]

According to American authorities the void for vagueness doctrine is based on two essential rationales: 1) a vague statute cannot serve as an adequate warning for people who may violate it; thus it does not satisfy the requirement of the essential of fair warning; 2) when its violation has to be ascertained such a statute fails to provide uniform criteria for law enforcement authorities, i.e., police, prosecutors and judges. In other words a vague statute implies arbitrary official decisions instead of decisions based on uniform criteria provided by the law.[53]

---

[50] Both clauses declare that no person can be deprived of life, liberty, or property without due process of law. The Fifth Amendment refers to Federal, the Fourteenth to state authorities.

[51] *International Harvester Co.* v. *Kentucky*, 234 US 216 (1914). See for an excellent survey of this doctrine Justice Stewart's dissent in *Parker* v. *Levy* 94 Sp. Ct. 2547 (1974) at p. 2570 ff.

[52] Usually a statute is declared void for vagueness in a context of a prosecution; however an injunction, although in exceptional cases, may be obtained. W. R. LaFave and A. W. Scott, op. cit., p. 84; *Dombrowski* v. *Pfister*, 380 US 479 (1965).

[53] P. A. Freund, "The Supreme Court and Civil Liberties", *Vanderbilt Law Review*, 1951, Vol. 4, p. 541; A. W. Scott, "Constitutional Limitations on Substantive Criminal Law", *Rocky Mountain Law Review*, 1957, Vol. 29, p. 288; A. G. Amsterdam, "Federal Constitutional Restrictions on the Punishments of Crimes of Status, Crimes of General Obnoxiousness, Crimes of Displeasing Police Officers, and the Like", *Criminal Law Bulletin*, Vol. 3, 1967, pp. 217, 221.

How can this vagueness, declared as unconstitutional, be measured? What criteria should be employed to establish whether or not the statute complies with the requirements of the due process clause?

The opinion of the Supreme Court in *Connally* v. *General Construction Company*[54] introduced a common intelligence test, repeated in several subsequent cases.[55] The test says: "...a statute which either forbids or requires the doing of an act in terms so vague that men of common intelligence must necessarily guess at its meaning and differ as to its application violates the first essential of due process of law".[56]

There are some exceptions to this rule. Statutes which use terms ununderstandable to a layman but bearing a definite meaning in the common law are not declared unconstitutional: the same applies to statutes addressed chiefly to certain narrow professional groups which use the terminology of the given profession.[57]

Furthermore it has been suggested that a vague statute amounts to an unconstitutional transmission of legislative power into the hands of the judges. Comp.: *James* v. *Bowman*, 190 US 127 (1903); *United States* v. *Reese*, 92 US 214 (1876). Besides such a statute violates the constitutional (Sixth Amendment) right of the defendant to be informed "of the nature and cause of the accusation". *United States* v. *Cohen Grocery*, 255 US 81 (1921). See Note, "Due Process Requirement of Definiteness in Statute", *Harvard Law Review*, 1948, Vol. 62, p. 78. However, today it is the void for vagueness doctrine which prevails. W. R. LaFave and A. W. Scott, op. cit., p. 83.

[54] 269 US 385 (1926).

[55] See *Lanzetta* v. *State of New Jersey*, 306 US 451 (1939); *Winters* v. *New York*, 333 US 507 (1948).

[56] 269 US 385, 391.

[57] *Conally* v. *General Constr. Co.*, op. cit., p. 391; *Hygrade Provision Co.* v. *Sherman*, 266 US 497 (1925); *United States* v. *Vuitch*, 402 US 62 (1971). Compare also *Parker* v. *Levy*, supra, wherein the US Supreme Court adapted a lesser standard of definiteness for military penal statutes. See also A. G. Amsterdam, op. cit., p. 218.

A statute can be saved from invalidation on grounds of vagueness by an authoritative judicial interpretation. That is why statutes declaratory of common law[58] and those used over a long period of time are seldom voided on grounds of vagueness. In this connection it seems that the common intelligence test cannot be understood in a literal sense. Rather the test requires that the given statute makes it possible for a person of common intelligence to discover its meaning by: 1) alerting him to the need of legal advice; 2) giving the lawyer some help in advising his client.[59] With the second condition fulfilled the requirement of proper evaluation criteria for the court is satisfied.

In the first period of its existence the void for vagueness doctrine was applied mainly to statutes regulating economic relationships.[60]

A later decision in *Lanzetta* v. *State of New Jersey* gained wide fame because it voided on grounds of vagueness a provision penalizing a rather curious offense of "known to be a member of any gang".[61]

Statutes relating to the sphere especially protected by the constitution and voided on grounds of vagueness constitute a separate group; these are statutes restricting the freedom of speech, of the press, of assembly, etc. In such matters the void for vagueness doctrine is applied not only when the words of the statute are vague but also when they are precise

---

[58] The common-law rules are frequently given a statutory form. Such statutes introduce no new elements into the body of the legal system. Since they simply repeat the common-law provisions they are known in the American terminology as statutes declaratory of common law.

[59] Note, "Due Process Requirement...", op. cit., p. 84.

[60] See for example the opinion in *U.S.* v. *Cohen Grocery*, 225 US 81 (1921) invalidating on grounds of vagueness Paragraph 4 of the Food Control Act enforcing penalties for unjust and unreasonable prices for staples.

[61] 306 US 451 (1939).

but use such over broad terms as to embrace also actions especially protected by the constitution.[62]

A statute may be declared void on grounds of vagueness because the text of the statute itself is vague: this is a statute void on its face;[63] or, because the way in which the court interpreted the statute made it ambiguous: this is a statute void as construed.[64] Therefore federal statutes as a rule are not declared void on grounds of vagueness. Federal courts, and especially the US Supreme Court, when dealing with an obscure federal statute attacked on grounds of vagueness, may provide a construction satisfying the requirement of the due process clause.[65]

The picture looks entirely different when a state statute is questioned on grounds of vagueness before a federal court. The final decision in matters concerning the meaning of state law belongs to the supreme court in the given state. The United States Supreme Court is not competent to modify the construction of state law. The U.S. Supreme Court must accept the statute in such form as was given to it by the state court and confront it with the constitutional requirement of precision and definiteness. Therefore the Supreme Court can exert no direct influence upon the application of analogy in the criminal law when a state court chooses to make use of it. The construction of state law constitutes the exclusive domain of these

[62] P. A. Freund, "The Supreme Court and Civil Liberties", op. cit., p. 450. Compare, for instance, *Winters* v. *New York*, 333 US 507 (1948); *Cox* v. *Louisiana*, 379 US 536 (1965); *NAACP* v. *Button*, 371 US 415 (1963): "Because First Amendment freedoms need breathing space to survive, government may regulate in the area only with narrow specificity."

[63] For example *U.S.* v. *Cohen Grocery*, op. cit.

[64] For example *Winters* v. *New York*, op. cit.

[65] It happens quite frequently that the Supreme Court supplements a federal statute to defend it against an attack on grounds of vagueness. And so, for instance, to comply with the requirement of fair warning, when interpreting a statutory crime, the Supreme Court may amplify it with scienter as an element of the offense. Comp.: *United States* v. *National Dairy Products Corp.*, 372 US 29 (1963).

courts. However the Supreme Court may question these effects of analogy which conflict with the Fourteenth Amendment due process clause. This attitude is reflected in *Bouie* v. *City of Columbia* in which the retroactive effect of the application of an analogy was questioned as inconsistent with the constitutional fair warning requirement, while the application of the analogy itself was not questioned at all.[66]

And so, although the federal courts cannot prevent the breach of the principle of *nullum crimen sine lege* when, in fact, it is broken by state courts, the federal courts still can eliminate some effects of the breach as, for instance, the retroactive penalization in *Bouie* v. *City of Columbia.*

---

[66] "While such construction is of course valid for the future it may not be applied retroactively..." (Emphasis added—SP). *Bouie* v. *City of Columbia*, op. cit.

Chapter 3

CREATING NEW OFFENSES IN THE ENGLISH COMMON LAW

The creating of new offenses by judicial legislation is the fundamental principle on which the English criminal law was founded.

Back in the Middle Ages the common law courts had already specified and defined the fundamental offenses against life, freedom and property, such as homicide, rape, assault, battery, arson, larceny and false imprisonment. At a later stage the courts and the Parliament laid down and developed the principles of responsibility for the commission of these offenses.[1]

This group of crimes constitutes the foundation of the English common law of crimes.[2]

The Court of Star Chamber had a very broad, almost unlimited, discretion to make criminal law and, in particular, to declare new crimes.[3] Under the jurisdiction of the Star Chamber (finally abolished in 1641) the following acts were declared to be crimes: unlawful assembly, riot, perjury, libel

---

[1] W. S. Holdsworth, *A History of English Law*, 4th ed., Boston, 1936, Vol. II, pp. 256–257, 357 passim; T. F. T. Plucknett, *A Consise History of the Common Law*, op. cit., p. 442. Compare also: G. Williams, *Criminal Law*, op. cit., p. 592.

[2] We will use henceforth the term "common law of crimes" for this part of the common law which constitutes an independent base of legal responsibility.

[3] W. S. Holdsworth, *A History of English Law*, Vol. V, 2nd ed., Boston, 1937, p. 213.

and criminal attempt of several crimes.[4] It is worth noting that the Star Chamber considerably extended the concept of criminal conspiracy which under the medieval common law was linked to offenses aimed at the obstruction of justice.[5]

Although the Star Chamber acted outside the common law system, the common law courts accepted its pattern of indictable offenses.[6]

The seventeenth century witnessed an upward trend in the law-making function of the courts; the best known among them was the Court of King's Bench which asserted itself as the rival and later the heir to the Star Chamber. In an opinion delivered in 1616 (before the Star Chamber was abolished) the Court of King's Bench claimed an undefined discretion to punish all wrongs tending to breach of the peace, or oppression of subjects, or to any matter of misgovernment.[7]

The common-law courts exercised the function of law-makers either by declaring new crimes *per analogiam*, i.e., by a liberal construction of precedents and statutes, or else by extension of the criminal law to include new offenses which did not appear to be warranted by existing precedents and statutes. This classification, as one excluding borderline cases, is bound to be somewhat arbitrary.[8]

The offense known as constructive treason, created by extending the meaning of treason, provides an example of the first form of the law-making function of the courts.[9]

---

4 Ibidem, p. 197, passim.

5 Ibid., pp. 203–205. For a comprehensive discussion on the subject see Chapter 5.

6 R. M. Jackson, "Common Law Misdemeanors", *Cambridge Law Journal*, 1937, Vol. 6, p. 194.

7 G. Williams, *Criminal Law*, op. cit., p. 593.

8 R. M. Jackson, op. cit., p. 194.

9 W. S. Holdsworth, *A History of English Law*, Vol. VIII, 2nd ed., Boston, 1937, p. 307. It should be stressed, however, that the broad construction of criminal statutes was very uncommon.

The second form of the courts' respective activities manifested itself in declaring a number of new crimes not warranted by proper authority; the courts acted simply in virtue of their generally recognized law-making function. And so blasphemy (in 1616), conspiracy (postponed for later consideration), sedition, forgery (in 1727) were declared to be crimes; criminal attempt was declared an offense in 1784 and incitement in 1801.[10]

A group of seventeenth and eighteenth century precedents dealing with morality and good manners demands our special attention for it paved a very handy way for the courts to create new offenses. The first well-known precedent is the case of *Rex* v. *Sedley* decided in 1664. Sir Charles Sedley appeared naked on a balcony in Covent Garden and further indulged in some indecent acts. He was arrested and punished for offending morality. In its decision the court declared itself to be the guardian of morality (*custos morum*) of all the king's subjects; the superintending of offenses against good manners served as the general premise for the conviction.[11]

Rex v. *Curl* (1727) evoked the *Sedley* precedent. In this case the conviction for obscene libel was involved.[12]

Two decisions made by the famous Lord Mansfield (in *Rex* v. *Deleval*, 1763, and in *Jones* v. *Randall*, 1774) asserted the broad authority of the court to punish offenses against good manners along with its function as *custos morum* of the king's subjects.[13] In *Rex* v. *Deleval* Lord Mansfield declared: "...this court is the *custos morum* of the people, and has the superintending of offences *contra bonos mores*: and upon this ground, both Sir Charles Sedley and Curl, who had been

---

[10] G. Williams, *Criminal Law*, op. cit., pp. 593–594. Compare also F. B. Sayre, "Criminal Attempts", *Harvard Law Review*, 1928, Vol. 41, pp. 835–836; R. M. Jackson, op. cit., p. 198.

[11] R. M. Jackson, op. cit., p. 195.

[12] Ibid. G. Williams, *Criminal Law*, op. cit., p. 593.

[13] G. Williams, *Criminal Law*, op. cit., p. 593.

guilty of offences against good manners, were prosecuted here".[14]

Recognized authorities on common law, Blackstone[15] and Russel,[16] expressed similar views.

Among the nineteenth century precedents there are at least three which continue the line started by *Sedley*, and they are: *Rex* v. *Crunden*, [17] *Regina* v. *Saunders*, [18] and *Regina* v. *Wellord*.[19]

Beside offenses against morality conspiracy is the second traditional area of common law which was and still is (as we will see later) a source of new offenses made by the judges.[20]

Conspiracy to produce public mischief was probably the broadest category of conspiracy, one which left most room for judges to create new offenses. It was first introduced in the *Rex* v. *Berenger* (1814)[21] decision to appear again in the twentieth century precedents. However it was recently rejected by the House of Lords in *Director of Public Prosecutions* v. *Withers*.[21a]

Conspiracy to corrupt the morals stands at the crossroads of the two aforementioned traditional trends in the law-making policy of the courts.[22]

---

[14] Quoted after the House of Lords in *Director of Public Prosecutions* v. *Shaw* [1962], AC 220, at pp. 286–287. See also Lord Mansfield's passage from *Jones* v. *Randall*, 98 E.R. 706 (1774): "Whatever is *contra bonos mores et decorum*, the principles of our law prohibit, and the King's court, as the general censor and guardian of the public manners, is bound to restrict and punish".

[15] W. Blackstone, *Commentaries on the Laws of England*, op. cit., Vol. II, Book IV.

[16] W. O. Russel, *Russel on Crime*, 12th ed. by J. W. C. Turner, London, 1964, p. 7.

[17] R. M. Jackson, op. cit., p. 196.

[18] (1875), 1 Q.B.D. 15.

[19] (1844), 14 Q.B.D. 63.

[20] For the genesis of this crime see Chapter 5.

[21] G. Williams, *Criminal Law*, op. cit., p. 703.

[21a] [1974] 3 W. L. R. 751.

[22] The opinion of Lord Tucker in *Shaw*, op. cit., ft. 14, p. 287.

It was however in connection with a case which involved neither conspiracy nor public morals that the judges most liberally extended the criminal law. In the earlier mentioned *Rex* v. *Higgins* (1801) Judge Lawrence speaking for the court claimed for the courts the right to punish "all offenses of a public nature, that is, all such acts or attempts as tend to the prejudice of the community..."[23] With no authority of a precedent, as it was unnecessary for the case before the court, Judge Lawrence's opinion was a mere *dictum*.[24] Therefore it remained unnoticed but would grow famous one hundred and thirty two years later.

This survey, taken by itself, may seem to suggest that the judges have freely extended the criminal law whenever it appeared to them to be expedient to do so. Such a conclusion would be erroneous. In fact, quite frequently the judges have simply refused to treat the criminal law as expansible claiming that it was the domain of the Parliament to make new offenses. This was the case with the offense of obtaining property by false pretences, and with embezzlement, which were made indictable by the Parliament in 1757 and 1799 respectively.[25]

We also have an indirect proof of the judges' reluctance to create new offenses that is the significant role played by statutory enactments in the criminal law; statutes held a much higher rank in this sphere of the law than in any other.[26]

It was however in the 19th century that a systematic opposition directed against what is known as judicial legislation emerged; for the first time this doubtlessly happened under the influence of modern Continental thought; the English approach toward the law grossly contradicted the principle

[23] Quoted after the opinion of Lord Hewart in *Rex* v. *Manley* (1933), 1 KBD, p. 529.

[24] W. Stallybrass, "Public Mischief", *Law Quarterly Review*, 1933, Vol. 49, p. 187.

[25] R. M. Jackson, op. cit., p. 199.

[26] R. M. Jackson, op. cit., p. 193; W. S. Holdsworth, *A History of English Law*, Vol. III, 6th ed., Boston, 1938, p. 277.

of *nullum crimen sine lege poenali anteriori.* The opponents of judicial legislation held that the judge-made law inevitably works retrospectively, creating an atmosphere of insecurity, whereas penalization for offenses which at the time of their commission were not illegal, was irrational and offensive to the sense of justice.

One of the first outspoken critics of the retroactive judge-made law was Jeremy Bentham. "Do you know how they make it?" wrote Bentham. "Just as a man makes law for his dog. When your dog does anything you want to break him of, you wait till he does it and then beat him. This is the way you make laws for your dog, and this is the way the judges make law for you and me."[27]

A Royal Commission appointed in 1833 to draft a criminal code recommended that all crimes not contained in the Code should be abolished. Another Commission made the same recommendation in its report in 1879.[28] The authors of the draft thus aspired to the full realization of the principle *nullum crimen sine lege.* They wanted not only to eliminate penalization of new offenses by judicial legislation but also to rule out criminal responsibility based on existing precedents and consequently to make statute law the only means of defining criminal offenses.

Judge Stephen, a prominent judge and legal historian and a member of the Codification Commission, called for a total abolition of uncodified offenses and for a maximum restriction of the law-making function of the courts.[29]

Charging the jury in *The Queen* v. *Price*[30] Stephen ex-

[27] J. Bentham, *The Works of J. Bentham,* Edinburgh, 1843, Vol. V, p. 235. Compare also Bentham's viewpoint concerning the retroactive penalization discussed in Introductory Remarks.

[28] G. Williams, *Criminal Law,* op. cit., p. 595.

[29] See J. F. Stephen, *A History of the Criminal Law of England,* London, 1883, Vol. III, pp. 358–360.

[30] (1883–1884), 12, Q.B.D. 247.

pressed his opinion that the act committed by the defendant does not constitute a crime: "...the great leading rule of the criminal law is that nothing is a crime unless it is plainly forbidden by law. This rule is no doubt subject to exceptions, but they are rare, narrow, and to be admitted with the greatest reluctance, and only upon the strongest reasons."[31]

As we see, Stephen, recognizing the right of the court to make new offenses, pointed out that this right should be narrowed down as much as possible, and this in two ways: (1) the exceptionally admissible extension of criminal law ought to be subject to the strongest reasons; this can be understood as a state of necessity caused by an offense particularly injurious to the society which for some reasons was not illegal at the time it was committed; (2) the scope of the new offense should be maximally restricted which is to say it should be narrowed down to the facts of the concrete case and not serve as a basis for making broad new categories of indictable offenses.[32]

It seems that Stephen's opinion was shared by the English judiciary at large since almost fifty years passed in which the judges refrained from extending the criminal law.[33]

This silent agreement was first broken in 1933 in *Rex* v. *Manley*.[34]

The defendant Elizabeth Manley made false allegations of assault and robbery to the London police thus causing them to make unnecessary investigations and exposing innocent individuals to suspicion. These allegations were not denied by the defendant who however pleaded not guilty submitting

[31] Ibid., p. 256.

[32] Such an interpretation of Stephen's view is supported both by his briefing for the jury in *Price* and by his 1884 opinion (Stephen was then already a Justice of the Crown Cases Reserved Court) in *Regina* v. *Stephenson* (13, Q.B.D. 331).

[33] With the only exception of making new punishable forms of conspiracy.

[34] (1933) 1 KB, 529.

that she had committed no offense known to the law. Convicted by the court of first instance she lodged an appeal. The Court of Criminal Appeal upheld the conviction with Lord Hewart expressing the judgment of the court: "The first (question) is whether it is true at the present day that there is a misdemeanour of committing an act tending to the public mischief. In our opinion that question ought to be answered in the affirmative. We think that the law remains as it was stated to be by Lawrence J. in *Rex.* v. *Higgins.*"[35]

The decision in *Rex* v. *Manley* was met with strong condemnation in legal circles.[36] Not only was the mere fact attacked that the defendant was convicted for an act which was not known to the common law, which is to say, not the mere principle of extending criminal law was attacked but the method of extending it: was found most objectionable because the decision declared that every act is indictable which effects public mischief or tends to effect it. The critics indicated that this formula leaves much room for the discretional power of judges making them free to punish all acts they might consider undesirable. They stressed further that vague and flexible as the concept of public mischief was, the decision threatened individual liberties and created an atmosphere of uncertainty in law which is intolerable in the sphere of criminal law.[37]

Referring to Stephen, Stallybrass recommended a cautious and carefully limited application of analogy in criminal law

[35] Ibid., p. 534.

[36] Compare, editorial note, *Law Quarterly Review*, 1933, p. 153; W. Stallybrass, op. cit.; R. M. Jackson, op. cit.; G. Williams, *Criminal Law*, p. 596; C. S. Kenny, *Kenny's Outlines of Criminal Law*, Cambridge, 1952, pp. 335–337; J. C. Smith and B. Hogan, *Criminal Law*, 3rd ed., London, 1973, p. 591.

[37] W. Stallybrass in his already quoted article, devoted wholly to the decision in re *Manley*, starts his criticism by quoting the principle of *nullum sine lege*, and goes on: "It now appears that the citizen of England, land of the free, is denied any such safeguards". W. Stallybrass, op. cit., p. 183.

and contraposed his own method to the opinion of the Court of Criminal Appeal.[38]

The decision in *Rex* v. *Manley* was strongly criticized also on account of other legal and logical errors.

Despite the outright condemnation the Manley decision influenced the British courts and was approved by the Scotch judicature.[39] In the English law the decision served as a basis for indictment for giving false information to the police;[40] also, it became a new stimulant for the prosecution of cases of conspiracy to produce public mischief.[41]

Let us now analyze a few more recent decisions of English appellate courts in order to present the actual scope of judicial power to create new offenses.

In October 1953 the Court of Criminal Appeal affirmed in *Regina* v. *Newland*[42] that a wide category of indictable offenses exists which is covered by conspiracy to produce a public mischief. Speaking for the court, Lord Goddard referred twice to the Manley decision, emphasizing that this decision was binding.[43] At the same time, however,

[38] W. Stallybrass, op. cit., p. 184.

[39] The *Manley* doctrine was applied in *Kerr* v. *Hill*, 1936, S.C. (J) 71; and *Gray* v. *Marrison*, 1954, S.C.(J) 31. This however is of small importance since the Scotch courts preserved their traditional broad power to make new crimes. G. Williams, *Criminal Law*, op. cit., p. 596, ft. 2.

[40] Thus the established practice limited the application of the *Manley* precedent; it was followed on its actual facts only. G. Williams, *Criminal Law*, op. cit., p. 599. See however J. C. Smith and B. Hogan, *Criminal Law*, op. cit. p. 592: "...until *Manley* is overruled it seems that public mischief exists as an independent misdemeanor".

[41] In the following cases: *Rex* v. *Leese*, *The Times*, 10 and 22 August, 1936; *Rex* v. *Young* (1944), 30 C.A.R. 57; and *Regina* v. *Newland* (1954), 1. Q.B.D. 156. See, however, *D.P.P.* v. *Withers*, supra note 21a.

[42] See supra, ft. 41.

[43] Ibidem, pp. 167–168. This opinion does not however constitute a precedent but a *dictum*, because *Newland* was a case of conspiracy not of individual crime. Besides, Goddard's remark is erroneous because

Goddard criticized the *Manley* decision as one rendering wide possibilities for judicial legislation in the realm of criminal law, a realm which should be, and in fact is, the domain of Parliament.[44] It is difficult indeed to guess how his statement on the binding character of the *Manley* decision can be reconciled with his recommendation to refrain from its application; Professor Glanville Williams quite properly called Goddard's a Delphic utterance.[45] Lord Goddard's opinion strongly tends, however, to restrict the application of the public mischief doctrine only to cases of conspiracy and to refuse judges the right to create new "individual" offenses within the wide terms of the Manley formula.

A common law misdemeanor of conspiracy "to effect public mischief", after having been reasserted not long ago by the highest judicial authority,[45a] was ultimately declared by the House of Lords to be "not known to law" in *Director of Public Prosecutions* v. *Withers*.[45b] The ground for rejecting conspiracy to effect public mischief as a common law crime seems to have primarily been, that it gave too much discretion to judges and to juries in defining criminal conduct, and, therefore, was offensive to the principle of legality as well as to the principle of separation of powers. At the same time Law Lords on several recent occasions have emphatically pointed out that the courts have no residual power to create new offenses.[45c] Does this mean that the power

according to the Taylor doctrine (1950) 2 K.B. 368, the precedents of the Court of Criminal Appeal could be overruled by this Court in favor of the defendant, hence the *Manley* precedent was not binding over the Court of Criminal Appeal.

[44] Ibid., p. 167.

[45] G. Williams, *Criminal Law*, op. cit., p. 597.

[45a] *Regina* v. *Kamara* (1974) A. C. 104 at pp. 123, 126.

[45b] Footnote 21a supra.

[45c] *Regina* v. *Knuller* (1973) A.C. 435; *D.P.P.* v. *Withers*, supra.

of the courts to create new offenses under English law, has been effectively eradicated? It does not seem that such a conclusion would be justified in spite of the Law Lords' pronouncements to the contrary. In order to make a fair assessment of the *status quo* it is necessary to examine the landmark case of *Director of Public Prosecutions* v. *Shaw*[46] and its recent applications.

The defendant Shaw was convicted by the Central Criminal Court of a misdemeanor of conspiracy to corrupt public morals.[47] He pleaded in the appellate court that such a crime is not known at the common law. The Court of Criminal Appeal upheld the conviction.

Since it presented a number of legal questions the case was finally taken to the House of Lords.

The judgment itself of the Court of Criminal Appeal was upheld but the legal status established therein was somewhat modified. Lord Tucker and Lord Reid each delivered a detailed opinion, making some interesting points, which deserve to be presented here:

1. Lord Tucker in his opinion joined by the majority indicated that the prosecution supported the conviction on two alternative grounds: (a) that conduct calculated and intended to offend public morals is an offense *per se* and consequently a conspiracy to this end is indictable as a conspiracy to commit a criminal offense; alternatively: (b) a conspiracy to offend public morals is indictable as a conspiracy to commit a wrongful, although not criminal *per se*, act which is calculated to cause public injury. The Court of Criminal Appeal based its decision on the first proposition. "I have, I hope, sufficiently

---

[46] (1962) A.C., 220.

[47] The defendant in this case made an agreement with a number of prostitutes to publish for advertisement purposes a booklet "*Ladies Directory*" containing names, addresses and pictures of the prostitutes, and a description of the services rendered by each.

indicated that I prefer to base my decision on the second (proposition), but in so saying I m u s t n o t b e t a k e n a s r e j e c t i n g t h e f i r s t",[48] (emphasis added) said Lord Tucker in his opinion.

According to this opinion the *Shaw* case constituted a precedent only in respect to the second proposition set forth by the prosecution, that is, only in respect to conspiracy. However, the first, further reaching proposition adopted by the Court of Criminal Appeal was not rejected either; we may even go as far as to say that it was indirectly upheld. It seems clear that an indictment for an act committed by an individual, with no conspiracy involved, but falling in the category of corruption of public morals may hold water.[49] It also seems that Lord Tucker considered conspiracy to corrupt public morals as a sub-category of conspiracy to effect public mischief: in this indirect way the *Newland* doctrine was endorsed.[50]

The category of offenses against public morals is very extensive because of the vagueness of the concept of morality: in particular it is not clear whether it is sexual morality and the related norms, or a broader notion of morality, which is concerned. Therefore we cannot but agree with Lord Tucker's critics who felt that he used in his opinion ambiguous words and phrases.[51]

---

[48] Ibid. p. 290.

[49] As a matter of fact the opinion of Lord Tucker is based on a still broader basis, i.e. on the premise that an agreement to commit an act even against the morality of an individual constitutes a common law crime; the criminal character of an act against public morality is deduced *a fortiori*. This proposition, however, does not have the authority of a precedent because it is based on hypothetical facts and is not necessary for the decision in *Shaw*.

[50] J. C. Smith and B. Hogan, op. cit., p. 592.

[51] J. Brownlie, D. G. T. Williams, "Judicial Legislation in Criminal Law", *Canadian Bar Review*, 1964, Vol. 42, p. 593.

There is no question that the *Shaw* decision re-asserted the concept of the courts as the *custos morum* of the people.[52]

2. The author of the dissenting opinion, Lord Reid, opposed the extension of criminal law by judicial legislation. His theses may be summed up as follows:

(a) the courts cannot create new offenses with respect to individual acts.[53]

(b) judges continue to extend penalization on new types of conspiracy. Therein it is said that there is no question of creating a new offense because there is only one offense of conspiracy under different forms. The difference is a matter of words. The essence of the matter is that a type of conduct for which there is no previous authority for punishment now for the first time becomes punishable solely by a decision of a court. Therefore to extend the criminal law to new types of conspiracy by a process of judicial decisions should not be tolerated on the same grounds as creating new individual offenses is not tolerated.[54]

The wide differences of opinion in the House of Lords betray the deep controversy concerning the scope, the methods and the substance itself of judicial legislation in criminal law. The *Shaw* decision was recently upheld by the House of Lords in *Regina* v. *Knuller*, op. cit., against the contentions of the defense urging its overruling and over a strong dissent by Lord Diplock. Lord Diplock indicated that the whole concept of conspiracy to corrupt public morals as a common law crime was incompatible with the principle of legality: "The vice of *Shaw*'s case was that it opened a wide field of uncertainty as to what other conduct was also criminal... As a result of

[52] This is said *expressis verbis* in Lord Hodsen's opinion in re *Shaw*, who shared the opinion of Lord Tucker in its entirety. It has been also correctly pointed out by Smith and Hogan that in *Shaw*, Lord Simonds used language which suggested that the House was asserting the right to expand the scope of criminal law. J.C. Smith and B. Hogan, op. cit. p. 187.

[53] *Director of Public Prosecutions* v. *Shaw*, op. cit., p. 274.

[54] Ibid., pp. 275–276.

Shaw's case it would seem that any conduct of any kind which conflicts with widely held prejudices as to what is immoral and indecent, at any rate if at least two persons are in any way concerned with it, may *ex post facto* be held to have been a crime".[54a]

It seems that the English judiciary has been traditionally and for a long time strongly committed to the idea of the enforcement of morals through the criminal law. An idea of the courts as *custos morum* of the king's subjects is very much a part of this tradition. The tradition itself may be traced back to the *Sedley* case and through the famous pronouncements by Lord Mansfield and the controversy between philosophies of Judge Stephen and J. S. Mill. In our time this tradition has clearly surfaced in *Shaw* and *Knuller* as well as in the dispute over the relationship of morality to criminal legislation; in this dispute the judiciary invariably supports the "moralization" of the criminal law.[54b] The aforesaid may serve at least as a partial explanationof the internal inconsistency shown by the House of Lords decision in *Knuller*: on the one hand emphatic statements that the courts have no residual power to create new offenses, on the other — continuing reliance on the *Shaw* doctrine which provides an excellent vehicle for such a power. Before drawing some tentative conclusions concerning the presently binding principles of the English law let us present briefly another decision of the House of Lords in *Board of Trade* v. *Owen* (1957).[55] The defendants were convicted by

[54a] *Regina* v. *Knuller*, supra, at p. 480.

[54b] H.L.A. Hart, "The Enforcement of Morality", in: *The Morality of the Criminal Law*, Jerusalem, 1964.

[55] (1957), A.C., 602. The defendant Owen and his codefendants were charged with "conspiracy to defraud the Government of the German Federal Republic". They conspired on English soil to cause the German government to grant export licenses by fraudulently representing the place of destination of the German exported goods, i.e. that the said goods will be supplied and consumed by Irish manufacturers, whereas, in fact, they were delivered to socialist countries, contrary to the German export policy.

a court of first instance but the sentence was reversed in the Court of Criminal Appeal on grounds that conspiracy to commit a crime abroad is not indictable in England unless the contemplated crime is one for which an indictment would lie in England (this had no bearing in the case of Owen and co-defendants). The House of Lords concurred with the opinion of the Court of Criminal Appeal, declaring that it is for the Parliament, not for the court, to create new types of conspiracy.

At first sight this opinion rather clearly deviates from Lord Tucker's opinion in *Shaw* and from the generally known flexibility of the courts in matters of conspiracy.

There is however one essential difference which cannot be ignored: in order to convict Owen the mere extension of criminal law on a new fact-situation would not be enough: it would be necessary to go beyond the existing conspiracy headings, i.e., beyond these categories of conspiracy indictable by previous laws *in genere* even in broad and vague terms.

Here a somewhat arbitrary distinction has to be drawn for it uses necessarily inexact and indefinite terms: the very existence of a given category of conspiracy, and particularly the classification of a given fact-situation in a certain category cannot but raise doubts. Therefore judicial extension of existing law and new offenses which do not appear to be warranted by precedent remain today largely a matter of discretion of the judges.

Against the background of doctrines and precedents discussed hitherto we may at best try to make some prognoses as to the trends likely to be adopted by the English courts:

1. Despite the emphatic pronouncements to the contrary conspiracy will most probably remain the vehicle for the extension of criminal law however used with some restraint.

It is not very likely that within the area of conspiracy new headings will be created (compare *Board of Trade* v. *Owen*).

2. The concept of the court as the *custos morum* is very

deeply rooted in the tradition of the common law of crimes; just as it is in the court's authority to punish offenses against public morality. There are reasons to assume on the basis of the precedents which were presented here that the courts are concerned first of all with offenses against sexual morality and/or related acts.

Despite a considerable opposition against creating new "individual" offenses by judicial legislation it may be assumed that it is legal to create new offenses following the doctrine that any act against public morality is indictable. Although there is no recent supporting precedent in this area still the *Shaw* case indicates that this doctrine was fully endorsed by the Court of Criminal Appeal and, willingly if cautiously, approved by the House of Lords.

3. There is no chance, however, for the extension of criminal law on grounds of the doctrine that any act effecting or tending to effect public mischief is indictable. The crushing criticism of the *Manley* decision both in academic and judicial circles corroborates this prediction. After the recent decision of the House of Lords in *D.P.P.* v. *Withers*, public mischief doctrine in the criminal law seems to be dead.

Chapter 4

TYPES OF COMMON LAW OFFENSES AND STATUTORY CRIMINAL LAW

THE DYNAMICS OF STATUTORY CRIMINAL LAW

From the vantage point of the binding authority of the common law of crimes all American jurisdictions[1] can be divided into two groups.

The first group embraces jurisdictions which accept the common law of crimes as an independent basis of criminal responsibility; the principle *nullum crimen sine lege* is not binding under these jurisdictions.

Within jurisdictions belonging to the second group the common law cannot constitute an independent basis of criminal responsibility; in theory, only a statute or a provision of a lesser order provides the ground for criminal proceedings.

There is only one state, and this is the State of Louisiana, where the common law (at least formally) never constituted an independent basis of criminal responsibility. In this state, as we pointed out in Chapter 1, the general reception of the English law did not take place at all. In the remaining states of the second group the process of a gradual derogation of the common law, not yet completed, was carried out throughout the 19th century. As it was correctly pointed out: "The trend in the twentieth century... is to enact comprehensive new

[1] There are at present 55 jurisdictions in the United States; for details see Chapter 1, ft. 10.

criminal codes, abolishing common law crimes in the process".[2] At present about 32 jurisdictions belong to the second group. We say "about" because the situation in a number of states is not yet clear: the common law as the basis for penalization was not explicitly abolished, and it would be presumptuous to imply that it was, in the absence of authoritative judicial decisions. The jurisdictions in this group are as follows: Arizona, California, Colorado, Georgia, Indiana, Iowa, Kansas, Louisiana, Minnesota, Montana, Nebraska, New York, Ohio, Oklahoma, Oregon, Puerto Rico, South Dakota, Texas, Utah, Wisconsin, Wyoming and North Dakota,[3] and the federal jurisdiction. Also federal Territories of Guam and Virgin Islands, and the State of Hawaii belong here.[4] In recent years six more states have joined this group: Illinois, Connecticut, Kentucky, New Hampshire, Delaware and Pennsylvania.[5] Among the aforementioned states it is primarily North Dakota which is con-

[2] W. R. LaFave and A. W. Scott, op. cit., p. 60. There are, however, some exceptions to this general trend represented by the states of New Mexico, Florida and Virginia whose new criminal codes retained common law crimes.

[3] *Model Penal Code*, Tentative Draft No. 4, Philadelphia, 1955, Comment, pp. 106–107; Note, "Common Law Crimes in the United States", *Columbia Law Review*, 1947, Vol. 47, p. 1332; Clark and Marshall, *A Treatise on the Law of Crimes*, 6th ed., Chicago, 1958, pp. 27–28.

[4] Compare: *The Penal Code of the Territory of Guam*, 1970, Paragraphs 6 and 15; *Virgin Islands Code*, 1964, Title 14, Para. I and "A Revision Note", Ibidem, Vol. 3, p. 4; *Hawaii Revised Statutes*, 1968, Sec. I-1.

[5] Compare: Illinois Criminal Code, 1961, Para. I-3 (*Illinois Revised Statutes*, 1967, Chapter 38); Connecticut Penal Code, 1969, Paragraphs 53a-4, 53a-24 (*Connecticut General Statutes Annotated*, Title 53a); Kentucky Penal Code, 1972 (effective 7.1.1974), Sec. 2 (*Acts of the General Assembly of the Commonwealth of Kentucky*, 1972, p. 1653); New Hampshire [New] Criminal Code, 1971 (effective 11.1.1973), Para. 625:6 (*Laws of the State of New Hampshire*, 1971; Delaware Criminal Code, 1973, Section 202 (Delaware Code Annotated, 1953, Title 11); Pennsylvania Crimes Code, 1972 (effective 6.6. 1973), Paragraph 107 (b) (Purdon's Pennsylvania Statutes Annotated, Title 18).

sidered as "uncertain",[6] but so is Wyoming[7] and Utah.[8] Not all sources place Montana among the states where the common law of crimes was abolished.[9]

The common law of crimes has been abolished mainly in two ways: (a) by a statute explicitely derogating the common law[10] as the basis of criminal responsibility and declaring that only an act clearly forbidden by a statute constitutes a crime;[11] (b) by implication, that is, by enforcing a criminal code which covers the whole area of criminal law.[12] As we pointed out earlier the second method is bound to create some confusion, at least until the court within the given jurisdiction delivers an opinion clarifying the point in question. This however might take quite a long time as in the case of North Dakota.

---

[6] All three sources quoted in ft. 3 consider this state as uncertain.

[7] From among the sources cited in ft. 3 neither Note, "Common Law Crimes in the United States" nor the commentary of the American Law Institute to the Model Penal Code list Wyoming among jurisdictions which abolished the common law of crimes; only Clark and Marshall included Wyoming among such jurisdiction, with the remark "inconclusive". See Clark and Marshall, op. cit., p. 28.

[8] We found reservations concerning Utah only in Clark and Marshall, p. 28. Other sources cited in ft. 3 list Utah without any reservations. The Common law of crimes has been abolished explicitly by the Utah Penal Code, 1973, Sec. 76-1-105.

[9] *Model Penal Code*, Tentative Draft No. 4, Comment, pp. 106–107. Compare also: W. R. LeFave and A. W. Scott, op. cit., p. 61.

[10] The Wisconsin Criminal Code of 1955 is an example of this type of derogation; see *West's Wisconsin Statutes Annotated* (1958), Paragraph 939.10.

[11] Compare the earlier quoted Para. 1-3 of the Illinois Criminal Code. The following states explicitely abolished the common-law offenses: California, Georgia, Indiana, Iowa, Kansas, Minnesota, Nebraska, New York, Ohio, Oklahoma, Texas, and Wisconsin. Hawaii, Illinois, Kentucky and New Hampshire should be also included among them. See above. See also Paragraph 22 of the former New York Penal Law.

[12] Such codes were drafted in: Arizona, Colorado, Montana, North Dakota, Oregon, South Dakota, Utah, Wyoming. Compare also Connecticut Penal Code.

Let us take a closer look at the two jurisdictions where common law offenses were abolished relatively early.

The first of these is Ohio. In Ohio at the beginning of the 19th century it was widely accepted that under a republican system of government nothing but a statute could constitute the basis of criminal responsibility.[13]

Although an opinion to the contrary was expressed in an 1817 decision,[14] it must be said that this was an isolated case, categorically rejected by later decision.[15]

From the end of the 18th to the early years of the 19th century the existence of the common law of crimes in the federal jurisdiction grew into a highly controversial question and belonged among the issues of political strife between the Federalists and their opponents.[15a] The Federalists fought for a stronger federal government with broad powers including a maximum extension of the jurisdiction of the federal courts.[16] Two trends can be traced in the decisions of the US Supreme Court of this period: a "federalist" trend which accorded to the federal courts the power to prosecute common law crimes, which however the fall of the Federalists brought to an end,[17] and an opposite trend, which denied the existence of the federal common law of crimes.[18] It was the latter which finally

[13] S. Glueck, L. Hall, *Criminal Law and its Enforcement*, Boston, 1958, p. 7; *Key* v. *Vattier*, 1 Ohio 132, 144 (1823).

[14] *Ohio* v. *Lafferty*, Tappan 113 (Ohio 1817).

[15] *Mitchell* v. *State*, 42 Ohio State 383 (1884).

[15a] C. Warren, *The Supreme Court in United States History*, Vol. I, Boston, 1923, p. 157ff; M.J. Horwitz, op. cit., p. 299ff.

[16] H. J. Stegmaier, "Federal Criminal Common Law", *Kentucky Law Journal*, 1933, Vol. 22, pp. 152–153.

[17] *U.S.* v. *Ravara*, 2 Dallas 297 (1793); *U.S.* v. *Meyer*, Wharton's Prec. 955 (1798). In the latter case the defendant was convicted for having violated the neutrality of the United States; and: *U.S.* v. *Willing*, Wharton's State Trials 652 (1804); *U.S.* v. *McGill*, 4 Dallas 426 (1806).

[18] This "anti-Federalist" line was commenced by the separate opinion of Judge Chase in *U.S.* v. *Worral*, 2 Dallas 384 (1798). Judge Chase held that the common law of crimes has never been adopted in the Federal

prevailed. From 1812 on, the United States Supreme Court invariably represented the view that legislation is the sole basis of criminal responsibility in federal courts. This doctrine is founded on the premise that federal jurisdiction is clearly defined by the Federal Constitution; an extension of this jurisdiction would entail the violation of the sovereignty of the states.[19] The decisions of various federal courts verified the

---

jurisdiction since there is no trace to this effect in the American Constitution—the only legal source of power for the Federal organs. Finally, the problem was authoritatively solved in *U.S.* v. *Hudson and Goodwin*, 7 Cranch 32 (1812) whose history runs briefly as follows: the editors of a Federalist oriented newspaper *Connecticut Currant* were indicted for a libel on the President and the Congress of the United States whom the defendants charged with having in secret voted two million dollars as a present to Bonaparte for leave to make a treaty with Spain. The defendants were charged with a common law crime. The judges of the first instance were evenly divided on the question of the existence of the federal common law of crimes. The U.S. Supreme Court agreed to hear the case in order to solve the basic legal question. The Attorney General, in behalf of the United States, and the counsel for the defendants, both declined to argue the case. It is easy to guess why; the prosecutor, a United States Government official, was *ex officio* an anti-Federalist; in the concrete legal question and in the given case his position played into the hands of the defendants. The counsel acting on behalf of the two eminent Federalists was bound to support a legal position which, in the given situation, was disadvantageous for his clients. Justice Johnson speaking for the unanimous Court, concluded: "Although this question is brought up now for the first time to be decided by this Court, we consider it as having been since long settled in public opinion... The legislative authority of the Union must first make an act a crime, affix a punishment to it and declare the court that shall have jurisdiction of the offense." See *U.S.* v. *Hudson and Goodwin*, op. cit., pp. 32 and 34. A few years later a futile attempt was made to overthrow the Hudson doctrine on the grounds that the decision was made in the absence and without hearing the parties in the case. The Supreme Court, however, reversed the conviction for a common law crime and confirmed the validity of the Hudson doctrine. See *U.S.* v. *Coolidge*, 1 Wheaton 415 (1816).

[19] H. J. Stegmaier, op. cit., p. 156.

Hudson doctrine many times.[20] Yet the rule still allows some exceptions. It should be remembered that in the areas under state jurisdiction, that is, in the better part of the United States, the federal criminal law plays but a secondary role. It is sort of second layer superimposed on the legal systems of the states. The situation in areas which are under the sole jurisdiction of the federal administration is different. There are two types of such territories: the District of Columbia and the federal enclaves. Each of these categories must be discussed separately.

The District of Columbia was created by an Act of Congress in 1801 on a part of the territory of the State of Maryland. It adopted the legal system of Maryland including the common law of crimes; since no act of Congress has ruled otherwise, it remains in force up to the present time though with some modifications and changes instituted by the federal courts of the District of Columbia.[21]

Within the federal enclaves the common law of crimes is enforced by Title 18 Section 13 of the United States Code.[22] According to its provisions, in a federal enclave located in a state where the common law may be the basis of criminal responsibility, the federal court may punish for an offense committed in the territory of the enclave according to the common law of that state.

Indeed, it would be difficult to suggest at the present stage that the principle of *nullum crimen sine lege* is fully implemented in the federal law; everything considered, it might be

---

[20] The following, well-known cases may be cited at this instance: *U.S.* v. *Eaton*, 144 US 677 (1892); *Jerome* v. *U.S.*, 318 US 101, 87 L. Ed. 640 (1943). More recently the Justices Black and Douglas (in *James* v. *U.S.*, 366 US 213; 1961) confirmed the validity of the Hudson doctrine.

[21] *U.S.* v. *Davis*, 71 F. Supp. 749, 751 (D.C. 1947).

[22] 18 U. S. C. Para. 13. According to W. R. LaFave and A. W. Scott (op. cit., p. 60, ft. 19) federal government owns almost half a billion acres which makes about 23% of the total land area of the continental United States.

submitted, that the principle is formally implemented within the extraterritorial reach of the federal law, which is to say, where the federal criminal law operates as a supplement to the state law and within federal territories of Guam and Virgin Islands. In its remaining territorial aspect the federal law varies too: the principle *nullum crimen sine lege* is binding neither in the District of Columbia nor in the federal enclaves located in states where the common law of crimes is in force. It is however binding on federal enclaves located in states which have abolished the common law of crimes. The progressing expansion of statutory law and the gradual abolition of the common law of crimes within state jurisdictions[23] thus have a double effect: the introduction of the principle *nullum crimen sine lege* in the state legal systems and, simultaneously, its fuller implementation in the federal law.

Many writers emphasize, not without reason, that even in states which had formally abolished common-law crimes their legislation adopts, in broadly worded statutes, not only specific offenses but entire groups of common-law crimes; furthermore, such states let the courts exercise discretion to no lesser degree than courts under jurisdictions which have preserved the common-law crimes, without such a clear legislative sanction.[24] Specifically, such traditional common-law crimes can be named here as conspiracy[25] and offenses against public order and

[23] During 1955–1975 (as of April) the common law of crimes was derogated in seven states: Wisconsin, Illinois, Connecticut, Kentucky, New Hampshire, Delaware and Pennsylvania. Compare criminal codes cited in this chapter, ft. 5, and Wisconsin Criminal Code, 1955, Para. 939.10 (*Wisconsin Statutes Annotated*, 1958, Chapter 939). A new criminal code of the State of Arkansas (1975) was not available to this writer as of August 1975.

[24] *American Jurisprudence*, op. cit., Vol. 21, p. 91; Note, "The Use of Analogy in Criminal Law", *Columbia Law Review*, 1947, Vol. 47, p. 624; Note, "Common Law Conspiracy as a Weapon Against Corrupt Political Organizations", *University of Chicago Law Review*, 1948, Vol. 15, p. 941. See also W. R. LaFave and A. W. Scott, op. cit., p. 61.

[25] The "catch-all" provisions are especially common where conspiracy is concerned. This will be discussed in more detail in Chapter 5.

good morals.[26] It is worth noting that these vague statutes are generally not held unconstitutional.[27] Moreover some states, including some of those rejecting common law crimes as such, often use common law terms in their statutes without defining them, in which case resort must be had to the common law for definition.[28] Such offenses may be put into an intermediate category: enforced by a statute they are not common-law offenses *sensu stricto*; it would be difficult however to consider them as plainly statutory crimes because of the blanket legislation instituting criminal responsibility. They may be likened to offenses created on grounds of blanket provisions with one reservation however: it is not a statute or a written law of a lower order that fills the blank but it is the common law.

---

[26] Compare, for instance, *North Dakota Century Code, 1960 (With 1971 Pocket Supplement)*, para. 12-22-01 which reads as follows: "Every person who willfully and wrongfully commits any act which openly outrages public decency and is injurious to public morals, although no punishment is expressly prescribed thereof, is guilty of a misdemeanor". Compare also: *South Dakota Compiled Laws, 1967 Annotated*, Para. 22-24-6, Article 133 of the Uniform Code of Military Justice, infra p. 205, and former *New York Penal Law*, Para. 43.

[27] M. G. Paulsen, S. H. Kadish, *Criminal Law and its Processes*, Boston–Toronto 1963, p. 503. The reference is made to unconstitutionality on grounds of vagueness.

[28] See: W. R. LaFave and A. W. Scott, op. cit., p. 61 and judicial decisions cited therein. And so, for instance, in *State* v. *Moore*, 196 La. 617, 199 So. 661 (1940) and in *State* v. *Dailey*, 191 Ind. 678, 134 N.E. 481 (1922) under the statutes punishing "murder", the common law "year and a day" rule was applied. In *State* v. *Potts*, 75 Ariz. 211, 254 P. 2d 1023 (1953) and in *State* v. *Anthony*, 179 Ore. 282, 169 P. 2d 587 (1946), where statutes punished "sodomy" and "the crime against nature" without defining them, the common law definitions applied, likewise in *Hogan* v. *State*, 441 P 2d 620 (Nevada, 1968). As to the most recent statutory law see: Kansas Criminal Code, 1969 (*1969 Session Laws of Kansas*, Chapter 180), Para. 21-3102(1): "No conduct constitutes a crime against the state of Kansas unless it is made criminal in this code or in another statute of this state, but where a crime is denounced by any statute of this state, but not defined, the definition of such crime at common law shall be applied".

The common law may constitute an independent basis of criminal responsibility in the following states: Alabama, Alaska, Mississippi, New Jersey, Nevada, New Mexico, Rhode Island[29] and Arkansas, Florida, Idaho, Maine, Maryland, Massachusetts, Michigan, Missouri, North Carolina, South Carolina, Tennessee, Vermont, Virginia, Washington, West Virginia, and the District of Columbia.[30]

In these jurisdictions the common law of crimes may be enforced provided that in the specific area it has not been derogated by a statute. Whether and to what extent it has been derogated is determined in different ways under different jurisdictions. It should be stressed that in principle in all jurisdictions criminal liability for felonies[31] and more common misdemeanors[32] has been regulated by legislation. The common law of crimes has been abandoned as a major instrument of criminal repression. It continues, nevertheless, as a reservoir of law to stop up the gaps left by the legislation and, as such, it still performs a vital function.[33]

The mere existence of a statute regulating criminal responsibility for a given crime or a given group of crimes does not mean that the common law of the respective area has been abolished. In Chapter 2, we discussed at length the general rule that without clear legislative intent the common law cannot be abrogated.[34] "Clear legislative intent" itself is not an

[29] In these jurisdictions the common law of crimes remained valid in virtue of explicit statutes to this effect.

[30] In these jurisdictions the common law of crimes remained valid because it was not abolished by the legislator. Clark and Marshall, op. cit., p. 28. As to Arkansas see footnote 23 supra.

[31] Note, "Common Law Crimes...", op. cit., p. 1333.

[32] Ibid. For the exact meaning of felony and misdemeanor see sub-section on the classification of crimes.

[33] Ibid., pp. 1334–1335.

[34] Compare Chapter 2.

unambiguous term: therefore the effect of a statute in derogation of a respective part of the common law of crimes is often uncertain.

The extreme traditional position had it that the common law was abrogated only if the statute said so *expressis verbis*;[35] on the other hand a considerable number of states recognized long since that the common law may be also abrogated by implication. In other words, it was accepted that a statute which deals with an entire subject matter abrogated the common law as to that subject.[36] The generally binding implication is that it was the legislatures intent to uphold the common law: and irrefutable proof to the contrary must be contained in the statute.

In order to better perceive the effects of the specific relationship of the statutory criminal law and the common law it is desirable to analyze a number of typical situations:

1. If a statute regulating the responsibility for a type of offense known at the common law defines its forms and the punishment, whereby the scope of the given crime is narrower under the statute than under the common law, then it is the common law that may become the basis of criminal responsibility for such forms of action which are not covered by the statute.

State v. *Dalton*[37] reflects this type of coincidence. The defendants in this case were indicted on grounds of conspiracy to induce a group of workers to go on strike unless the man who employed the workers gave the defendants a certain sum of money.

The liability for conspiracy was regulated in Missouri by the same type of statute that is binding in California (compare Chapter 5). The offense committed by the defendants was not

[35] This opinion is sometimes expressed in modern textbooks. It is based, however, on older decisions.

[36] *American Jurisprudence*, op. cit., Vol. 21, p. 92.

[37] 114 S.W. 1132 (1908).

covered by the statute. The court of first instance dismissed the case declaring that conspiracy was a statutory crime exclusively. The court of appeal reversed the judgment declaring that the common law concerning conspiracy was not abolished because the statute embraced only some forms of conspiracy whereas others remained under the rule of the common law.[38]

The more recent decisions tend to express similar views.[39]

2. It occurs frequently that, as was already mentioned, the statute without defining the offense uses the common law term but the statutory punishment differs from that provided by the common law. The decisions on this point are divergent. Some courts hold that in such a case the common law sanction is repealed and replaced by a statutory sanction.[40] Some other courts are of the opinion that in such a situation the common law sanction is applicable cumulatively with the statutory punishment.[41]

3. There are also different solutions when an act violates the statute and simultaneously is a common law offense. In some jurisdictions the offender will be liable for two offenses: the statutory and the common law one;[42] in other states he might be indicted for the statutory offense only.[43]

---

[38] In its opinion, the court of appeal elaborated the question of abolishing the common law of crimes within a given area. The common law may be, according to the opinion, abolished: a) explicitly, b) in case of conflict between the statute and the common law, c) when the entire subject is fully regulated under a statute.

[39] *State* v. *Cantwell*, 126 Conn. 1, 81A 2d 523 (1939); *Redolick* v. *State*, 219 Md. 95, 148 A. 2d 384 (1959).

[40] *State* v. *One Ford Auto*, 151 Arkansas 29, 235 S.W. 378 (1921).

[41] *Commonwealth* v. *Wiman*, 308 Ky. 565, 215 S.W. 2d 283 (1948); comp. also: F. Wharton, *Wharton's Criminal Law and Procedure*, by R. A. Anderson, Rochester, New York, 1957, Vol. I, p. 22.

[42] *Lutz* v. *State*, 167 Md. 12, 172 A. 354 (1934).

[43] *Commonwealth* v. *Ackerman*, 176 Pa. Super. 80, 106 A. 2d 886 (1954). Compare also *People* v. *Amore*, 369 Ill. 245 (1938); *People* v. *Curran*, 186 Ill. 302 (1919). Both Illinois and Pennsylvania have since abolished, common law crimes. See footnote 23, supra.

The fact that the common law dealing with a certain subject matter was not abrogated by statute is a necessary but not sufficient ground for its implementation. There also must be found (and this is the second indispensable condition) that the common law rule is applicable to the local conditions of the given state.

The criteria of the applicability of the common law to the local conditions of the given state were outlined in Chapter 1. Therefore we will point out at this juncture only two interesting cases in which the American courts rejected the English precedents as inapplicable; in effect, the charges against the defendants were dismissed.

The first case is of great historical interest because it is connected with the beginnings of the American trade unions. In 1841 a group of Boston shoemakers organized a club. It was against the rules of the club to work for an entrepreneur who employed workers who were not members of the club. All members of the club were consequently charged with conspiracy on grounds of a famous English precedent.[44] The Boston municipal court found the defendants guilty. The Massachusetts Supreme Judicial Court reversed the judgement ruling that the English precedent was inapplicable in the State of Massachusetts.[45]

In *People* v. *Lefkowitz*[46] the court declared that a failure to report a felon, (misprision of felony) long known to be an offense at common law, was absolutely inapplicable under American conditions. The judgment of the court of first instance was reversed and the defendant discharged.[47]

---

[44] *King* v. *Journeymen Tailors*, 8 Mod. 10 (1721).

[45] *Commonwealth* v. *Hunt*, 45 Mass. 111 (1842).

[46] *People* v. *Lefkowitz*, 293 N.W. 642 (1940) (Michigan).

[47] See also, Note, "Misprision of Felony", *Harvard Law Review*, 1941, Vol. 54, where the opinion is expressed that this crime should be considered as obsolete both in the United States and in England. Compare also Florida District Court of Appeal decision in *Holland* v. *State*, 16 Cr. L. 2206 (1974), holding misprision of felony inapplicable in Florida.

In conclusion we may say that in these jurisdictions where the common law of crimes was not generally abrogated it may become an independent basis of criminal responsibility provided that in the given area it was not invalidated by a statute and it was not declared inapplicable by the court.

Both the problem of the derogation of the common law and its applicability are solved in a casuistic way. Therefore in regard to jurisdictions which preserved the common law of crimes it is difficult to define the exact dimensions of the violation of the principle *nullum crimen sine lege.*

THE CLASSIFICATION OF COMMON LAW OFFENSES. THE PROBLEM OF SANCTIONS

Under the ancient English common law all crimes fell into three categories: treason, felony and misdemeanor.[48]

The most serious offense, treason, was of two kinds: high and petty. High treason consisted of the betrayal of the king as the highest sovereign (only a subject of the Crown could be guilty of the offense),[49] while petty treason consisted of the slaying of a master by his servant or the slaying of a husband by his wife. In the last case the act of murder was coupled with a breach of fidelity and loyalty.[50] One common element in both kinds of treason was the breach of fidelity toward the feudal sovereign who in the case of high treason was the king, that is, the highest sovereign in the feudal rank: in the case of petty treason it was the king's subject but in the feudal hierarchy the offender's master.[51] The American common law never

[48] Kenny, op. cit., pp. 92–93; Clark and Marshall, op. cit., p. 95; J. F. Stephen, op. cit., Vol. II, p. 92.

[49] W. Blackstone, op. cit., Book IV, p. 74.

[50] Ibidem.

[51] Kenny, op. cit., p. 312.

adopted the crime of petty treason;[52] the American "treason against the United States", which is a federal statutory crime[53] is the equivalent of the English high treason.

The evolution of the concept of felony and its application in the United States is much more complicated.[54]

The characteristic feature of felony under the early English common law was that it produced a forfeiture of the offender's lands, goods, or both, beside other forms of punishment. It was forfeiture which made a felony significantly different from a lesser offense, that is, from a misdemeanor.[55] A felony was not necessarily punished with death.[56] Still the idea of capital punishment became so closely associated with that of felony that somehow they became inseparable and, in effect, an offense declared by statute as a felony made it capital if only by tacit implication.[57]

The traditional common law felonies included murder, manslaughter, burglary, larceny, rape, robbery, arson.[58]

The difference between felony and misdemeanor, following the criteria of forfeiture and capital punishment, was removed

---

[52] J. P. Bishop, *A Treatise on Criminal Law*, 9th ed., Indianapolis, 1923, Vol. II, p. 893. It is worth noting that petty treason, as a separate crime, different from murder, was abolished in England in 1828 (9 Geo. IV. c. 31, p. 2).

[53] Treason against the United States is the only crime explicitly listed in the Constitution of the United States (Article III, Section 3). For full statutory definition see 18 U.S.C.A., Para. 2381.

[54] The etymology itself of the word felony is controversial. In any case felony is a fèudal conception, originally applied to a crime accompanied by the breach of the fidelity and loyalty due to the feudal master. T.F.T. Plucknett, op. cit., p. 442.

[55] W. Blackstone, op. cit., Book IV, p. 94.

[56] Ibidem, p. 69; J. F. Stephen, op. cit., Vol. II, pp. 192–193; Kenny, op. cit., p. 94; J. P. Bishop, op. cit., Vol. I, p. 447.

[57] Kenny, op. cit., p. 94. Stephen seems to share the view that "roughly speaking" felony was a crime punishable with death. J. F. Stephen, op. cit., Vol. II, p. 193.

[58] Kenny, op. cit., p. 93.

by several acts of Parliament which created new felonies which occasioned neither forfeiture nor death, or abolished these punishments in respect to some of the old felonies leaving the classification itself intact.[59] These acts of Parliament originating from the time prior to the reception of English law became a part of the American common law and instantly produced chaos in the classification of offenses on the new continent.[60]

Misdemeanor, the third category of crimes, is defined by a negative criterion: offenses not amounting to felonies are misdemeanors.[61]

At common law a misdemeanor was punishable by deprivation of freedom or by fine or both at the discretion of the judge.

Since forfeiture was not adopted in the United States the traditional criteria of classification of crimes into felonies and misdemeanors proved useless;[62] yet the classification itself was preserved. In the absence of a commonly applicable common law criterion which would draw the line between the two classes of crimes the problem is generally solved by the legislation.[63] Several statutory types of classification may be discerned:

Type I: offenses punishable by death or by imprisonment in a state prison or penitentiary, are felonies: all others, including those punishable by imprisonment in the county jail, are

---

[59] J. F. Stephen, op. cit., Vol. II, p. 193; *American Jurisprudence*, op. cit., Vol. 21, p. 101.

[60] *American Jurisprudence*, op. cit., Vol. 21, p. 101. Compare also: *State* v. *Clark*, 83 Vt. 305, 75 A. 534 (1910).

[61] W. Blackstone, op. cit., Book IV, p. 4. In the modern English law all distinctions between felonies and misdemeanors have been abolished by Sec. I of The Criminal Law Act 1967. Comp.: J. C. Smith and B. Hogan, op. cit., p. 23f.

[62] J. P. Bishop, op. cit., Vol. I, p. 447.

[63] *American Jurisprudence*, op. cit., Vol. 21, p. 101.

misdemeanors.[64] Where the statute characterizes an offense as a misdemeanor it is an indication that the county jail must be the place of confinement;[65]

Type II: Whether a criminal act is to be classed as a felony or as a misdemeanor depends on the statutory limits of punishment, not on the place of confinement. This rule of classifying offenses is adopted in the federal law and accordingly an offense punishable by death or imprisonment over a year is a felony, whereas all other crimes are misdemeanors.[66]

Type III: Some jurisdictions classify offenses regardless of the punishment prescribed by a statute but depending on the punishment actually inflicted by a court.[67]

In a related type of classification the statute leaves to the discretion of the court the decision to punish the offense as a felony or as a misdemeanor: before the sentence is passed the offense is always regarded as a felony and then classified as a misdemeanor if the punishment is appropriate for a misdemeanor.[68]

Type IV: Under some jurisdictions it is the terminology of the statute that determines the classification of an offense: if the statute terms a certain offense a felony or a misdemeanor then the legislative designation is decisive while the general criteria have only an auxiliary function.[69] Directly opposed to this is an approach that legislative nomenclature is of secon-

---

[64] Ibidem, pp. 101–103. This type of statutory classification is very common. Among modern American criminal codes this pattern is represented by the Kansas Criminal Code, Para. 21-3105.

[65] *Gherna* v. *State*, 16 Arizona 344, 146 P. 434 (1915).

[66] U.S.C., Title 18, Para. I. This type of statutory classification is also very popular. Comp., for example, new criminal codes of Connecticut, Georgia, Minnesota, and New Mexico.

[67] *State ex rel. Anderson* v. *Fousek*, 91 Montana 448 (1932).

[68] *People* v. *Hamilton*, 33 Cal. 2d 45, 198 P. 2d 873 (1948).

[69] *Eckhart* v. *People*, 126 Colo. 18, 247 P. 2d 673 (1952).

dary importance and must give way to the classification corresponding to the nature of the offence.[70]

Type V: In some jurisdictions the common law classification is still used: in the absence of a clear statute classifying the offense either as a felony or as a misdemeanor and regardless of the punishment, only such offenses are felonies which belonged to this class under the English common law of the time of the reception.[71]

The classification of a criminal act as a felony or as a misdemeanor is not only an indicator of the gravity of the crime. There is a number of questions which are solved depending on whether the offense was classed as a felony or as a misdemeanor, and they are as follows:

1. Is the offender who caused death liable for murder or manslaughter? If the act which caused death is a felony the offender is liable for murder; if it is a misdemeanor he is liable for manslaughter;[72]

2. Is the arrest of the offender legal without a warrant?

3. Is a killing committed to prevent a crime or to prevent a criminal from running away legal? If the attempted crime is a felony or if the fugitive earlier committed a felony, killing as a means of defense or as a preventive measure may not be punishable;

4. Must the bill of indictment be signed by a grand jury (which often is indispensable in the case of a felony), or is a less formal mode of accusation, i.e., an information sufficient?[73]

LaFave and Scott also discuss several other legal consequences of a very serious nature depending upon the classifica-

---

[70] *State* v. *Kelly*, 218 Minn. 247 (1944).

[71] *Dutten* v. *State*, 23 Md. 373 (1914). Compare also J. P. Bishop, op. cit., Vol. 1, p. 448; W. R. LaFave and A. W. Scott, op. cit., p. 63.

[72] This treatment is connected with the so-called felony-murder rule, a medieval common-law rule, applied until present in the American law. The felony-murder rule was, at least formally, abolished in England.

[73] S. Glueck, L. Hall, op. cit., p. 12.

tion of an offense as a felony or a misdemeanor. For the purposes of substantive criminal law the following should be mentioned here:

1. A burglary is defined at common law as breaking and entering another's dwelling house at night with intent to commit a felony;

2. There exists a common law crime of compounding of felony, which is committed by one who for a consideration agrees not to prosecute for, or to keep quiet about, a felony (but not a misdemeanor) he knows has been committed;

3. At common law parties involved in felonies are divided into principals and accessories, whereas with misdemeanors all parties are considered principals.[74]

Outside the field of criminal law classifying a crime as a felony or as a misdemeanor is also of importance. Conviction for felony usually: 1) disqualifies a convicted person from holding a public office; 2) deprives him of rights to vote, to serve as a juror, to practice as an attorney and to practice medicine; 3) constitutes a ground for divorce.[75]

The Model Penal Code introduced a classification somewhat different from the traditional one.[76]

How does the problem of common law offenses in American law present itself in the light of the hitherto discussed rules of the classification of crimes?

An analysis of the methods of penalization provides an answer to this question. If there is no distinct statutory regulation, a common law misdemeanor under American law is ordinarily punished with either a fine or imprisonment, or both, at the discretion of the court.[77] In some states the dis-

[74] W. R. LaFave and A. W. Scott, op. cit., p. 27.

[75] Ibidem, p. 28.

[76] *Model Penal Code* (Proposed Official Draft), 1962, Section 1.04, M.P.C.

[77] J. P. Bishop, op. cit., Vol. I, p. 693. Compare also *State* v. *Coolidge*, 106 Vt. 183 (1934).

cretional power of the judges has been restricted by the courts themselves. For instance, in Pennsylvania prior to the abolition of common law crimes there was a judicially established rule by which the punishment for a common-law offense must correspond with the punishment for a similar statutory offense.[78]

There is a rather popular institution known as maximum punishment provisions which imposes statutory restrictions on the discretional power of the court. In fact, it amounts to a statutory definition of the maximum punishment for a common-law offense. Paragraph 22-107 of the District of Columbia Code illustrates this point. "Whoever shall be convicted of any criminal offense not covered by the provisions of any section of this code, or of any general law of the U.S. not locally inapplicable in the District of Columbia, shall be punished by a fine not exceeding one thousand dollars or by imprisonment for not more than five years, or both". The provision does not contain the term "common law crime" but doubtlessly refers to it.[79] In some jurisdictions the maximum punishment provisions explicitly specify the common law offenses.[80]

When comparing the statutory definitions of misdemeanor and felony and the punishments which may be inflicted for committing common law offenses in various jurisdictions, we may draw the following conclusions:

1. Under some jurisdictions all common law offenses are reduced by statute to the rank of misdemeanor;[81]

---

[78] It was also established that the penalty for an attempt and conspiracy punishable on the basis of the common law cannot be heavier than the optimal penalty for the committed crime. See N. Kessler, "Common Law Offenses and Penalties in Pennsylvania", *Temple Law Quarterly*, 1960, Vol. 33, p. 421 and the decisions cited therein.

[79] *District of Columbia Code Encyclopedia*. Completely Annotated.

[80] Compare, for instance, *Nevada Revised Statutes*, Paragraph 193.180; *Mississippi Code*, 1942, Annotated with 1971 Cumulative Supplement, Para. 2562.

[81] Note, "Common Law Crimes in the United States", op. cit., p. 1333.

2. Under other jurisdictions common law offenses may be treated as felonies.[82] In the District of Columbia all common law offenses are felonies.[83]

CRIMINAL OFFENSES UNDER THE AMERICAN COMMON LAW

Given the diversity of the American legal systems it would be extremely difficult to state precisely what offenses are punishable in the United States under the common law for in order to do so twenty-three systems must be examined in detail. It seems however that it is both feasible and sufficient to review the typical spheres governed by the common law and to present some characteristics of the system.

It is in the sphere of conspiracy[84] that the common law retained most firmly its effective hold.

Because of the specific character and considerable practical meaning of the institution of conspiracy we devoted a separate chapter (Chapter 5) to it.

The common law misdemeanor doctrine and contempt of court are also discussed in a separate chapter; this doctrine, like conspiracy, are closely connected with the highly controversial problem of judge-made new offenses.

Below the crimes are discussed which, as a rule, have been punishable on the basis of precedent.

---

[82] According to the author of the Note, "Common Law Crimes in the United States" op. cit. this is the case in the following states: Colorado, Connecticut, Delaware, Idaho, Maine, Maryland, Massachusetts, Michigan, Nevada, New Hampshire, New Mexico, North Carolina, Pennsylvania, Rhode Island, South Carolina, Tennessee, Vermont, Virginia, West Virginia and, probably, Wyoming. Connecticut, New Hampshire, Delaware and Pennsylvania no longer belong to this group.

[83] The above quoted provision defining penalties for common law offenses put together with the definition of felony contained in the USC (Title 18, Para. 1), which makes every crime punishable with death or more than one year imprisonment a felony, leads to this conclusion concerning the District of Columbia.

[84] *Model Penal Code*, Tentative Draft No. 4, Comments, pp. 106–107.

Attempt and Solicitation

In several states an attempt to commit a crime as well as a solicitation to commit a crime have been held punishable solely on the ground of common law.[85]

Even more recently an attempted murder was prosecuted as a common law crime in Maryland.[86]

Breach of the Peace

Breach of the peace constituted a traditional part of the English criminal law.[87] This general denomination embraced such crimes as affray, unlawful assembly and riot, forcible entry, carrying weapons, spreading false news, false prophecy, challenging to fight, libel.[88]

In the United States the majority of these acts are at present statutory crimes, in several jurisdictions however they remain common law offenses.

Among the common law offenses are the following:

1. Unlawful assembly and riot—a crime whose definition is very vague. As a rule three or more persons must meet together to make an assembly. It seems that the necessary element of breach of the peace is that the persons who take part in an unlawful assembly act in such a way as to

---

[85] As to an attempt compare: *Nider* v. *Comm.*, 140 Ky. 684, 13 SW 1024 (1910); *Commonwealth ex rel. Swisher* v. *Ashe*, 145 Pa. Super. 451, 21 A. 2d 479 (1941).

As to a solicitation compare: *State* v. *Schleifer*, 99 Conn. 432 (1923); *Commonwealth* v. *Flag*, 135 Mass. 545 (1883); *Commonwealth* v. *Randolph*, 146 Pa. 83 (1892). See, however, new criminal codes enacted in Connecticut, Kentucky and Pennsylvania, note 5 supra.

[86] Arthur H. Bremer was prosecuted, among other charges, for an attempt to murder Governor George C. Wallace. This crime, according to the common law of the state of Maryland was a felony carrying no fixed penalties and could have resulted upon conviction in the death penalty. *The New York Times*, May 24, 1972, p. 35.

[87] See W. Blackstone, op. cit., Book IV, Chapter XI, "Of offenses against the public peace".

[88] Ibidem, pp. 141–152.

give rational men ground for fear, etc.[89] Inciting others to riot and uttering inflammatory remarks during a "period of excitement"[90] is also an indictable offense;

2. The conducting of a dangerous or noxious business;[91]

3. Exhibition of an effigy calculated to provoke the anger and resentment of the populace;[92]

4. Public utterances alarming or calculated to alarm the public at large;[93]

5. Allowing any dangerous animal to go at large to the terror of the public;[94]

6. Malicious disturbance of a meeting;[95]

7. The circulation of a false or alarming report (about an enemy invasion, or the outbreak of a contagious disease) calculated to excite fear in the minds of the people;[96]

8. Obstruction of public highway;[97]

9. Maintaining a "disorderly house" on whose premises the law (not necessarily the criminal law) was systematically violated.[98]

10. Public drunkenness.[99]

11. Creating a public nuisance.[100]

---

[89] *State* v. *Lustig* (New Jersey), 13 N. J. Super 149, 80 A. 2d 309 (1951). *State* v. *Butterworth*, 104 N.J.L. 579, 142 A. 57, 58 Al.R. 744 (1928).

[90] N. Kessler, op. cit., p. 425. In a case known as *Jones*'s case, 2 DR 538 (1892) the defendant was convicted for uttering "inflammatory remarks" during a period of excitement attending a labor strike, in addressing a justice of the peace.

[91] N. Kessler, op. cit., p. 423.

[92] Ibidem, p. 424.

[93] *Cantwell* v. *Connecticut*, 310 US 296 (1940).

[94] N. Kessler, op. cit., p. 425.

[95] Ibidem, p. 427.

[96] *Commonwealth* v. *Cassidy*, 6 Phila. (1865).

[97] N. Kessler, op. cit., p. 428.

[98] *State* v. *W.U.Tel.Co.*, 13 N. J. Super. 172, 80 A. 2d 342 (1951); compare also *State* v. *Reade*, 98 N.J.L. 596, 121 A. 288 (1923).

[99] *Willard* v. *State*, 174 Tenn. 642, 130 S.W. 2d 99 (1939).

[100] *State* v. *Quin*, 217 Miss. 567, 64 So. 2d 711 (1953).

Misconduct in Office

A "general" offense of misconduct in office, like that under Article 246 of the Polish Criminal Code or that of Article 170 of the Russian Soviet Federal Socialist Republic Criminal Code, is not known to the American law (but, compare Paragraph 33-3 of the Illinois Criminal Code, 1961). Therefore it seems that the common law performs a significant function in this sphere for it contains a general doctrine that a federal, state or municipal officer, who fails in his duties, can be punished under the common law for an offense called malfeasance in office.[101] Besides other offenses the following have been indictable under the common law:

1. Negligence in office as, for instance, when an officer charged with legal custody of a prisoner, permits his charge to escape;[102]
2. Bribery not provided for by statute;[103]
3. Extortion by public officers in the taking of fees not allowed by law;[104]
4. Some forms of fraud in the election of public officers.[105]

Obstruction of Justice

Crimes against the administration of justice constituted a very broad area of the English common law.[106] Some of them still exist in the American common law and for want of another technical term are sometimes gathered together under the common denomination "obstruction of justice". The following acts have been considered as forms of obstruction of justice:

---

[101] *Commonwealth* v. *Miller*, 94 Pa. Super. 499 (1928); *State* v. *McFeeley*, 136 N.J.L. 102, 54 A. 2d 797 (1947).

[102] *U.S.* v. *Davis*, 71 F. Supp. 749 (1947).

[103] N. Kessler, op. cit., p. 422.

[104] Ibidem, p. 424.

[105] Ibid.

[106] Compare W. Blackstone, op. cit., Book IV, Chapters IX and X.

1. To wilfully hamper and obstruct a legitimate investigation of corruption in the administration of justice;[107]

2. Obstructing a sheriff proceeding to investigate a complaint;[108]

3. Attempts to influence jurors or a sheriff in making the selection of jurors for a trial;[109]

4. A juror voluntarily becoming intoxicated so as to disqualify himself for the discharge of duties;[110]

5. To wilfully mislead and defeat a court by presenting false and fraudulent depositions.[111]

A separate offense consists in withholding information that a felony was committed as a result of an amicable settlement or corrupt rewards (compounding of felony).[112]

The courts differ in their approach towards a crime known at common law as misprision of felony. Under the common law misprision of felony is a crime of neglect of duty consisting of either the failure to prevent a felony, or else of the failure to report the commission of a felony. Misprision of felony differs from compounding of felony in that it is an ordinary concealment of an offense by mere failure to report, while compounding of felony is a concealment in exchange for financial gains.[113]

In earlier American precedents misprision of felony was a crime.[114] But in the well-known opinion in *People* v. *Lefko-*

---

[107] *Commonwealth* v. *Evans*, 190 Pa. Super. 179 (1958).

[108] *Commonwealth* v. *Baltr*, 11 D. & C 2d 235 (Pa. 1957).

[109] N. Kessler, op. cit., p. 428.

[110] Ibid.

[111] *State* v. *Harton*, 47 R.I. 341, 133 A. 236 (1926).

[112] *Pearl Assurance Co.* v. *Nat. Agency*, 150 Pa. Super. 265 (1941).

[113] *Corpus Juris Secundum*, Brooklyn, N.Y., 1939, Vol. 15, p. 703.

[114] *State* v. *Wilson*, 80 Vt. 249, 67 A. 533 (1907): "The common law as to misprision of felony is a part of law of this state". Compare also Note, "Misprision...", op. cit., and the decisions cited therein. *State* v. *Wilson* is still cited as the decision authoritative for the State of Vermont.

witz[115] (1940) the Michigan Supreme Court categorically dismissed the charge of misprision of felony declaring the respective common law absolutely inapplicable in the State of Michigan.[116] The legal literature at large endorsed this opinion.[117] In recent years legislation and the courts tend to punish only an active concealment of a felony as accessorship after the fact.

It would be fair to say that misprision of felony as a common law crime cannot be held as entirely derogated but its status seems rather unsettled.

It should also be mentioned here that American courts enjoy a very broad power to punish for contempt of court; this subject cannot be dealt with here; because of its complex nature it requires more detailed and separate discussion. (See Chapter 6)

Offenses Against Property

The following offenses belong to this group:

1. To take money or other property from a person by the threat of criminal prosecution;[118]

---

[115] 293 N.W. 642 (Michigan 1940).

[116] Ibid. See also *Holland* v. *State*, supra note 47 at 2207 "We agree... that the crime of misprision of felony is wholly unsuited to American criminal law. While it may be desirable, even essential, that we encourage citizens to ›get involved‹ to help reduce crime, they ought not be adjudicated criminals themselves if they don't. The fear of such a consequence is a fear from which our traditional concepts of peace and quietude guarantee freedom. We cherish the right to mind our own business when our own best interests dictate. Accordingly, we hold that misprision of felony has not been adapted into, and is not a part of, Florida substantive law." Misprision of felony, as a common law misdemeanor, has been abolished in England by the *Criminal Law Act* 1967. Compare: J. C. Smith and B. Hogan, *Criminal Law*. 3rd ed., London, 1973, p. 597.

[117] See Note, "Misprision...", op. cit. See, however, a contrary opinion: G. Goldberg, Misprision of Felony — Shadow of Felony: An Old Concept in New Context. A.B.A.J., Vol. 52 (1966).

[118] *State* v. *Morrissey*, 11 N. J. Super. 198, 78 A. 2d 329 (1951).

2. Cheating affecting the public or a large number of individuals, in particular by the use of false weights and measures;[119] selling forged goods;[120]

3. Wilful damage of property;[121]

4. The receiving of more than lawful interest;[122]

Offenses Against Morality

Here we must examine a little more closely the offenses against good morals.

According to the traditional doctrine of the common law every act against public morals constituted a crime. This broad and flexible doctrine contained an essential restricting criterion, namely the public character of the act. Ordinarily the common law did not concern itself with immoral acts committed in the privacy of one's home.[123] Thus, under the common law neither fornication nor adultery was an offense *per se* if not committed in public.[124] The same act became an offense when committed publicly, e.g. in the public square or anywhere else in public.[125]

There were three exceptions to this general rule. Blasphemy, offensive acts with respect to dead bodies, and sodomy were indictable under the common law whether committed in private or in public.[126]

We can trace down several changes by comparing the present American criminal law concerning crimes against morals with the traditional concept of the common law.

---

[119] N. Kessler, op. cit., p. 423.

[120] *Commonwealth* v. *Hickey*, 2 Persons 317, 1 Clark 436 (1843).

[121] *Commonwealth* v. *Voodran*, Clark 202 (1847).

[122] N. Kessler, op. cit., p. 430.

[123] Compare: J. Thompson, "Common Law Crimes Against Public Morals", *Journal of Criminal Law, Criminology and Police Sciences*, 1958, Vol. 49, p. 351.

[124] *Anderson* v. *Commonwealth*, 16 Am. Dec. 776 (1827).

[125] *Carotti* v. *Mississippi*, 42 Miss. 334 (1868); *Redd* v. *State*, 7 Ga. App. 575, 67 SE 709 (1910).

[126] J. Thompson, op. cit., p. 352.

The majority of offenses against morals are now statutory offenses. The criterion drawing the line between acts punishable and unpunishable, that is, the "public" versus the "private" test, has been abandoned. Acts of private immorality which the common law did not punish are now made criminal by statute.[127]

The concept of blasphemy underwent essential change. According to Blackstone, the Christian religion was an integral part of the common law so, naturally, blasphemy was not limited to speaking contemptuously of the Christian religion but the negation of the foundations of Christianity, as for instance, the negation of the existence of God, constituted an offense.[128] The early American decisions basically accepted Blackstone's concept, treated the Christian religion as part of the law of the land and consequently punished any utterance against Christianity as blasphemy.[129]

However it was commonly accepted at a relatively early date that the mere denial of the truth of Christianity was not enough to constitute the offense of blasphemy because this was in violation of the constitutionally guaranteed freedom of religion. Increasingly, the mode and manner in which the words of criticism were spoken, and not merely the substance, became the designation of the offense. Blackstone's argument that Christianity was an integral part of the law of the land gradually lost its validity. It has been held that assailing Christianity

---

[127] Ibid. And so—according to J. Thompson—fornication constitutes a statutory offense in sixteen states; illicit cohabitation in twenty-one states, adultery in twenty-seven states. The trend of excessive penalization of sexual life, characteristic for American criminal law in general has been, in principle, sustained by some modern criminal codes. Compare, for instance, provisions punishing adultery in criminal codes of Connecticut (Para. 53a-81), Georgia (Para. 26-2009); Kansas (Para. 21-3507).

[128] W. Blackstone, op. cit., Book IV, p. 59.

[129] *Updegraph* v. *Commonwealth*, 11 S and R 394 (Pa. 1824); *American Jurisprudence*, op. cit., Vol. 12, pp. 375–376.

in a land where it is the belief of most of the people was an asocial act like breach of the peace.[130]

Under the modern law blasphemy is treated as an offense against the religious sentiments of the fellow-countrymen. Therefore even the most basic elements of the Christian faith can be attacked and negated provided that no profane language is used. In order to constitute the offense of blasphemy the accused must have been actuated by a wilful and malicious intent in exposing the principle of Christian religion to contempt and ridicule. This intent is excluded *ex definitione* if the anti-Christian argument was made in the course of a scholarly dispute.[131] In many states blasphemy is a statutory crime but the statutory wordings and their judicial construction make the offense in no way different from its common law concept.[132] In some states blasphemy has long remained only a common law offense (Alabama and Tennessee),[133] in others it has been both a statutory and a common law offense.[134]

Blasphemy charges are extremely rare in practice. The last reported conviction took place in 1921 in *State* v. *Mockus*, op. cit. The most recent attempt at prosecuting blasphemy failed. The Court of Special Appeals of Maryland found that: "Blasphemy statute making it a crime for any person to blaspheme or curse God, whether orally or in writing, or to write or utter profane words concerning Jesus Christ or the Trinity violated First Amendment prohibition of laws respecting an establishment of religion or prohibiting free exercise thereof".[135]

Also in the recent legal literature on the subject matter

---

[130] *People* v. *Ruggles*, 8 Johns 290, 5 Am. Dec. 335 (1811); *State* v. *Chandler*, 2 Del. 353 (1838).

[131] *American Jurisprudence*, op. cit., Vol. 12, pp. 375–376; Thompson, op. cit., p. 354.

[132] Note, "Blasphemy", *Columbia Law Review*, 1970, Vol. 70, p. 694. See also *Commonwealth* v. *Kneeland*, 37 Mass. (20 Pick) 206 (1838).

[133] *Goree* v. *State*, 71 Ala. 7 (1881); *State* v. *Steele*, 2 Heisk 135 (1810).

[134] *State* v. *Mockus*, 120 Me. 84, 113 A. 39, 14 A.L.R. 87 (1921).

[135] *State of Maryland* v. West, 263 A. 2d 602 (1970) (a headnote).

a position was taken that blasphemy laws violate the First Amendment of the Federal Constitution.[136]

At common law the offense called sodomy consisted of copulation *per anum* between man and man or man and woman.[137] In 1964 sodomy was reported an indictable offense in all states[138] except for Vermont but in comparison to the English law the definition of sodomy was expanded by American courts to include also the oral-genital copulation.[139]

It seems therefore that "unnatural" sexual intercourse is punished at present only by statutory law, hence in the United States it is not a common law offense.[140]

---

[136] "Blasphemy laws are one of the last remnants of an established church, and in protecting religions from verbal affront they significantly curtail the freedom of expression...", Note, "Blasphemy...", op. cit.

[137] *Regina* v. *Allen*, 169 Eng. Rep. 282; J. Thompson, op. cit., p. 352.

[138] St. John-Stevas, *Life, Death and the Law*, Cleveland–New York, 1964, p. 198 and passim. Also compare the statutes of the particular states—ibidem, p. 311 and passim.

[139] J. Thompson, op. cit., pp. 354–355. According to Thompson, *coitus oralis* is punishable as so-called crime against nature in 41 states, i.e., in all states except for Colorado, Kentucky, Michigan and New Jersey; probably also in South and North Carolina and in Rhode Island (the situation in the last three states is not quite clear in the absence of authoritative decision of the court). It is worth mentioning that in some cases married couples were convicted for *coitus oralis*. *Smith* v. *State*, 150 Ark 265, 234 SW 32 (1921); *Commonwealth* v. *Wiesner*, 21 Lehnigh L.J. 284 (Pa. 1945). *Coitus oralis* is also a crime in the states recently admitted to the Union, i.e. in Alaska and Hawaii, which are not listed by Thompson. Statutes punishing sodomy are used also to punish intercourse with animals. Female homosexuality is punishable only in some states (as, for instance, Arizona and Mississippi). The punishability of homosexuality creates enormous possibilities for blackmail, which in the United States rose to a grave problem. See *New York Times*, March 3, 1966, describing a huge blackmailing ring operating especially among homosexuals. Compare also new criminal codes of the states of Connecticut (Para. 53a-65(2)), Georgia (Para. 26-2002), Kansas (Para. 21-3505); providing for punishments for the crime of "sodomy".

[140] The interpretation of St. John-Stevas (erroneous, in my opinion) is different, see: op. cit., p. 199.

In spite of an immensely strong interference by legislation in the sphere of offenses against sexual morality there are some long remained common-law offenses, such as:

1. Indecent assault upon a person for the purpose of sexual liberties;[141]

2. Obscene or indecent public exhibitions or the public exhibition of obscene pictures;[142]

3. The public exposing of one's naked body;

4. The use of foul language uttered in public in a loud tone of voice;[143]

5. Any acts punishable under the general doctrine[144] of the common law according to which acts injurious to public morals constitute offenses.

Suicide

In England suicide originally fell under the jurisdiction of ecclesiastical courts.[145] By the middle of the 14th century it was settled that a person of sound mind who intentionally took his own life was guilty of felony punishable by the common courts with forfeiture of land or goods. The rule was consistently followed by the major legal common law authorities like Coke, Hale and Blackstone.[146]

Forfeiture was abolished in 1870[147] by an act of Parliament.

---

[141] J. P. Bishop, op. cit., Vol. II, pp. 27–28. See also *Commonwealth* v. *De Gerange*, 97 Pa. Super. 181, 186 (1929).

[142] *Commonwealth* v. *Blumenstein*, 395 Pa. 417 (1958).

[143] N. Kessler, op. cit., p. 429.

[144] *Barker* v. *Commonwealth*, 19 Pa. 412 (1852); N. Kessler, op. cit., p. 428.

[145] Commonwealth v. Mochan, 177 Pa. Super. 454 (1955). For details see Chapter 6.

[146] St. John-Stevas, op. cit., p. 233; Blackstone, Book IV, op. cit., p. 189.

[147] 33 and 34 Vic., Ch. 23, Para. 1 (1870).

Under the present English law, since 1961 when the Suicide Act was passed,[148] suicide and attempted suicide are not treated as criminal acts.[149]

The American common law did not follow the English prototype. Forfeiture, except during the life of the person attainted,[150] was abolished very early, and this fact accounted for the basic difference. At common law forfeiture was the only penalty which could be inflicted on a dead person; thus its abolition made suicide innocent.[151] In this situation in the United States suicide was always held not punishable.[152] Some states however treat suicide as an illegal or even criminal act but by its nature unpunishable.[153] There are some states which seem to share the former English point of view making suicide an unpunishable felony.[154] In the majority of states attempted suicide is not punishable either.[155] In those juris-

---

[148] 9 and 10 Eliz. 2, Ch. 60, Para. 1

[149] J. C. Smith and B. Hogan, op. cit., p. 238. See also: D. S. Markson, "The Punishment of Suicide: A Need for Change", *Villanova Law Review*, 1969, Vol. 14, p. 465f.

[150] Article III, Section 2 of the Constitution of the U.S., and 1 US Statutes at Large, 117, Act of April 30, 1790, Para. 24. Compare also J. P. Bishop, op. cit., Vol. 1, p. 718.

[151] J. P. Bishop, op. cit., Vol. I, p. 375.

[152] St. John-Stevas, op. cit., p. 241. From the judicial decisions compare, for instance, *Grace* v. *State*, 44 Texas Cr. R. 193, 69 SW 529 (1902); *Burnet* v. *People*, 204 Ill. 208, 68 NE 505 (1903). The sole exception to this rule was Massachusetts, where suicide was punished by "unholly internment in the common highway" (statutory rule of 1660). This practice was early abandoned and the rule itself finally repealed by the 1823 statute. D. S. Markson, op. cit., p. 465.

[153] *Penn. Mutual Life Ins. Co.* v. *Cobbs*, 23 Ala. App. 205, 123 So. 94 (1929); *State* v. *La Fayette*, 15 N.J. Misc. 115, 188 Atl. 918 (1937).

[154] For instance Massachusetts, North Carolina (St. John-Stevas, op. cit., p. 242).

[155] St. John-Stevas, op. cit., p. 242. The following states belong to this group: Indiana, Iowa, Illinois, Maine, Massachusetts, Ohio, Pennsylvania and Texas.

dictions where suicide has not been held a crime the unpunishability of attempted suicide follows as a logical consequence.[156] In those states where suicide is a common-law offense (although unpunishable) there are three different ways of treating attempted suicide:

1. In Massachusetts, where suicide is an unpunishable felony, attempted suicide is nonetheless not punishable, since statute law on attempted crimes does not include it;[157]

2. In other states where suicide is criminal but not punishable, attempted suicide is a common law misdemeanor;[158]

3. Finally, in a number of states attempted suicide is a separate statutory offense.[159]

Other Offenses

Various offenses were long known at common law under the common denomination of p u b l i c m i s c h i e f. These were acts which amounted to intentional and malicious mischief or the wilful injury to a person as, for instance, bodily injury

---

[156] See *Commonwealth* v. *Wright*, 26 Pa. County Ct. 666 (Pennsylvania, 1902).

[157] *Commonwealth* v. *Dennis*, 105 Mass. 162 (1870).

[158] *State* v. *Carney*, 69 N.J.L. 478, 55 A. 44 (1903); *State* v. *La Fayette*, 15 N.J. Misc. 115, 188 A. 918 (1937); *State* v. *Willis*, 255 N.C. 473; 121 SE 2d 854 (1961). In 1972, N. Jersey abolished attempted suicide as a crime (N.J.S.A. Sec. 2A: 85-S.1), and in 1973 the crime of suicide was abolished in N. Carolina (G.S.N.C. Sec. 14-17-1).

[159] Markson, op. cit., lists among these states Nevada, New Jersey, North Dakota, Oklahoma, S. Dakota, Washington. Such statutes typically provide that attempted suicide is punishable by imprisonment in the state penitentiary for a period up to 2 years, a fine up to 1000 dollars, or both. D. S. Markson, op. cit., p. 466.

For criticism of statutes punishing attempted suicide see: *Model Penal Code*, Tentative Draft Np. 9, Philadelphia, 1959, Comment to Sec. 201.5; D. S. Markson, op. cit., p. 470.

with intent to disfigure a person,[160] the malicious disturbance of the peace,[161] or wanton cruelty to animals.[162]

Offenses against the peace and harmony of family and community life may be gathered in a separate sub-category. A certain specific status (in contrast to an act) was punishable under the common law and thus was the status of "being a common scold". Liable to indictment were troublesome people who because of their habit of scolding and brawling become a nuisance to the neighborhood, village or hamlet.[163]

The common law also recognized various crimes such as disturbing the peace of a dwelling house, the secret breaking and entering of a house with intent to disturb the peace[164] or eavesdropping.[165]

---

[160] N. Kessler, op. cit., p. 426; *Commonwealth* v. *Musky*, 1 DR 561 (1892).

[161] *Commonwealth* v. *Cramer*, 2 Pearson 441 (1870). Note that when Pennsylvania adopted its present "Crimes Code" all such common law offenses were abolished.

[162] N. Kessler, op. cit., p. 426.

[163] *People* v. *Smith*, 17 Berks. 40 (Pa. 1924).

[164] N. Kessler, op. cit., p. 425, and p. 429.

[165] Ibidem, p. 424.

Chapter 5

CONSPIRACY DOCTRINE AS A FORM OF VIOLATION OF THE PRINCIPLE OF LEGALITY IN THE CRIMINAL LAW

In the Introduction we distinguished essentially two forms of the implementation of the common law of crimes: one requires a specific precedent in order to impose responsibility, the other requires a general doctrine only. Both violate the principle *nullum crimen sine lege*. The first however jeopardizes the rights of the individual to an incomparably lesser degree than the second.

Penalization based on precedent constitutes a violation of *nullum crimen sine lege* but it leaves the principle of legality only slightly abused. The punishable fact-situations it involves are defined and known; the accused has, at least in theory, the possibility to have knowledge of the illegality of his intended or actual act; retroactive punishment is prohibited. Making the decision the court follows criteria contained in the precedential opinion so that the danger of an arbitrary judgment is eliminated.[1]

---

[1] It should be noted here that the question of punishability on the grounds of a precedent has not been dealt with by American courts in a uniform way. Some courts held that in order to punish conduct as a common law crime it is necessary to find an English judicial precedent originating from the period preceding the reception date of the English common law. Compare, for example, *People* v. *Dolph*, 124 Colo. 553, 239 P. 2d 312 (1951); in this case the court could find no English precedent earlier than 1625 supporting indictment for criminal attempt, and in effect charges against the defendant were dismissed. 1607 was

The principle of legality is violated in its entirety under the second form of penalization, that is, when general doctrines are applied. In this case it is not only the monopoly of the statute (as the source of penalization) that is broken, but the most elementary principles of safety under law and of the predictability of punitive measures as well. The general doctrines outlined in loose and extremely flexible words leave ample room for the courts to make new laws and, to create appearances that "old rules are applied to new facts".

Penologists who advocate (both in literature and in the judiciary) that the principle of legality be adhered to in the criminal law, usually do not question the existence itself of the common law of crimes; they only suggest that precedents should be limited to those already known and that only such acts should be punished which were earlier adjudged criminal.

The supporters of the traditional trend want the courts to preserve the right to create new crimes—if such necessity arises. So, the whole argument revolves around the following question: does punishability under the common law mean that an offense may be punished only on the basis of a precedent, or—does it mean that it may also be punished in the absence of a precedent on the basis of a general doctrine?

Two prominent American criminal law writers assert that: "Most states accepting common law crimes, however, would agree that the common law can expand to meet a new situation hitherto unknown".[2]

At the contemporary American law and at the English law there are two doctrines which serve the court as a virtual spring board when it creates new offences: they are the doctrine of

held a reception date for the State. Comp. also *Aetna Gas Co.* v. *Commonwealth*, 106 Ky. 864, 51 SW 624 (1899).

On the other hand there are some American decisions to the effect that the test may also be satisfied by later English precedents or by precedents from other American jurisdictions. W. R. LaFave and A. W. Scott, op. cit., p. 66.

[2] W. R. LaFave and A. W. Scott, op. cit., p. 67.

conspiracy and contempt of court doctrine (more of the last one in Chapter 6).

Conspiracy comes to the forefront of judicial practice because of its scope, its frequency and the serious influence it exerts on the shaping of the principle of responsibility for conspiracy under the statutory criminal law.

The origins of conspiracy are buried deeply in the history of the common law. Originally conspiracy was an offense against the administration of justice. First during the seventeenth century the doctrine of conspiracy expanded in two directions: *primo*, it became a crime of "pure agreement" (i.e., without any required overt act), *secundo*, it embraced combinations to commit all crimes of whatever nature.[3]

During the eighteenth century the doctrine developed further and far-reaching consequences followed; it was then that it became a rule that an agreement to commit an act, not criminal *per se*, may also fall in the category of criminal conspiracy.[4] Since then the English common law created several

---

[3] Under medieval statutes (the first was passed by Edward I in 1285—13 Edw. I, c. 12, 1285) conspiracy consisted originally of a criminal confederacy to make a false accusation. The accusation and the subsequent acquittal of the falsely accused person were *conditiones sine qua non* of the crime of conspiracy. F. B. Sayre, "Criminal Conspiracy", *Harvard Law Review*, 1921, Vol. 35, pp. 395–398.

For elaboration on conspiracy in England see: R. S. Wright, *The Law of Criminal Conspiracies and Agreements*, Philadelphia, 1887 (the first English edition appeared in 1873) and G. Williams, *Criminal Law*, op. cit., p. 663 and passim.

[4] As early as the end of the XVIIth century the idea was born to also include under the doctrine of conspiracy such agreements which were made in order to commit non-criminal acts. These suggestions, made by some lawyers, were systematically refuted by the courts. F. B. Sayre, "Criminal Conspiracy", op. cit., p. 401; R. S. Wright, op. cit., pp. 31–33. Hawkins is believed to have laid down the first authoritative formulation of the modern doctrine of conspiracy. It is said, however, that he had based his proposition on misinterpretation of authorities (F. B. Sayre, "Criminal Conspiracy", op. cit., p. 402). The first edition of *Pleas of the Crown* by Hawkins appeared in 1716. Therein Hawkins said: "There can be no

categories of indictable agreements to commit acts which are not criminal or even not unlawful *per se*.[5] For many years the conspiracy doctrine was used to repress workers' organizations in England.[6]

The conspiracy doctrine met with wide recognition in the United States and in the other common law systems. It constitutes one of the peculiarities of these systems but is unknown to the Continental law.[7]

The early intervention of the criminal law, at the stage when the agreement to commit an act is made, is usually rationalized on two grounds:

---

doubt but that all confederacies whatsoever, wrongfully to prejudice a third person, are highly criminal at common law". W. Hawkins, *A Treatise on the Pleas of the Crown*, London, 1824, p. 446. Shortly after Hawkins' proposition was adopted by the courts, the first indictment for an agreement to commit a non-criminal act was made in the well-known *Rex* v. *Journeyman Tailors*, 8 Med. 320 (1721). In this case a group of migratory tailors were tried on an indictment of criminal conspiracy for having agreed together not to work except for higher wages. Significantly, the first indictment for an agreement to commit an act which was not illegal concerned an organization aiming at the defence of the class interests of workers.

[5] G. Williams specifies the following categories of conspiracy to commit non-criminal acts: conspiracy to defraud, conspiracy to commit other torts, conspiracy to commit or produce a breach of contract and conspiracy to produce public mischief. G. Williams, *Criminal Law*, op. cit., pp. 688–710. Compare also in Chapter 3 the remarks concerning decisions in: *Regina* v. *Newland*, *Board of Trade* v. *Owen*, *D.P.P.* v. *Shaw*, *R.* v. *Knuller* and *D.P.P.* v. *Withers* passed in the years 1953–1974.

[6] G. Williams, *Criminal Law*, op. cit., pp. 699–700. Compare also the following passage from Karl Marx: "Nicht zufrieden mit diesem Verrat, erlaubte die 'grosse liberale Partei' den im Dienst der herrshenden Klassen allzeit schweifwedelnden englischen Richtern, die verjährten Gesetze uber 'Konspirationen' wieder auszugraben und sie auf Arbeiterkoalitionen anzuwenden". K. Marx, *Das Kapital*, op. cit., Vol. I, p. 769.

[7] W. Wagner, "Conspiracy in Civil Law Countries", *Journal of Criminal Law, Criminology and Police Sciences*, 1951, Vol. 42, p. 171 and passim; T. Cyprian, J. Sawicki, *Prawo norymberskie* (The Nürnberg Law), Warszawa–Kraków, 1948, pp. 395–404.

When two or more make an agreement there is ample proof of their firm intent to accomplish a purpose: an agreement, once it is made, makes it more difficult for the parties to back out, and gives them a sense of power based on the strength of mutual cooperation; in other words, it increases the probability of accomplishing the end. It is not only that inherent in the collective action is the increased probability of committing the wrong itself but also the probability that its scope may be extended. These are the components (specific object rationale) projected toward the specific object of conspiracy.

There are other components which transcend the object and which are considered to be indicative of the general tendencies underlying the action of groups uniting to accomplish an unlawful purpose. It is highly probable, the argument runs, that a group of people united by a common criminal purpose may expand its activity and commit further offenses in or with no connection with the original purpose. Therefore the mere existence of such a group endangers the public order regardless of whether or not the original purpose of the agreement was accomplished (general danger rationale).

The enormous success of the doctrine of conspiracy in the United States rests chiefly on its flexibility; pliable as it is, it has become an effective weapon to deal with group crime. The elasticity of its substantive and procedural attributes has made it useful for the prosecution; it enables prosecution of agreements whose objects are legally neutral (sometimes not even involving civil sanctions) and, it introduces the principle of collective responsibility since each participant is liable for an act committed by any one of them.

In conspiracy cases the prosecution enjoys also several advantages of a procedural character which can put the defense in a difficult position or make the conviction easier. Some of the more important ones should only be mentioned here: a) co-conspirators may be tried in any district where an agreement was concluded or where any overt act in furtherance of a conspiracy was committed; this rule affords the prosecution an opportunity to select a district inconvenient to the defendant or one in which a jury may be more disposed to convict; b) hearsay, usually inadmissible in criminal trials is allowed under certain conditions; c) a co-conspirator's out-of-court confession may be factually used against co-defendants, although with somewhat "ritualistic" instruction to the jury to disregard it with respect to all defendants but a person who confessed; d) joint trial of co-conspirators limits to a certain degree individual rights of the defendants; e) "The greatest danger, however", as LaFave and Scott put it, "is that the probability of an individual defendant being convicted may be greatly enhanced by his association through joinder with the others".[8]

If we keep in mind the generally known fact that organized crime is a plague in the American scene, it becomes clear why and how conspiracy is useful and helpful for the prosecution.

Still the elasticity of the doctrine of conspiracy seriously jeopardizes individual rights, especially as it is used as a weapon against the non-conformist groups and political parties, as for example, the communists. This is why conspiracy is the most entangled, uncertain and most severely criticized branch of the criminal law both in the United States and in England.

Let us put aside the procedural problems which go beyond our considerations and consider the substantive aspects of conspiracy. As a common law crime, in the United States conspiracy is also a crime of a "pure agreement" with no overt act required. This is to say that it is accomplished the moment two or more have agreed that they will carry out a certain act in

---

[8] See generally: "Developments in the Law—Criminal Conspiracy", *Harvard Law Review*, 1959, Vol. 72, p. 975ff.; W. R. LaFave and A. W. Scott, op. cit., p. 456ff.; *Krulewitch* v. *United States*, 336 US 440 (1949). See also: M. T. Yawn, "Conspiracy", *Military Law Review*, 1971, Vol. 51.

Using co-conspirators out-of-court confessions in criminal trials was recently severely limited by the U.S. Supreme Court ruling in *Bruton* v. *United States*, 391 US 123 (1968).

the future. The object of conspiracy may be a criminal or a non-criminal act.[9]

As far as an criminal act *per se* is concerned conspiracy would simply mean that some forms of preparation are punishable, if not for the fact that ordinarily there is a separate sanction for the offense ultimately aimed at and another for the agreement itself. Furthermore the penalty for conspiracy is sometimes more severe than that for the act agreed upon.[10]

As for non-criminal objects of conspiracies this category is so broad and flexible that it defies definition.[11] It leaves ample room for the judge to extend the liability on a new type of conduct—by his own individual standards. All that can be said with certainty about this category of acts is, that had they been committed single-handedly they would not be punishable; they become punishable only when an agreement has been entered on by two or more persons.[12] The considerable number of convictions for conspiracy renders a basis for some kind of classification within this category. To put it in general terms such acts may be discerned which are unlawful (and hence roughly speaking may be a ground for a civil action), and such which do not even give rise to civil action but in view of some general criteria of an ethical and social nature are recognized as reprehensible by the court.[13]

---

[9] *American Jurisprudence*, op. cit., Vol. 16, p. 129. Compare also: *Truax* v. *Corrogan*, 257 US 312, 66 L.Ed. 254 (1921). Note, "The Conspiracy Dilemma: Prosecution of Group Crime or Protection of Individual Defendant", *Harvard Law Review*, 1948, Vol. 62, p. 277; F. B. Sayre, "Criminal Conspiracy", op. cit.

[10] This problem will be more comprehensively treated later on.

[11] This question is also elaborated on later.

[12] Note, "The Objects of Criminal Conspiracy", *Harvard Law Review*, 1955, Vol. 68, p. 1059; Note, "The Conspiracy Dilemma...", op. cit., p. 285; Clark and Marshall, op. cit., pp. 504–512.

[13] See: *State* v. *Buchanan*, 5 Harris and J. (Md.) 317, 9 Am. Dec. 534 (1821); Clark and Marshall, op. cit., pp. 504-512; "Developments", op. cit., p. 941.

Upon a closer analysis cases involving conspiracies to commit non-criminal acts may be classified as follows:

1. Conspiracy to defraud. Under this heading fall various deceitful practices, not punishable *per se*, calculated to lure an individual into conduct desired by the offender. Various illegal fraudulent dealings for the purpose of cheating an individual out of his property or otherwise involving property rights belong to this group as well.[14] Usually such dealings are not punishable *per se* because under the common law cheats not of public nature were seldom held indictable.[15] Deceitful practices which fall under the heading conspiracy to defraud are not limited to property rights but can also be directed against political and administrative authorities.[16]

2. Conspiracy to commit a civil wrong other than fraud. This class includes such acts as: to injure somebody's property,[17] to slander,[18] to obstruct a person from exercising his profession,[19] to ruin a tradesman's business,[20] to receive more than lawful interest,[21] etc.

---

[14] Compare Clark and Marshall, op. cit., pp. 508–509.

[15] Under the common law only, cheating by means of false scales and measures constituted a criminal act. From among the enormous number of cases of indictment for conspiracy to defraud in which the object of conspiracy was not a punishable offense the following are worth noting: to charge the public admission to spiritualistic seances where "materializing" spirits are also demonstrated (*People* v. *Filman*, 121 Michigan 187, 1899); to make a person intoxicated and then to cheat him at cards (*State* v. *Hounger*, 12 N.C. 357, 1827); to get goods from a merchant with no intention of paying him (*Commonwealth* v. *Eastman*, 1 Cash (Mass.) 189 (1848); to dispose of the property, in view of a bankruptcy, so as to harm the creditors (*U.S.* v. *Rabinowitch*, 238 US 78, 1915).

[16] *Hammerschmidt* v. *United States*, 265 US 182 (1924).

[17] *Wilson* v. *Commonwealth*, 96 Past. 56 (1880).

[18] Clark and Marshall, op. cit., pp. 509–510.

[19] *Crump* v. *Commonwealth*, 84 Va. 927, 6 S.E. 620 (1888); *State* v. *Huegin*, 110 Wis. 189, 85 N.W. 1046, 62 A.L.R. 700 (1901).

[20] Clark and Marshall, op. cit., p. 510.

[21] *Commonwealth* v. *Donoghue*, 250 Ky. 343, 63 SW 2d 3, 89 A.L.R. 819 (1933).

The quoted examples of conspiracy seem to lead to the conclusion that actually any agreement to commit an unlawful act, even a non-criminal one, may be punished as conspiracy.[22] Still some penalists hold that not every agreement of this kind constitutes a crime.[23]

3. Conspiracy to corrupt public morals. The object of conspiracy need not be a criminal or even unlawful act. An immoral object suffices to make a conspiracy indictable.[24] This doctrine is perhaps most tangible in *Smith* v. *People*[25] where three were charged with conspiracy to procure a young girl to have sexual intercourse with one of the defendants. The Illinois Supreme Court dismissed the defendant's appeal declaring: "Conspiracy to accomplish such an object as this (the destruction by seduction, of any young girl)... whether the means to be used be unlawful or criminal or not, is a crime..."[26]

4. Conspiracy to commit public mischief. Although the American courts do not use this term the American law contains a wide doctrine which corresponds to the English conspiracy to produce public mischief. Some writers call this class "conspiracy to do acts prejudicial to the public generally".[27] It

---

[22] Compare *Commonwealth* v. *Donoghue*, op. cit.

[23] *Commonwealth* v. *Donoghue*, op. cit., *Smith* v. *People*, 25 Ill. 17 (1860), p. 23. Nevertheless none of the decisions quoted here contain criteria to draw a distinction between illegal acts which may or may not constitute an object of punishable conspiracy. For an attempt to outline such a distinction see: *R.* v. *Kamara*, [1974] A.C. 104.

[24] Clark and Marshall, op. cit., p. 506; *State* v. *Buchanan*, 5 Harris and J. (Md.) 313, 9 Am. Dec. 534 (1821); *Smith* v. *People*, 25 Ill. 17 (1860); *State* v. *Continental Purchasing Co., Inc.*, 195 A. 827 (1938).

[25] *Smith* v. *People*, op. cit., pp. 17, 23, 24.

[26] Ibidem, p. 17. Conspiracy to commit an immoral act (according to Paragraph 8–12 of the Penal Code) does not constitute an offense at present in Illinois. From the more recent decisions see: *Baker* v. *Commonwealth*, 204 Ky. 420 (1924); *State* v. *Cheveneek*, 127 N.J.L. 476 (1941); compare also *Corpus Juris Secundum*, op. cit., Vol. 15, p. 1095.

[27] Clark and Marshall, op. cit., p. 511.

includes: a malicious scheme to drive a man out of his employment,[28] falsification of registration lists,[29] enforced collection of money by means of intimidation and oppression,[30] conducting a public auction with sham bidders,[31] a conspiracy to cause incorrect government crop reports to be issued,[32] a conspiracy to limit bids on public works,[33] and many others.

This brief review shows that common law conspiracy is so vague, loose and elastic that it practically defies definition.[34] This leads some American writers to advance the opinion that conspiracy permeates the criminal law with uncertainty and creates wide possibilities for the extension of responsibility to meet the exigencies of new cases.

The danger inherent in this practice is that it is under the shield of conspiracy that the doctrine is extended, and so to all appearances no new crime is prosecuted and punished.

Naturally the conspiracies of non-criminal objects cause most apprehension. In the first place, indicates Sayre, more often than not there are no rational reasons for a punitive action in such cases. The sum total of non-criminal elements may justify criminal sanction only when the effect of group action is socially more injurious than the effect of an individual act. However if the group action produces exactly the same

[28] *State* v. *McFeely*, 52 A. 2d 823 (1947).

[29] *Mitchell* v. *State*, 27 So. 2d 30 (1945).

[30] *State* v. *Continental Purchasing Co.*, 119 N.Y.L. 257, 195 A. 825 (1938).

[31] Clark and Marshall, op. cit., p. 511.

[32] *Haas* v. *Henkel*, 216 US 462, 30 S.Ct. 249 (1940).

[33] *People* v. *Strauch*, 240 Ill. 60, 130 Am.St.R. 255 (1909).

[34] Justice Jackson in *Krulewitch* v. *U.S.*, 336 US 440 (1949), at p. 445: "The modern crime of conspiracy is so vague that it almost defies definition". Compare also S. Glueck, L. Hall, op. cit., p. 359, and O. G. Judd, "Judge Learned Hand and the Criminal Law", *Harvard Law Review*, 1947, Vol. 60, p. 419. G. Williams renders a similar assessment of conspiracy in the English law, G. Williams, *Criminal Law*, op. cit., p. 711. See also judicial dicta to this effect in recent English cases e.g. *Regina* v. *Knuller*, op. cit.; *Regina* v. *Kamara*, op. cit.

effect as an individual act there is no reason for punishing conspiracy.[35]

In the American common law any act deemed either unlawful or immoral or injurious to public life, may become the object of criminal conspiracy; this creates, of course, unlimited possibilities for criminal repression. Under such a doctrine everyone who has made any kind of agreement may some day land in prison depending upon the personal predilections of the prosecutor and of the judge, who have general discretion to declare any object morally wrong or socially dangerous. In effect, under the shield of the old doctrine new crimes are made and new offenses punished which, at the time they were committed, were not illegal. Furthermore the constitutional separation of powers is violated once the court encroaches upon the legislature's province.[36] Sayre, with a great amount of reason, emphasized that conspiracy may become a very real danger especially during periods of reaction: a formidable weapon in the hands of the judges, it may be turned against associations which stir up the prejudices of the social class in which the judges have been bred.[37]

American decisions give ample proof that Sayre's misgivings were well justified. In the nineteenth century the conspiracy doctrine was used against organized labor;[38] also some

---

[35] F. B. Sayre, "Criminal Conspiracy", op. cit., pp. 410–411.

[36] Ibidem, pp. 412–413; Note, "The Objects...", op. cit., p. 1067; "Developments...", op. cit., pp. 941–942; W. R. LaFave and A. W. Scott, op. cit., p. 473.

[37] F. B. Sayre, "Criminal Conspiracy", op. cit., p. 413.

[38] In the case of the Philadelphia Cordwainers (1806) a group of shoemakers was tried on an indictment of criminal conspiracy to go on strike until their demands of higher wages were met. Similar cases were tried and workers sentenced in New York in the years 1809 and 1823 and in Philadelphia in 1815. *American Cases on Conspiracy*, Philadelphia, 1887, pp. 144–151. In *State* v. *Donaldson*, 32 N.L.J. 151 (1867) a group of workers was found guilty and sentenced for conspiracy to threaten their employer with work stoppage if he failed to fire persons named by the participants

more recent decisions in this field are most objectionable on legal and moral grounds.[39]

Let us review now briefly the development of conspiracy in the various states.

Almost all states which have not abrogated the common law of crimes have retained the common law of conspiracy.[40] In some of these the common law is the only general indicator marking the boundaries of the punishability of conspiracy;[41] in others, with broadly defined statutory provisions, it is generally accepted that where there is no explicit statute to the contrary the common law conspiracy has not been abrogated. Under

---

of the conspiracy. Also compare more recent: *State* v. *Dalton*, 134 Mo. App. 517, 114 S.W. 1132 (1908). It is worth noting that in *Commonwealth* v. *Carlisle*, Brightly's N.P. Rep. (Pa.) 36 (1821), the court dismissed an accusation of conspiracy against the owners of shoe-workshops who made an agreement to lower the workers' wages. It is clear that the doctrine of conspiracy was flexible enough as to achieve entirely different effects in analogous fact-situations. It should be emphasized, however, that in effect of the statutory regulation of labor relations the doctrine of conspiracy lost its meaning in the worker-employer relationship. Therefore the cases cited in this footnote have only a historical significance.

[39] *Winkler* v. *State*, 194 Md. 1 (1949); in this case the Maryland courts found the defendants guilty of conspiracy to organize a tennis match between white and black players. Compare also, "Developments...", op. cit., p. 941. There is no doubt that today such a conviction would be invalidated as unconstitutional.

Compare also: W. R. LaFave and A. W. Scott, op. cit., p. 455 and the literature cited therein; H. L. Packer, "The Conspiracy Weapon", in *Trials of the Resistance*, The New York Review, 1970; Ch. Goodell, *Political Prisoners in America*. New York, 1973, p. 208ff.

[40] Note, "The Objects...", op. cit., p. 1059.

[41] This is the case in the following states: Maryland, Massachusetts, North Carolina and Rhode Island. It is assumed that the new state—Alaska—can be also included in this group because the common law of crimes was not abolished there and the legislation does not contain a general definition of conspiracy.

these jurisdictions conspiracy is generally both a statutory and a common law offense.[42]

It becomes increasingly clear that the common law is still well established as an independent basis for responsibility for conspiracy. It should also be pointed out that the common law conspiracy exerted a strong influence on the legislation. Except for states which have no statury definition of conspiracy (although they have retained conspiracy as a common law offense), and with the exception of Ohio, and West Virginia which have no crime of conspiracy (except for several specified, narrow provisions), all other states have enacted some kind of a broad statutory definition. Several states[43] employ almost uniform provisions listing as objects of conspiracy: (a) the commission of any crime, (b) a false accusation and an act to cause to be arrested under false charges, (c) to maintain a suit

[42] Note, "The Objects...", op. cit., p. 1059; Paulsen and Kadish, op. cit., p. 503; *Berman* v. *Lecal*, 237 F. Supp. 767 (1964).

[43] Note, "The Objects...", op. cit., pp. 1057–1058, lists seventeen of them: Alabama, Arizona, California, Florida, Idaho, Minnesota, Mississippi, Missouri, Montana, Nevada, New Jersey, New York, North Dakota, Oklahoma, Tennessee, Utah and Washington. Since the Note was published two of these states enacted new criminal codes, which slightly changed this general picture. The new Minnesota Criminal Code limited the objects of criminal conspiracy to two categories of acts only: 1) to cause false arrest or prosecution, 2) to commit a crime (Para. 609.175). The revised New York Penal Law limited conspiracy objects only to acts criminal *per se*. Compare also Para. 182 of The Penal Code of The Territory of Guam containing a broad criminal conspiracy statute. The Missouri amended conspiracy statute (1973) no longer includes as the objects of conspiracy civil fraud and acts injurious to public health or morals. Missouri Annotated Statutes, Sec. 556. 120 (Vernon, 1949). The New Jersey conspiracy statute does not explicitely include as conspiracy objects or acts injurious to public health and public morals. New Jersey Statutes Annotated, Sec. 2A: 98-1. The new Florida Criminal Code of 1974 limits criminal conspiracy objects to "offenses", including also "violations" i.e. civil offenses. The Florida Criminal Code of 1974, Para. 7767.04 (3). The same solution is offered by the new Hawaii Penal Code of 1972. Comp. sections 107 and 520,

falsely, (d) any fraud punishable *per se* and any fraud not punishable *per se* in which civil damages may result, (e) any act injurious to public health or morals or which obstructs or perverts justice and the due administration of the laws.[44]

Of these several states, five also make criminal a conspiracy to hinder or prevent by force or intimidation the doing of a lawful act, or the engaging in a lawful occupation or employment.[45]

Four of these five[46] further include conspiracy to do an unlawful act, or a lawful act by unlawful means.[47] The entire statutory definition of conspiracy in one state was embodied in a section similar to the last one.[48]

Two other states, though using different words and forms, have broad provisions similar to those listed in footnote 43.[49]

Twenty-one states limit the statutory offense to conspiracy to commit a crime; in eight of these[50] only felonies are objects

---

[44] Compare, for instance, California Penal Code, Para. 182.

[45] Alabama, Mississippi, Nevada, North Dakota and Washington. As to Minnesota, Florida, and New York listed in the Note, see above footnote 43.

[46] The Penal Codes of Alabama, Mississippi, Nevada and Washington. Note, "The Objects...", op. cit., p. 1058.

[47] This is a literal adoption of Lord Denman's epigrammatic "definition" employed in *Rex* v. *Jones*, 110 Eng. Rep. 485, 487 (1832). The term "unlawful" has been traditionally construed in a broad way. See: *State* v. *Burnham*, 15 N.H. 396, 403 (1844).

[48] Pennsylvania. Note, "The Objects...", op. cit., p. 1058 Pennsylvania "Crimes Code" (1972) limited conspiracy objects to criminal acts only. The definition of criminal conspiracy in Connecticut was changed by its new Criminal Code (Para. 53a-48). At least two states: Michigan and South Carolina define a criminal conspiracy as an agreement to commit an offense or "an illegal act" or "a legal act in an illegal manner". That amounts to no more than a statutory form of Lord Denman's statement in Jones. Comp.: Michigan Penal Code, Sec. 750. 157a (Mich. Compiled Laws Ann., 1968); South Carolina Code of Laws, 1962, Sec. 16–550.

[49] Iowa and Maine. Kentucky, listed in the Note, does not belong here according to its new Criminal Code.

[50] Arkansas, Indiana, Nebraska, New Mexico, Texas, Vermont, Virginia. Note, "The Objects...", op. cit., p. 1058, ft. 15; New Mexico Criminal

of conspiracy (in Vermont only specified, more serious felonies), one state[51] also included most serious misdemeanors, and twelve others conspiracies to commit any crime.[52]

South Dakota, District of Columbia, and Minnesota solve the problem of conspiracy in a different way.[53]

Federal legislation limited the objects of conspiracies to committing another federal crime or to defrauding the United States.[54]

The above survey shows the formidable influence of the

Code, Para. 40A-28-2. Oregon listed by the Note no longer belongs to this category, see ft. 51, infra., whereas Wyoming omitted by the Note does (see Wyoming Statutes, 1957, Sec. 6–16.1. The new Virginia Criminal Code of 1975 includes also conspiracy to commit a trespass. Comp. Para. 18.2–23.

[51] See Oregon Criminal Code, 1971, sec. 59(1). (*Oregon Laws* 1971, Chapter 743).

[52] This includes: Colorado (Colorado Criminal Code, 1971, Sec. 40-1-20(1); *Colorado Revised Statutes,* 1963, 1971 Permanent Cumulative Supplement, Chapter 40); Connecticut (Connecticut Penal Code, Para. 53a-48(a)); Delaware (Del. Crim. Code, 1973, Secs. 511–513) Del. Code Ann; petty offenses are however excluded: Georgia (Criminal Code of Georgia, Para. 26-3201); Illinois (Illinois Criminal Code, Para. 8-2); Kansas (Kansas Criminal Code, Para. 21-3302); Kentucky (Kentucky Penal Code, Sec. 53(1)); Louisiana; New Hampshire (New Hampshire Criminal Code, Sec. 629:3); New York (New York Revised Penal Law, 1965, *Gilbert Criminal Law and Procedure,* 1971, Paragraphs 105.00-105.15); Pennsylvania (Crimes Code, Sec. 903, Purdon's Penna Statutes, Ann, 1972); Wisconsin (Wisconsin Criminal Code, Sec. 939.31).

[53] South Dakota and District of Columbia have, statutory definitions similar to the federal law. See, Note, "The Objects...", op. cit., p. 1058, ft. 15. For the provisions of the new Minnesota Criminal Code, see ft. 43 in this chapter.

[54] U.S.C., Title 18, Para. 371. It should be stressed, however, that beside the broad and general definitions of conspiracy in the common law and in the statutes (the most typical of them were already discussed) there is a great number of special federal and state statutes which enact the punishability of conspiracy. See also Para. 1004 of A Proposed New Federal Criminal Code which restricts conspiracy objects to the conduct criminal *per se.*

common law on the statutory definition of conspiracy. The majority of statutes adopted the basic idea of the common law that a conspiracy to do a non-criminal act may be indictable. Furthermore, the majority of the statutes simply repeat the common-law doctrine either specifying, in broad and vague terms, the typical objects of conspiracy known under the common law, or retaining the loose formula about unlawful purposes and unlawful means.[55] It is doubtful whether such statutes implement the principle *nullum crimen sine lege* with respect to conspiracy even under jurisdictions where the common law of crimes is not in force.[56] Rather, the essence of the common law doctrine is retained under the disguise of a statute since legally neutral acts, phrased by the legislator in loose and vague terms, still remain the objects of conspiracy. What is provided in effect is some kind of a general instruction to punish acts directed against some legal objectives, but the decision, as to which acts are and which are not punishable, remains in the hands of the prosecutor, the judge and the jury. Consequently, under the rule of such a statute, the courts retain no less authority than under the common law, to make new offenses under the shield of conspiracy. Nonetheless the statutory form of the old common-law doctrine is not without meaning as far as the principle of legality is concerned because of the constitutional protection against vague criminal legislation (compare Chapter 2).[57]

---

[55] Compare ft. 47.

[56] Note, "Common Law Conspiracy as Weapon...", op. cit., p. 941. Compare also Note, "The Objects...", op. cit., p. 1067; *American Jurisprudence*, op. cit. Vol. 21, p. 91.

[57] The void for vagueness doctrine is, in principle, also applicable to common law crimes. However in practice invalidation of a conviction for a common law crime on the ground of vagueness is extremely rare. Comp. *Ashton* v. *Kentucky*, 384 US 195 (1966); W. R. LaFave and A. W. Scott, op. cit., p. 84.

Some statutes introduce significant modifications to the common law definition. These modifications consist mostly in *a sui generis* game with the code fixed by the common law and they focus upon maneuvering the two following elements of crime:

1. One of them is the objects of conspiracies known to the common law. Handled accordingly some objects can be adopted while others can be eliminated. The most consistent legislations limit the objects to acts criminal *per se*. In a jurisdiction where the common law may not be an independent basis of responsibility such a statute usually leaves no room for the court to make new offenses under the shield of conspiracy. Modern codifications usually limit the objects of conspiracy by this method.[58]

The leading case, in which typical conspiracy statute was held void for vagueness is *Musser* v. *Utah*, 333 US 95 (1948) and *State* v. *Musser*, 118 Utah 537, 223 P2d 193 (1950). "However—as LaFave and Scott pointed out—most state courts have upheld their rather broad conspiracy statutes in the face of similar due process objections. Statutes making combinations "to pervert justice or the due administration of the laws" have been upheld because such acts were defined at common law and in the statutes. Similarly, a statute prohibiting conspiracies to injure trade or commerce has been held not to be vague, and the same result has been reached as to legislation prescribing conspiracies to perform any act injurious to the public health, morals, or to obstruct justice.... Notwithstanding such decisions, it is... a fair conclusion that most such provisions fail to provide a sufficiently definite standard of conduct to have any place in a penal code." W. R. LaFave and A. W. Scott, op. cit., pp. 473–474.

[58] Compare provisions of the new criminal codes listed in the footnote 52, supra, and Sec. 1004 of A Proposed New Federal Criminal Code. See also Sec. 5.03 (1) of the Model Penal Code which evidently influenced modern state codifications. Compare also: W. R. LaFave and A. W. Scott, op. cit., p. 473; N. R. Sobel, "The Anticipatory Offenses in the New Penal Law: Solicitation, Conspiracy, Attempt and Facilitation", *Brooklyn Law Review*, 1966, Vol. 32, p. 263; R. G. Lawson, "Criminal Law Revision in Kentucky: Part 2—Inchoate Crimes", *Kentucky Law Journal*, 1970, Vol. 58, pp. 711–714. Traditionally broad definitions of conspiracy objects (comp. ft. 43) have been, however, retained by the new criminal codes

It should be emphasized that legal theorists have long since suggested the restriction of the objects of conspiracy to acts punishable *per se*.[59]

Some statutes seriously reduce the catalogue of the objects of the conspiratorial agreement, however, they still retain the principle that an innocent act may become punishable as an object of conspiracy.[60]

2. The second element rests on the introduction of another component of the crime beside the agreement itself. This is an act to effect the purpose agreed upon, known as an overt act. It is immaterial whether or not the overt act accomplished the end but it must pursue the end. This condition is met and the participants held responsible for conspiracy, as soon as at least one of them has done anything to carry out the design.[61]

Evaluating the doctrine of conspiracy from the vantage point of the principle of legality it becomes obvious that the least objectionable form of conspiracy is that which requires an object criminal *per se*. But even this form tends to expand and it shows a strong tendency to increase the scope of criminal responsibility. This is manifested on the one hand in the

---

of North Dakota, Montana and Utah. For the different position taken by the new Minnesota Criminal Code, see ft. 43 in this chapter. It should be also noted that the Proposed Criminal Code of Massachusetts (Chapter 263 Para. 48(a) (2)) provides for broadly worded non-criminal objects of criminal conspiracy.

[59] F. B. Sayre, "Criminal Conspiracy", op. cit., pp. 412–413 and 416; comp. also Note, "The Conspiracy Dilemma...", op. cit., p. 285.

[60] U.S.C., Title 18, Para. 371; the Florida Criminal Code, supra ft. 43.

[61] The federal statute as well as the majority of modern criminal codes (at least thirteen out of twenty-five) contains a requirement of an "overt act". The Model Penal Code (Para. 5.03(5)) excepts conspiracies to commit felonies of the first and second degree from the overt act requirement. The law of ten other states and the District of Columbia also requires an overt act as an element of criminal conspiracy. "The function of the overt act in a conspiracy prosecution is simply to manifest that conspiracy is at work." *Yates* v. *United States*, 354 US 298, 334 (1957).

separate indictability of the conspiracy and of its criminal object and, on the other, in the specific form of collective responsibility. Both questions must be separately examined.

What is the relationship of this form of conspiracy and its criminal object and, in particular, will the doer of the wrongful act be charged with one or with two crimes?

Under an old rule of English common law a lesser offense was absorbed into the greater. Thus, if conspiracy is a crime of a lesser degree than the completed offense, the former is "absorbed" by the latter (merger doctrine).[62] This doctrine was never very popular in the United States.[63] At one time some jurisdictions applied the merger doctrine both to statutory and common law offenses.[64] The merger doctrine was gradually abandoned however and conspiracy punished as a separate offense.

Some modern American codifications which tend to narrow the doctrine of conspiracy and to reduce it to the inchoate crime, exclude the responsibility for conspiracy once the conspirator is indicted for the object-crime.[65] They usually follow, in this respect, a pattern established by the Model Penal Code.[66]

There is one generally recognized exception to the rule of punishing conspiracy and its criminal objects separately; this is when the substantive offense is so defined that its commission is virtually impossible without some kind of agreement between two or more persons. Then the punishment for conspiracy is as if included in the penalty for the substantive offense.

---

[62] *People* v. *Tavormino*, 177 NE 317, 257 N.Y. 84 (1931); "Developments...", op. cit., p. 968.

[63] J. P. Bishop, op. cit., Vol. I, p. 580; *Pinkerton* v. *United States*, 328 US 640 (1946); See also *Callanan* v. *United States*, 364 US 587 (1961) and "Developments...", op. cit., pp. 968–969.

[64] *Corpus Juris Secundum*, op. cit., Vol. 15, p. 1108.

[65] Illinois Criminal Code, Para. 8–5; Oregon Criminal Code, Sec. 64(3).

[66] Comp. Section 5.04(3) in connection with Sec. 1.07.

This is the so-called Wharton rule.[67] Furthermore, the participant necessary to accomplish the criminal object of the agreement is not liable for conspiracy if he is a member of a legislatively protected class.[68]

Some writers suggest that sentences should be cumulative only if the combination poses a serious danger of further unlawful activity, that is, when the danger generated by conspiracy is greater than that inherent in the specific offense itself.[69]

The separation of conspiracy from a substantive offense (its object) also emerges in the sphere of criminal sanction and, sometimes, with rather absurd overtones. Granted that under the American common law and under typical statutes conspiracy constitutes a separate offense, independent from its criminal object, it is nevertheless a quite specific offense whose gravity depends on the criminal act which in each concrete case was the purpose of the agreement. It is clear to every reasonable person that a conspiracy to commit murder carries a different weight than a conspiracy to hunt or fish in a closed season. Unfortunately, however, no such distinction is made by the common law; whatever the substantive offense, conspiracy is still a misdemeanor punishable with fine or imprisonment or both at the discretion of the court.[70]

Several statutes also have treated conspiracy in this uniform way. Regardless of its quality or form the punishment remains the

---

[67] Dueling, bigamy, adultery, and incest are considered as classical examples of the application of the Wharton rule. "Developments...", op. cit., pp. 954–955. In practice the Wharton rule is also applied in cases when the number of offenders does not follow *ex definitione* from the nature of the offense. Ibid., p. 955. Comp. also new Kentucky Penal Code, Sec. 54(4).

[68] *Gebardi* v. *U.S.*, 287 US 112 (1932). In this case a woman was transported from one state to another for purposes of prostitution. A participant necessary to accomplish the crime can still be held responsible if he or she was actively participating in the achievement of the goal. *U.S.* v. *Holte*, 236 U.S. 140 (1915).

[69] "Developments...", op. cit., p. 685.

[70] G. Williams, *Criminal Law*, op. cit., p. 685.

same. In effect paradoxical sentences were imposed: in a case of conspiracy to commit a crime punishable by a maximum of twelve months detention the defendant was sentenced to seven years' imprisonment;[71] a conspiracy to commit a misdemeanor was punished like a felony;[72] in a conspiracy to commit a crime punishable by a 20 dollars fine the defendant was sentenced to three to five years of prison.[73] It seems that in actual fact this is an indirect way of violating the principle *nulla poena sine lege.*

In order to prevent such situations as described above some statutes distinguish various types of conspiracies and consequently make different types of criminal sanctions, as is the case of the federal statute and several new state criminal codes.[74]

Before we proceed to the problem of collective responsibility for complicity on the ground of conspiratorial relationship we propose to examine briefly the subjective side of conspiracy. It seems that because of the looseness and pliability of the

---

[71] *Scarlet* v. *State*, 201 Md. 310 (1953). Defendant Scarlet, a Negro from Baltimore, was originally indicted for the violation of the so-called lottery law and subsequently released for lack of evidence. Some time later he was accused for conspiracy to commit an act which was included in the earlier non-guilty verdict. This time, however, Scarlet was pronounced guilty and sentenced to 7 years imprisonment and a $2000 fine, on grounds of a statute declaring conspiracy, an offense punishable by a maximum imprisonment of ten years and by a fine of $2000. The defendant appealed arguing an abuse of discretion by the sentencing judge. The court of appeals upheld the sentence, dismissed the defendant's argument concerning the abuse of discretional power from the part of the court of the first instance, and emphasized, furthermore, that in view of the upper limit of the sanction, the punishment was not excessive.

[72] *People* v. *Cansley*, 299 Mich. 340 (1941). The court substantiated its thesis with a long list of precedents from many different states.

[73] *State* v. *Collidge*, 106 Vt. 183 (1934).

[74] Compare, USC Title 18, Section 371(2); see also, for example: Wisconsin Criminal Code, Sec. 939.31; New York Penal Law, Paragraphs 105.00-105.15; New Hampshire Criminal Code, Sec. 629:3.IV.

doctrine of conspiracy its subjective side (*mens rea*) would be its most stable element. There never was any doubt under the American law that the essential element of conspiracy is *mens rea.*[75] Moreover the analysis of the relevant judicial decisions leads to the conclusion that in order to convict for conspiracy it is necessary to prove such a form of *mens rea* which corresponds at least with the Continental *dolus directus.*[76] We say "at least" for a number of decisions, particularly recent ones, require something even more than *dolus directus.* These decisions leave no doubt that the participant joined the conspiracy in order to commit a crime or, in a conspiracy with a non-criminal object, that he joined it with some other specific purpose in mind, as for instance, in order to injure public life or to molest a person in connection with his professional occupation. It was frequently pointed out both in judicial decisions and in literature that the mere knowledge of the unlawful design is not in itself sufficient. It must be established that there was a unity of intent and a unity of purpose on the part of the participants of conspiracy.[77]

Case law does not treat this question in a uniform way. Besides decisions stressing the necessity of the specific purpose[78] there are decisions founded on nothing but mere intention.[79]

---

[75] A. J. Harno, "Intent in Criminal Conspiracy", *University of Pennsylvania Law Review*, 1941, Vol. 89, p. 634.

[76] A. J. Harno, op. cit., p. 635.

[77] Ibidem, p. 633, p. 637 and p. 643; H. Wechsler, W. K. Jones, H. L. Korn, "The Treatment of Inchoate Crimes in the Model Penal Code of the American Law Institute", *Columbia Law Review*, 1961, Vol. 61, p. 968.

[78] A well-known decision representative for this type was pronounced by the Federal Court of Appeals (Second Circuit) in *U.S.* v. *Falcone*, 109 F. 2d 579 (1940). From the more recent decisions see, among others, *People* v. *Bernhardt*, 222 Cal. App. 2d 622 (1963).

[79] *Quirk* v. *U.S.*, 250 F. 2d 909 (1958). This tendency comes through also in the decision in *Direct Sales Co.* v. *U.S.*, 319 US 703 (1943).

It seems, however, that it is the first trend which is predominant.[80]

Conspiracy requires a specific purpose regardless of whether or not the specific purpose is the necessary element in the crime which is an object of conspiracy.

The singular problem of the "subjectivity" of conspiracy is also reflected in the common found requirement that even those elements of the contemplated crime which constitute the objective conditions of responsibility for the substantive crime itself must be covered by intent if responsibility for conspiracy should lie.[81]

Finally it is worth noting that some jurisdictions allow ignorance of the unlawfulness of the crime as a defense to prosecution for conspiracy in cases of conspiracy to commit *mala prohibita* (wrongs merely because they are prohibited and punished by statute).[82]

Let us look now at the peculiar institution called the vicarious liability of parties to a conspiracy.

If several persons conspire to commit a crime, each is re-

---

[80] *Seales* v. *United States*, 81 S.Ct. 1469 (1961). As W. R. LaFave and A. W. Scott correctly pointed out: "... it may generally be said that the mental state required is an intent to achieve a result which is criminal or which though non criminal is nonetheless covered by the law of conspiracy". W. R. LaFave and A. W. Scott, op. cit., p. 465. Several modern state criminal codes included an "intent" or "purpose" to commit a crime as an essential element of the crime of conspiracy. Compare for example New Hampshire Criminal Code, Sec. 629:3.1: "A person is guilty of conspiracy if, with a purpose that a crime defined by statute be committed, he agrees with one or more persons to commit or cause the commission of such crime...". The same will be true for criminal codes of Connecticut, Illinois, Louisiana, New Mexico, New York and Wisconsin. On the other hand some new criminal codes seem not to require specific intent; see, for example, criminal codes of Georgia (Para. 26-3201) and Kansas (Para. 21-3302).

[81] See *Abott* v. *U.S.*, 239 F. 2d 310 (1956). But see a contrary opinion in *United States* v. *Feola*, 95 Sp. Ct. 1255 (1975).

[82] *People* v. *Powell*, 63 N.Y. 88 (1875).

sponsible as an accessory for an act committed by any one of them. What is the nature of responsibility for an act other than the object of the conspiracy agreed upon, merely committed by one in connection with the common purpose? In this situation each participant is responsible for the act done by one of the conspirators, provided it was done in the process of executing the agreement and was "reasonably foreseeable".

The leading authority for this proposition is the U.S. Supreme Court decision in *Pinkerton* v. *United States* (328 US 640, 1946). The Pinkerton doctrine although never generally accepted has been adopted in several jurisdictions by legislation and by judicial decisions.[83]

What we are dealing with here is an extremely broad form of collective responsibility—sometimes, a responsibility where no actual guilt is involved. This is what happens when the medieval principle *versanti in re illicita*, which is still effective in the American law (suffice it to mention the commonly used felony-murder rule and misdemeanor manslaughter rule), is driven to its extreme.

The American literature points out that these rules have introduced in an extra-legislative way a new, considerably broader—both in respect to intent and causality—crime of complicity, regardless of the fact that the forms of complicity are regulated by statute both under federal and many state legal systems.[84] Therefore, leaving aside the specifics of the Pinkerton doctrine (and its counterparts in state law) it is submitted that this doctrine is a relatively new form of using the conspiracy doctrine to violate the principle *nullum crimen sine lege*.

It should be noted, however, that the opposition to Pinkerton doctrine has grown significantly in recent years.[85] The

[83] Among others compare *Anderson* v. *Superior Court*, 78 Cal. App. 2d 22 (1947), *People* v. *Cohen*, 68 N.Y.2d 140 (1947); Minnesota Criminal Code, Para. 609.05; Wisconsin Criminal Code, Para. 939.05(1) (c).

[84] "Developments...", op. cit., p. 995.

[85] W. R. LaFave and A. W. Scott, op. cit., p. 515.

Model Penal Code has rejected this doctrine[86] and was followed by the draftsmen of the proposed federal criminal code.[87]

[86] *Model Penal Code*, Tentative Draft No. 1, Philadelphia, 1953, Comment to Para. 2.04(3): "The most important point at which the draft diverges from the language of the courts is that it does not make "conspiracy" as such a basis of complicity in substantive offenses committed in furtherance of its aims" (pp. 20–21).

[87] A Proposed New Federal Criminal Code, Comment to Para. 401. As to the rejection of the Pinkerton doctrine by recent state decisions comp. *Commonwealth* v. *Perry*, 357 Mass. 149, 256 NE 2d 745 (1970).

Chapter 6

THE COMMON LAW MISDEMEANOR DOCTRINE AND CONTEMPT OF COURT

THE COMMON LAW MISDEMEANOR DOCTRINE

The English common law misdemeanor doctrine was received in the United States as it stands in Blackstone's *Commentaries*. The *Commentaries* played an extremely significant role in the reception of the English law in the United States.[1]

Blackstone's broad definition of crime, which holds that any act injurious to public life constitutes a crime, and distinguishes civil injury (as that done to individuals),[2] is firmly entrenched in the American law.[3] The American, like the English common law misdemeanor doctrine, is besides conspiracy, a particularly drastic means of violating the principle *nullum crimen sine lege*. It creates in theory unlimited possibilities of penalization for it allows the courts to declare criminal any act injurious to public order, health or morality and any act obstructing justice. There is a marked decrease on the part of the courts, especially in recent years, in exercising this power. In the wake of a gradual abrogation of the common

[1] R. Pound, *Criminal Justice in America*, New York, 1930, pp. 106–112; R. David and J. Brierly, *Major Legal Systems in the World Today*, London, 1968, p. 279.

[2] W. Blackstone, op. cit., Vol. II, Book IV, pp. 3–4.

[3] Blackstone's doctrine was frequently quoted both by American authors and judicial decisions. Compare J. P. Bishop, op. cit., Vol. I, p. 153 and p. 155 and the decisions cited therein. For an early formulation of the doctrine in the U.S. see *Respublica* v. *Teischer*, 1 Dall. 335 (1788).

law as an independent basis of responsibility the hold of the doctrine naturally shrinks; this happened, recently (1973), after Pennsylvania, whose courts strongly supported the doctrine, abolished the common law of crimes. The question whether a concrete precedent or just a general doctrine is needed to penalize a common law offense is still highly controversial.

The advocates of the common law misdemeanor doctrine are backed above all by the tradition embodied in the old cases and literature.[4] They advance the following arguments[5] in support of the doctrine:

1. Lacunae must appear even in the best code. It is in the interest of public safety that they be precluded by the general principles of the common law. Granted that there could be complete legislation it is impossible that it could anticipate the inventiveness of the modern criminal mind which needs an immediate social reaction; there would be no time then for the legislation to be formally amended. This is where the common law misdemeanor doctrine proves irreplaceable. Its main value is its elasticity and ability to adjust to new, unforeseeable situations.[6]

---

[4] Compare the English decisions and literature discussed in Chapter 3, and: J. P. Bishop, op. cit., Vol. I, p. 15; *Commonwealth* v. *Taylor*, 5 Binn 277 (Pa. 1812); *Respublica* v. *Teischer*, 1 Dallas 335 (1788); *Commonwealth* v. *McHale*, 97 Pa. 397, 408 (1881).

[5] Arguments in the defense of the doctrine are contained in works quoted in further footnotes. It does not follow, however, that all these authors advocate the law-making power of the courts. In actual fact, it is only F. Kaftan, from among the quoted authors, who explicitly supports the doctrine; S. Kline seems to lean toward this view; the remaining authors discuss the pros and cons, and either oppose the idea or do not take a direct stand.

[6] F. Kaftan, "Judicial Power to Find Common Law Crimes in Wisconsin", *Wisconsin Law Review*, 1939, pp. 307–309; Note, "Common Law Crimes in the United States", op. cit., p. 1336; S. Kline, W. H. Hitchler, "The Common Law Misdemeanours Doctrine", *Dickinson Law Review*, 1955, Vol. 59, p. 350.

2. The "crime-creating" doctrine does not abuse the principles of fair play for it is infrequently resorted to and only in cases when the moral norms are violated. Hence the punishment is consonant with the society's image of justice.[7]

Supporting arguments are that the doctrine is used where the offense is minor and the penalty slight—not sufficiently important to merit legislative treatment. In this situation a certain departure from the principle of legality is justified or at least should be tolerated.[8]

3. The right of the court to punish new types of acts has a deterrent effect on the potential wrongdoer who will weigh his chances before trespassing the "borderline" between acts punishable and unpunishable but socially injurious.[9]

4. The uncertainty resulting from the court's law-making function is not greater than that resulting in the interpretation of statutes. The argument that this doctrine has an *ex post facto* effect is inaccurate insofar as it may be applied to every bit of the common law which in the nature of things is retroactive.[10]

The opponents of the doctrine present distinctively stronger arguments. They challenge the doctrine on the grounds of both legality and effectiveness. Above all they question the rationality of the adverse criticism. They hold groundless the argument of the social utility of the doctrine as one effectively precluding the lacunae in statutory and case law. Experience shows, they argue, that criminal justice administration rarely suffers from the lack of laws, rather from lack of discovery of criminal conduct, lack of detection, lack of complaint and inefficiency in prosecution. By comparison with these common deficiencies a gap in the penal law is an exceptional event.[11]

---

[7] F. Kaftan, op. cit., pp. 307–309; Thompson, op. cit., p. 355.

[8] J. Hall, *General Principles...*, op. cit., pp. 52–54.

[9] S. Kline, W. H. Hitchler, op. cit., p. 350.

[10] Ibidem.

[11] J. Hall, *General Principles...*, op. cit., pp. 50–51.

Apart from this the adaptability of the common law is limited. It proved to be inadequate and unable to cope with the complexities of the new types of crime in the modern industrialized society.[12] Besides, the modern techniques of legislative procedure make it possible to react immediately with a new statute in response to new socially injurious acts.[13] The restriction of allowing the courts to extend punishability to include "only" misdemeanors is purely illusory since this category of offenses is the most common one.[14] There is ground for some doubts as to whether the power granted to the court will be used with sufficient caution and restraint.[15]

The following basic arguments may be presented against the "crime-creating" power of the courts.

1. At the foundation of the rule of law lies the safety and predictability of the judicial process. The law should be known and certain—this is the fundamental principle of the criminal law recognized by the whole civilized world. The formula *nullum crimen sine lege* is nothing else but the expression of fair play, the protection of the individual against unwarranted repression.

The common law misdemeanor doctrine coupled with that of conspiracy, allowing the punishment of acts, which were not illegal at the time they were committed, puts the accused in a position of dependency on the individual standards, pre-

---

[12] Note, "Common Law Crimes in the United States...", op. cit., p. 1336.

[13] Thompson, op. cit., p. 355. As an example Thompson cites five statutes drafted by Indiana, Illinois, Delaware, Mississippi and Tennessee, which hold punishable an act for which a Pennsylvania court convicted the defendant Mochan in *Commonwealth* v. *Mochan* on the grounds of the general doctrine (the case is discussed later in this chapter).

[14] Note, "Common Law Crimes...", op. cit., p. 1336.

[15] J. Thompson, op. cit., p. 355; S. Kline, W. H. Hitchler, op. cit., pp. 349–350. Compare below: the critical assessment of the decision in *Commonwealth* v. *Mochan*.

dilections and biases of the judge.[16] The common law misdemeanor doctrine is apparently very similar to analogy in criminal law, a rather ill-famed method.[17]

2. The U.S. Constitution provides that there should be no *ex post facto* legislation.[18] Although this does not apply directly to the judicial law-making[19] one hardly can escape the conclusion that judicial *ex post facto* penalization is analogous to a retroactive statute.[20]

3. It is the legislator's and not the judge's authority to make new laws. Since the application of the doctrine means that the legislator's province has been encroached by the judiciary[21] it follows that the doctrine is unconstitutional.

4. There is a constitutional guarantee in the American law of safety under the law, predictability of judicial procedure and certainty of what is legal and what is punishable. Against the background of the due process clauses (the Fifth and the Fourteenth Amendments)[22] the Supreme Court of the United States and the state courts have enforced the principle that the statutory definition of crimes must be so phrased that people of common intelligence are left with no doubt as to what

---

[16] Note, "Common Law Crimes...", op. cit., S. Kline, W. H. Hitchler, op. cit., pp. 349–350; Thompson, op. cit., p. 355; J. Hall, op. cit., p. 51; Sayre, "Criminal Conspiracy", op. cit., pp. 412–413. See also the literature cited by J. Brownlie and D. G. T. Williams in "Judicial Legislation in Criminal Law", *Canadian Bar Review*, 1964, Vol. 42, p. 579, ft. 110.

[17] Note, "The Use of Analogy in Criminal Law", *Columbia Law Review*, 1947, Vol. 47, p. 624.

[18] The Constitution of the United States, Article I, Sections 9 and 10.

[19] Compare: Chapter 1.

[20] J. Thompson, op. cit., p. 355; S. Kline, W. H. Hitchler, op. cit., pp. 349–350.

[21] Note, "Acts not Formerly Criminal at Common Law Held Punishable as Injurious to Public Morals", *University of Pennsylvania Law Review*, 1955, Vol. 103, p. 1094; W. Jentes, "Criminal Law—Immoral Practices and Conduct", *Michigan Law Review*, 1956, Vol. 64, p. 420; S. Kline, W. H. Hitchler, op. cit., p. 350.

[22] The doctrine void for vagueness is elaborated in Chapter 2.

is permitted or prohibited under the law. The common law misdemeanor doctrine employs equally vague phrases as statutes invalidated on grounds of vagueness.[23]

On the other hand the U.S. Supreme Court has invalidated a conviction for common law offenses on the grounds of unconstitutionality.[24] As we see the common law enjoys no immunity against constitutional attack.

All this considered, many authors conclude that although there has been no explicit precedent hitherto, which applied the void for vagueness or the fair warning doctrine to the common law formulations, still in view of the present state of the law such a utilization would be but a logical conclusion. The conclusive argument is that the extension of criminal responsibility on the basis of the general doctrines of the common law should be invalidated on the grounds of unconstitutionality.[25]

5. The common law misdemeanor doctrine is also attacked in respect to the ultimate purpose of punishment. The argument runs as follows: one of the purposes of the criminal sanction is to deter the potential offender from committing a prohibited act. It is clear that this end cannot be accomplished if the addressee has no knowledge of the object and the scope of the prohibition. In other words the deterrent function of the punishment is not performed when an individual has no

[23] Compare, for instance, *Commonwealth* v. *McHale*, 97 Pa. 397, 408 (1881): "We are of opinion that all such crimes as especially affect public society are indictable at common law. The test is not whether precedent can be found in the books, but whether they injuriously affect the public policy and economy".

[24] *Cantwell* v. *Connecticut*, 319 US 296 (1940).

[25] This opinion is supported by the American Law Institute, see *Model Penal Code*, Tentative Draft No. 4, 1955, Comment, pp. 106–107. As a matter of fact such an application of void for vagueness doctrine followed several years later in *Ashton* v. *Kentucky*, 384 US 195 (1966) A definition of a common law crime of libel as "the publication of a writing calculated to disturb the peace" was held vague, and the conviction void as unconstitutional.

knowledge of what is prohibited nor that he will be punished, when doing a certain act.[26]

Although the arguments against the common law misdemeanor doctrine seem to be sound and serious the doctrine can still be applied at the discretion of the judge, and this state of affairs will remain unchanged unless an explicit law is passed or the constitutional fair warning doctrine firmly enforced.

Counter to the optimistic expectations of the American Law Institute the common law misdemeanor doctrine is or at least has been until recently still alive in the United States. Although in actual fact it seldom occurs, the chance still exists for a man to be convicted for doing an act not formerly criminal at common law.[27]

What have been the guidelines followed by the American courts? The common law misdemeanor doctrine was doubtlessly most firmly entrenched in Pennsylvania judicial decisions, in fact, more firmly than in England,[28] as some authors suggest. Starting with the early nineteenth century decisions,[29] rein-

[26] J. Thompson (op. cit., p. 355) calls absurd the argument of the advocates of the doctrine, that the power of the court to extend legal responsibility to include new offences has a deterrent effect.

[27] Note, "Common Law Crimes...", op. cit., p. 1335; Note, "The Use of Analogy...", op. cit., p. 624; Note, "Acts not Formerly...", op. cit., pp. 1092–1093; W. Jentes, op. cit., p. 419; N. Kessler, op. cit., p. 419; S. Kline, W. H. Hitchler, op. cit., p. 344. Compare the opinion expressed by LaFave and Scott: "A majority of jurisdictions still recognizes the power of courts to create common law crimes, though they differ somewhat as to the extent of this power...". Most states accepting common law crimes, however, would agree that the common law can expand to meet a new situation hitherto unknown. W. R. LaFave and W. A. Scott, op. cit., p. 57, 67.

[28] S. Kline, W. H. Hitcher, op. cit., p. 347. Discussing here Pennsylvania decisions as a good illustration of the doctrine we should keep in mind that since June 1973 common law crimes have been abolished in this jurisdiction. See Ch. IV.

[29] *Commonwealth* v. *Taylor*, 5 Binn. 276, 281 (1811). Compare also *Commonwealth* v. *Sharpless*, 2 S and R 91 (Pa. 1815).

forced by the late nineteenth century decision in *Commonwealth* v. *McHale*,[30] down to the present day[31] the Pennsylvania courts generally observed the rule that an act may be punished under common law where no precedent or statute applies.

The famous decision in *Commonwealth* v. *Mochan*[32] deserves special attention.

In April 1954 the Court of Quarter Sessions of the Allegheny County convicted one Michael Mochan of committing an act not formerly criminal under statutory or common law. Throughout 1953 the defendant made repeated telephone calls to a married woman, a stranger to him, in which he used obscene language and suggested "sodomy".[33] The court pointed out that the defendant had telephoned the complainant on party line so any one on the line could have listened in on the conversation, thus, potentially at least, the appellate court declared, the defendant's act injuriously affected public morality.[34] The defendant unsuccessfully appealed claiming that

---

[30] *Commonwealth* v. *McHale*, op. cit. The Court of Appeals used the following argument: "The test is not whether precedents can be found in the books, but whether they injuriously affect the public policy and economy". Ibid., p. 410.

[31] *Commonwealth* v. *De Grange*, 97 Pa. Super. 181 (1929); *Commonwealth* v. *Miller*, 94 Pa. Super. 499 (1928). Other decisions made prior to 1955 which accepted the McHale doctrine are, among others, the following: *Com.* v. *Orris*, 136 Pa. Super. 137, 7 A. 2d 88 (1939); *Com.* v. *Glenny*, 54 Pa. D. and C. 633 (Erie Q. S. 1945); *Com.* v. *Sherman*, 72 Pa. D. and C. 66 (1950). In all these cases the defendants were convicted for common law offences on the grounds of the McHale doctrine, although there was no precedent available.

[32] 177 Pa. Super. 454, 110 A. 2d 788 (1955).

[33] It was emphasized in the decision that the defendant employed a particularly scurrilous and filthy language, and besides harassed not only the woman with his telephone calls but also the members of her family.

[34] The court evidently took it for granted that the users of the party ine listened in on each other's conversations.

the court of first instance convicted him for an act which was not criminal under the common law.

The majority opinion of the appellate court judges makes a classical presentation of the traditional common law misdemeanor doctrine as laid down by Blackstone and Russel. And so we learn that, "it is of little importance that there is no precedent in our reports which decides the precise question here involved. The test is not whether precedents can be found in the books but whether the alleged crimes could have been prosecuted and the offenders punished under the common law."[35] The decision favorably quotes the formulations contained in *Commonwealth* v. *Miller* and *Commonwealth* v. *De Grange*.[36] The decision was instantly rebutted by two judges from the court of second instance who dissented from the majority opinion. "The majority", asserted Judge Woodside in his dissenting opinion, "is declaring something to be a crime which was never before known to be a crime in this Commonwealth...

...Under the division of powers in our constitution it is for the legislature to determine what "injures or tends to injure the public". One of the most important functions of the legislature is to determine what acts "require the state to interfere and punish the wrongdoer". There is no reason for the legislature to enact any criminal laws if the courts delegate to themselves the power to apply such general principles as are here applied to whatever conduct may seem to the courts to be injurious to the public... we are making an unwarranted invasion of the legislative field when we arrogate that responsibility to ourselves by declaring now, for the first time, that certain acts are a crime."[37]

---

[35] Supra note 32 at p. 790.

[36] Compare ft. 31. Also the following formulation from *Commonwealth* v. *De Grange* is quoted: "Whatever openly outrages decency and is injurious to public morals is a misdemeanor at common law".

[37] Supra note 32, at p. 791.

The *Mochan* decision was also criticized in literature. Beside the standard arguments against making new crimes by the judges the critics indicated that the decision was erroneous even within the framework of the common law misdemeanor doctrine mainly because Mochan's conduct came within the statutory prohibition against solicitation to commit sodomy.[38] Besides Mochan did not act in public, hence the condition necessary to make it a common law misdemeanor was missing.[39] In spite of this criticism the Pennsylvania appellate courts relied upon the *Mochan* decision a number of times, though using it only as a *dictum*, because there was no such case in which an act not formerly criminal was punished.[40]

Concerning other American jurisdictions there was a case in Maine in 1939 when an act was punished which was not earlier held criminal, viz. the famous *State* v. *Bradbury*.[41] The accused was convicted for having burned his sister's dead body in a furnace. The act was not illegal either under the statutory or the common law. The Maine Supreme Court upheld the conviction concurring with the opinion of the court of first instance that "acts which are highly indecent, and hence *contra bonos mores*, are crimes".

Notably, there is another trend in the judicial decisions which derives its name from the eminent judge and legal scholar Stephen.[42] Courts following the Stephen's line hold that there is no common law offense without a precedent. The Wisconsin court, where the common law of crimes was

---

[38] Note, "Acts not Formerly Criminal...", op. cit., p. 1094; J. Thompson, op. cit., p. 355.

[39] Ibidem.

[40] Compare in particular: *Commonwealth* v. *Cano*, 133 A. 2d 800 (Pa. Super. 1956). Compare also *Com.* v. *Evans*, 190 Pa. Super. 179, 154 A. 2d 57 (1958); *Com.* v. *Gary*, 163 A. 2d 696 (Pa. Super., 1960).

[41] 9 A. 2d 656 (1939).

[42] J. Stephen, himself a judge and criminologist, was in principle opposed to the law-making power of the court. Compare Chapter 3.

abrogated as recently as 1955, has never created new crimes nor has it ever passed on the precise question.[43]

There are decisions available which show Alaska's and Tennessee's negative attitude toward the law-making function of the court.[44] The New Jersey courts have followed the Stephen's line led by the Supreme Court Chief Justice Weintraub.[45]

Some of the U.S. Supreme Court Justices[46] also have been adverse to the so-called judicial legislation in criminal law and consequently to the common law misdemeanor doctrine.

Finally, it is worth mentioning that in a related system where the common law could be an independent basis of responsibility, i.e., in Canada, the accused could not be convicted on the grounds of the general doctrines of the common law where no exact precedent was found.[47]

CONTEMPT OF COURT

The judicial power to punish a great variety of acts or omissions which in some way disrupt, obstruct or otherwise jeopardize the judicial process ("criminal contempt") and to apply personal and economic coercion to ensure compliance

---

[43] F. Kaftan, op. cit., p. 304.

[44] *Hotch* v. *U.S.*, 212 F. 2d 280 (1954, C.A. 9 Alaska); *Goff* v. *State*, 209 S.W. 2d 13, 186 Tenn. 212 (1948).

[45] *State* v. *Cohen*, 32 N.J. 1, 158 A. 2d 497 (1960).

[46] Compare the separate opinion of Justices Black and Douglas in *James* v. *U.S.*, 366 U.S. 213 (1961), p. 225.

[47] *Frey* v. *Fedoruk*, [1950] Canadian Supreme Court 517, 3 D.L.R. 513 (1950). The defendant was convicted for peeping into the bedroom of a woman who was a stranger to him. The defendant appealed the conviction which indeed was reversed by the Supreme Court on the following ground: "We have been referred to no reported case, in which the conduct of a peeping Tom was held to be a criminal offense. I think it safer to hold that no one shall be convicted of a crime unless the offense with which he is charged is recognized as such in the provisions of the criminal code, or can be established by the authority of some reported case as an offense known to the law." Let us add, in this instance, that shortly after this ruling the common law offenses were entirely abolished in the amended Canadian Criminal Code. Compare, Criminal Code 1964, Article 8a.

with court orders ("civil contempt") is a distinctive feature of common law systems.[48] It represents a vast and complex topic which has generated a large number of legal writings.[49] American writers as well as American courts, have recently focused primarily on the procedural and constitutional issues related to the contempt power. These brief remarks will be limited only to those substantive aspects of the contempt power which are relevant to the principles *nullum crimen, nulla poena sine lege.*[50] From this vantage point judicial power

[48] A. Pekelis, "Legal Technique and Political Ideologies". Michigan Law Review, 1943, Vol. 41, p. 665ff.; D. Dobbs, "Contempt of Court: A Survey", Cornell Law Review, 1971, Vol. 56, p. 184f.

[49] See for example: S. C. Smith, "Bibliography; The Contempt Process-Selected Writings". Yale Law Library, March 1970 (unpublished) which includes 102 items. See also some of the more recent authorities cited in footnote 50 infra.

[50] The reader who wishes to study the subject more extensively is referred to the following basic publications: R. L. Goldfarb, *The Contempt Power*, New York, 1963; D. B. Dobbs, supra footnote 48; P. A. Freund, "Contempt of Court", Human Rights, 1970, Vol. 1; A. E. Sutherland, "Contempt by Publication", North Dakota Law Review, 1967, Vol. 43. For a recent comprehensive discussion on the law of contempt in England see G. Borrie and N. Lowe, *The Law of Contempt*, London, 1973. From earlier writings see: J. H. Beale, "Contempt of Court, Criminal and Civil", Harvard Law Review, 1908, Vol. 21; W. Nelles, "The Summary Power to Punish for Contempt", Columbia Law Review, 1931, Vol. 31; E. M. Dangel, *Contempt*, Boston, 1939. A survey of American court decisions in contempt cases is given in *American Jurisprudence*, 2nd ed., Rochester, N.Y.–San Francisco, 1964, Vol. 17. For a historical discussion of contempt of court in England see: J. Ch. Fox, *The History of Contempt of Court. The Form of Trial and the Mode of Punishment*, Oxford, 1927. For a discussion of contempt of court in the United States and in England from the comparative point of view see: A. Pekelis, footnote 48 supra; M. Damaska, "Comment by Dr. Mirjan Damaska Comparing Study Draft of Proposed New Federal Criminal Code to European Penal Codes". In: *Working Papers of the National Commission on Reform of Federal Criminal Laws*, Washington, D.C., 1971, Vol. III; U. Rubens-Laarman, *Die Gerichtsberichterstattung im englischen Recht unter vergleichender Betrachtung des deutschen Rechts*, Münster, 1969.

to punish for acts labeled "contempt of court" is particularly interesting for at least four reasons:

1. American courts have long and successfully claimed "the inherent power" to punish for contempt, i.e. the power entirely independent from legislative authorization.

2. The concept of criminal contempt is so vague, that it defies any meaningful definition, thus conferring upon the judiciary a broad discretionary power to punish for almost any acts or omissions they choose to label criminal.

3. The limits of the criminal sanction for contempt remain undefined in many jurisdictions and hence left for discretionary determination by judges.

4. Conduct may be punished as contempt of court even though it clearly falls within the wording of a more specific criminal statute. Therefore the limits of a criminal penalty authorized by the legislature can be easily circumvented by a willing judge.

Criminal contempt is a common law crime inherited from England[51] and largely developed in the U.S. by judicial decisions.[52] Among common law crimes, however, it occupies a unique position insofar as it is punishable notwithstanding any legislative regulation even in those jurisdictions which in principle have not recognized common law crimes.[53] The "inherent" power of courts to punish for contempt has been energetically asserted by judges against legislative interference. More than once American judges have declared that the legislature "cannot... deprive the courts of this power or unduly interfere with its exercise".[54] It is worth noting that

---

[51] Compare: W. Blackstone, op. cit., Book IV, p. 283ff.; W. R. LaFave and A. W. Scott, op. cit., p. 42; E. M. Dangel, op. cit., p. 15.

[52] D. B. Dobbs, op. cit., p. 185.

[53] D. B. Dobbs, op. cit., p. 185; W. R. LaFave and A. W. Scott, op. cit., p. 42.

[54] *Ex parte* McCown, 139 N.C. 95, 51 S.E. 957 (1905); *La Grange* v. *State*, 238 Ind. 689, 153 N.E. 2d 593 (1958).

legislative attempts at imposing limitations on the sanctions applied for criminal contempt have been declared unconstitutional as "materially interfering with the administration of justice".[55] Contempt of court has gained a unique position through explicit legislative recognition. For example several modern criminal codes, having abolished common law crimes, nevertheless have retained an explicit exception for contempt of court. Thus contempt of court seems to be the only major characteristic of common law crimes which can live through criminal law reforms.[56]

Contempt of court has been variously defined, but hardly any of these definitions seems satisfactory. Indeed all of these try to synthesize such an enormous diversity of judicial practice that one can hardly expect any clarity and guidance from them. Thus, contempt has been defined as "a despising of the authority, justice, or dignity of the court";[57] as "any conduct that tends to bring the authority and administration of law into disrespect or disregard";[58] and as "an act or omission substantially disrupting or obstructing the judicial process...".[59] It seems that Justice Black's criticism expressed in his dissent in *Green* v. *United States*[60] was entirely well founded. He

---

[55] *Taylor* v. *Hayes*, 494 S.W. 2d 737 (Ky. 1973); *Arnett* v. *Meade*, 462 S.W. 2d 940 (Ky. 1971).

[56] And so, for example, Sec. 2 of the 1972 Kentucky Penal Code provides in relevant parts: "(1) Common law offenses are abolished and no act or omission shall constitute a criminal offense unless designated a crime or violation under this code or another statute of this state... (2) This provision shall not affect the power of a court to punish for contempt...". Similar provisions are fairly typical for new American state criminal codes; they also may be found in other common law jurisdictions. See for example the Crime Act of New Zealand 1961, Sec. 9.

[57] *American Jurisprudence*, op. cit., Vol. 17, p. 6f.

[58] Oswald, Contempt of Court, 3rd ed., 1911, p. 6, quoted after Justice Black's dissenting opinion in *Green* v. *United States*, 356 US 165 (1958) at p. 200.

[59] D. B. Dobbson, op. cit., p. 185.

[60] Footnote 58 supra at p. 199f.

indicated that "the substantive scope of the offense of contempt is inordinately sweeping and vague" and called it "the offense with the most ill-defined and elastic contours". Statutory definitions do not usually bring much improvement either. For example, the federal contempt statute[61] provides as follows:

"A court of the United States shall have power to punish by fine or imprisonment, at its discretion, such contempt of its authority, and none other, as—

(1) Misbehavior of any person in its presence or so near thereto as to obstruct the administration of justice;

(2) Misbehavior of any of its officers in their official transactions;

(3) Disobedience or resistance to its lawful writ, process, order, rule, decree, or command."

If there is any doubt as to the amorphous nature of those acts classified as contemptous, it can be swiftly dispelled by even the most cursory review of past convictions for contempt.[62] At times, the contempt sanction has been employed to punish such widely disparate and doubtfully criminal conduct as one "discourteous" response to a question by a defendant toward the trial judge,[63] an attorney's failure to appear on time for a scheduled hearing,[64] a defense attorney's "disrespectful" tone of voice and manner toward the court and toward a witness for the prosecution,[65] the attempt by a defendant's counsel

---

[61] 18 USC., Sec. 401.

[62] For a full review, see D. B. Dobbs, op. cit., supra footnote 48.

[63] *Champion* v. *State*, 456 P. 2d 571 (Okla. Crim. App. 1969).

[64] *In re Niblack*, 476 F. 2d 930 (D.C. Cir. 1973); see also *Knajdek* v. *West*, 278 Minn. 282, 153 N.W. 2d 846 (1967).

[65] *Taylor* v. *Hayes*, supra, the defendant was held to have been disrespectful toward the court in one count of contempt for having said "I'll certainly keep that in mind, your Honor", and in another count for referring to a certain police officer as "this nice police officer". Such words were clearly not offensive in and of themselves, and could only have acquired their offensiveness through the personal sensitivity of the judge.

to cite U.S. Supreme Court decisions in a lower Massachusetts court,[66] failure to follow a court imposed dress code, e.g., an attorney's wearing an open-necked shirt and no tie,[67] and finally, for an attorney's allegedly insolent colloquy with the trial judge in moving for a mistrial,[68] in this case it was necessary for the defendant to go all the way to the Supreme Court of the State of California before he could get a reversal. The contempt sanction also makes it possible for a judge to turn an otherwise innocent act into a violation of the criminal law through his injunctive powers. He need merely enjoin the legitimacy of its occurrence, e.g., in *Peck* v. *Stone*[69] a New York trial judge unsuccessfully attempted to prohibit a woman attorney from wearing a mini-skirt in his courtroom through use of the injunctive power under the penalty of contempt. Speaking to the potential for abuse of such unrestrained discretionary power, Chief Justice Warren, dissenting in *Frank* v. *United States*,[70] remarked "(the trial judge) can simply issue a blanket injunction against an unpopular group, (and) cite its members for contempt *en masse* for the slightest injunction violation...".

Common law, as well as many criminal statutes (for example the federal statute quoted above), establishes no limit on the punishment which may be imposed on a defendant found guilty of contempt. In some jurisdictions[71] the duration of imprisonment and amount of fine is left entirely to the discretion of the trial judge, in others, the judge is free to both

---

[66] R. Harris, "Annals of Law. In Criminal Court I", *New Yorker*, April 14, 1973, p. 88.

[67] See *Beardon* v. *State*, 458 P. 2d 914 (Okla. Crim. App. 1969) and *Crumb* v. *State*, 458 P. 2d 909 (Okla. Crim. App. 1969).

[68] *In re Hallinan*, 71 Cal. 2d 1179, 459 P. 2d 255 (1969); see also D. B. Dobbs, op. cit., at 204ff.

[69] 304 N.Y. 2d 881 (1969).

[70] 395 U.S. 147, 153 (1969).

[71] 18 USC., Sec. 401.

invent and apply new kinds of punishments not formerly provided for by law.[72]

Conduct falling well within the wording of a specific criminal statute, such as perjury for example, may at the same time, for the same offense, be punished as contempt of court.[73] Thus the contempt power can be instrumental in circumventing maximum penalties explicitly provided for by the legislature. Justice Rutledge dissenting in the celebrated case of *United States* v. *United Mine Workers* accurately pointed out that by using the contempt power the lower federal court had effectively multiplied the maximum penalty established by Congress for the particular offense involved in that case.[74]

Finally, it should be noted that notwithstanding its pervasiveness and viability the judicial power to punish for contempt has recently been subject to growing criticism and substantial limitation by the U.S. Supreme Court. Characteristically for American legal development, the limitations have been introduced gradually and through procedural devices.[75]

---

[72] D.B. Dobbs, op. cit., p. 282.

[73] W. R. LaFave and A. W. Scott, op. cit., p. 43.

[74] 330 US 258 (1947)

[75] Until recently "direct contempt", i.e. contempt committed in the presence of the court, was without exception punishable by instant action from the trial judge in a summary procedure. In summary contempt a judge could all at once, cite, convict, and sentence a defendant without a further hearing. This way of disposing of direct contempt cases was recently severely limited by the U.S. Supreme Court ruling in *Bloom* v. *Illinois*, 391 US 194 (1968). There, it was held that the Constitution requires a jury trial for criminal contempt citations except those in the "petty offense" category; the borderline between a petty and serious offense is determined by the penalty either potentially applicable under a statute or actually imposed in a given case if the statute does not provide for maximum punishment. Compare: *Baldwin* v. *New York*, 399 US 66 (1970). See also *Mayberry* v. *Pennsylvania*, 400 US 455 (1971).

Chapter 7

ATTEMPTS TO MITIGATE THE EFFECTS OF VIOLATION OF THE PRINCIPLE *NULLUM CRIMEN SINE LEGE*

The opponents of the so-called judicial legislation have always been most disturbed by its retroactive effects. Suffice it to mention the biting irony with which Bentham attacked the subject. The retroactivity of precedent which entails punishment for a new fact-situation becomes particularly annoying in view of American law, that is, in view of the constitutional prohibition of *ex post facto* legislative penalization (Article I, Sections 9 and 10 of the U.S. Constitution). The characteristic duality of this approach which has its historical roots in English law (compare the Introductory Remarks) finds its doctrinal justification in the declaratory theory of precedent. This theory holds that precedent is not the source but the proof of pre-existent law. The change of precedent therefore does not mean that the law underwent a change but that the false evidence was replaced by a real one. The fiction of the declaratory theory masks the retroactivity of the common law.

Although the American courts often follow the declaratory theory, in practice they modify some of its effects by restricting in some categories of cases the retroactivity of precedent. And so some rules have been fixed which put time limits on the operation of precedent in criminal cases which protect the defendant against unfair, *ex post facto* penalization.[1]

[1] This trend being predominant in the American judge-made law is not without some exceptions. Compare *State* v. *Mellenberger*, 163 Or. 233, 95 P. 2d 709 (1939), in which the Oregon court overruled its earlier

These rules perform a function related to that of the provisions prohibiting retroactive penalization in the Continental European penal codes. However, the two functions do not run exactly parallel. The prospective limitations of precedents do not protect the defendant against every kind of retroactive, disadvantageous changes in judge-made law. The time limit bars only the most extreme effects of retroactivity, that is, the transition from explicit non-punishability of a certain type of conduct to punishability of the same type of conduct.[2]

The technique of prospective limitation of judicial precedents declaring new types of acts criminal was further developed by the U.S. Supreme Court in *Bouie* v. *City of Columbia* (supra, Chapter 2). This decision represents an important step forward in at least two respects:

1) Judicial retroactive penalization was declared impermissible not only when certain conduct has been clearly held not punishable by a past judicial decision, but also when the law had remained silent.

2) For the first time, the Supreme Court of the U.S. based the prohibition of *judicial* retroactive penalization on constitutional grounds. Consequently, the prospective limitation

decision [*State* v. *Alexander*, 76 Or. 329, 148 P. 1136, 1915] and sent the defendant to jail, although the defendant may have relied on the earlier precedent declaring his act innocent. Compare also *Ginzburg* v. *United States*, 383 US 463 (1966), majority opinion. For criticism of this decision see: Justice Black's dissenting, ibidem at p. 477; A. M. Bickel, *The Supreme Court and the Idea of Progress*, New York, 1970, pp. 50–54.

[2] On the other hand at least some continental European penal systems have not created any satisfactory rules aimed at the protection of a defendant against retroactive effect of unfavorable judge-made changes in substantive criminal law. This was criticized in legal writings. Compare for example: S. Pomorski, "Z problematyki tzw. normotwórczej funkcji sądów w prawie karnym" (Problems of so-called judicial law-making in criminal law), *Państwo i Prawo*, 1969, Nos. 8–9; W. Strassburg, "Rückwirkungsverbot und Änderung der Rechtssprechung im Strafrecht", *Zeitschrift für das gesamte Strafrechtswissenschaft*, 1970, Heft 4.

of precedent which creates new offenses has become a rule of constitutional dimension.

The rule announced in *Bouie* has not always been consistently followed by the U.S. Supreme Court. For example, a new obscenity test established in *Miller* v. *California* 413 US 15 (1973) was later applied retroactively (*United States* v. *Orito* 413 US 139 (1973).

The rules governing the operation in time of precedent in criminal cases were mainly established in the context of the construction and implementation of the statutory criminal law, not of the common law of crimes. It would be difficult to explain exactly why this has happened in this way. Perhaps again it was the influence of the declaratory theory of precedent which has always had a stronger hold in the common law than in precedents which involved the construction of statutory law. In other words common law was perceived as a fixed body of rules which judges only "discover". One might venture still another hypothesis: statutory construction has undergone far more rapid change than the common law of crimes. Possibly it was against the background of statutory constructions that the courts were confronted with an extreme change of values in assessing certain kinds of conduct; naturally, such cases rendered the pressing need to lay down the rules under discussion.

Although the rules were established chiefly in the field of statutory interpretation, it does not follow that they may not be applied to the common law of crimes.[3] There is no such

[3] See: *Stinett* v. *Commonwealth*, 55 F. 2d 644, 647 (1932) where the U.S. Court of Appeals having rejected prosecution's claim that the common law rule concerning use of deadly force by an officer performing arrest should be changed and a new rule applied in the case at hand, commented upon the issue: "It is clear... that, as the rule of the common law has not been changed by statute in Virginia, this defendant is entitled to its protection, and that courts may not change the rule, because they may not agree with it, and thus make defendant guilty of a crime because of an act which was no crime when committed. *State* v. *Bell*, 136 N.C. 674, 49 S.E. 163".

restriction in their content or nature. They are applicable when the scope of punishability is judicially changed regardless of whether the act was punished by statute or by common law. It is the course of events rather than a matter of legal principles that hitherto they were applied in cases decided under statutory law.

Finally, it should be indicated that the rules of the temporal operation of precedent were introduced with no legislative action. A distinctive product of judicial decisions they constitute a part of the common law. We present them below, on the basis of two different types of situations:

Type I: The judicial decision declares some type of conduct to be of a non-criminal nature. The decision is binding for a certain time, then it is changed to the effect that the type of conduct formerly held non-punishable now is declared punishable. There are no simultaneous changes in the legislation. The question arises as to how the new rule will treat acts committed under the earlier decision.

It should first be pointed out that in such situations the American courts have usually restricted and keep restricting prospectively operation of new precedent (so-called prospective overruling). The courts were confronted with only a handful of such cases, all of which were concerned solely with a new and broader construction of the statute. The first noted case was the decision in *North Carolina* v. *Bell* (1904),[4] followed by a series of related cases[5] and closing with the well-known opinion of the Supreme Court of the United States in *James* v. *U.S.*[6]

---

[4] 136 N.C. 674, 676, 49 SE 163, 166 (1904).

[5] *People* v. *Maughs*, 149 Cal. 253, 86 Pac. 187 (1906); *State* v. *Longino*, 109 Miss. 125, 133, 67 So. 902 (1915); *State* v. *Simanton*, 100 Mont. 292, 49 P. 2d 981 (1935); *Wilson* v. *Goodin*, 291 Ky. 144, 163 SW 2d 309 (1942); *Commonwealth* v. *Trousdale*, 297 Ky. 724, 181 SW 2d 254 (1955).

[6] 366 US 213 (1961).

The state of the law may be considered as fixed only in relation to the principle itself because in all these cases the extension of criminal responsibility for acts which were earlier non-criminal did not work retroactively. However, legal opinions which served as the rationale for the prospective limitation were not uniform. In the earliest precedent *North Carolina* v. *Bell*, the North Carolina Supreme Court in reversing the conviction simply referred to the principles of just and proper judgment. The opinion indicates that the defendants could have acted in reliance upon a precedent not yet overruled,[7] so it would be an injustice to try them by the new law.

The Mississippi Supreme Court in *State* v. *Longino*[8] referred not only to the principles of "what is right and just", but also to constitutional principles. The decision brings forth an interesting concept, i.e. that the punishment of an act declared by the highest court of a state to be innocent at the time of its commission violates the Eighth Amendment because such punishment would be "cruel and unusual". Besides the Court ruled that the interpretation of criminal statutes should have a prospective effect since this applies the same principle as the constitutional prohibition of *ex post facto* legislation.[9] The arguments against retroactivity based on constitutional law, and in particular on the prohibition of *ex post facto* laws, as in the *Longino* case and earlier related cases, do not reappear in later decisions. This was probably effected by the authoritative decisions of the Supreme Court of the U.S. in the 1913–1915 cases which held that the constitutional prohibition of *ex post facto* laws refers only to legislation.[10] In the spectacular *State* v. *Jones*[11] case (a much later case than Longino) the court

[7] *N. Car.* v. *Bell*, op. cit., p. 164.

[8] Compare ft. 5.

[9] *State* v. *Longino*, op. cit., p. 903.

[10] Compare, *Ross* v. *Oregon*, 227 US 150 (1913); *Frank* v. *Mangum*, 237 US 309 (1915).

[11] *State* v. *Jones*, 44 N. Mexico 623, 107 P. 2d 324 (1940).

departed from its former opinion and adopted a new broader interpretation of the statute. It refused, however, to give the decision retroactive operation. Again, "the plainest principles of justice"[12] were quoted as the base of the judgment.

Since the *Sunburst* (1932) decision (compare Chapter 1) the possibility of prospective overruling was not again to engage the attention of the U.S. Supreme Court until 1961[13] in *James* v. *U.S.*[14]

The defendant James was convicted in the U.S. District Court of willfully attempting to evade federal income taxes by failing to include embezzled funds in his gross income.[15] The Court of Appeals affirmed. On certiorari the Supreme Court reversed the judgment. The defendant based his defense upon the holding in *Commissioner* v. *Wilcox*[16] that embezzled funds do not give rise to taxable income and that the alleged crime took place during the period in which *Wilcox* was not yet overruled.[17]

The two questions before the Supreme Court were: whether the *Wilcox* precedent should be overruled and whether the defendant was guilty of the offense of willfully attempting to evade the tax as long as the *Wilcox* case was not overruled. The answer to the first question was in the affirmative as a rule

[12] Ibid., p. 329.

[13] Note, "Prospective Overruling and Retroactive Application in the Federal Courts", *Yale Law Journal*, 1962, Vol. 71, p. 923.

[14] 366 US 213, 6 L.Ed. 2d 246 (1961).

[15] It was an offense under Paragraph 145(b) Title 26 of the United States Code.

[16] *Commissioner* v. *Wilcox*, 327 US 404 (1946).

[17] It may seem incomprehensible that courts of two instances upheld the accusation in view of an explicit precedent corroborating the discharge of the defendant. The explanation, it seems, rests on the fact that the *Wilcox* precedent has not been explicitly overruled but its meaning as a precedent was considerably weakened by the decision in *Rutkin* v. *U.S.*, 343 US 130 (1952) holding that money acquired by extortion is taxable.

was laid down that embezzled funds are taxable.[18] The answer to the second question was negative following the line started in *State* v. *Bell.*

The Supreme Court laid down a new substantive rule that embezzled funds are taxable and that a failure to include them in one's gross income is criminal; it did not however apply this rule to the defendant James, employing the technique of "pure prospectivity". However as the Justices differed so widely in their reasons for the reversal of the conviction, the law remained unclear.[19]

Read in the broadest sense the opinion might seem to suggest that *James* should have prospective effect only, and that *Wilcox* should govern all taxpayer conduct until the decision in *James* was made. Hence, by adhering to *Wilcox* the taxpayer remained within law and was liable neither criminally nor civilly.[20]

---

[18] Six Justices voted for overruling *Wilcox.*

[19] "The Supreme Court 1960 Term", *Harvard Law Review*, 1961, Vol. 75, p. 196. Three justices who asserted their belief in the correctness of *Wilcox* and voted for it, declared that James had not committed a crime for he acted within the law. The Justices, however, presented an interesting argument against the prospective limitation of the new rule. The six Justices who overruled *Wilcox* divided into two groups: Warren together with Stewart and Brennan held that since the defendant had acted when *Wilcox* was binding, the requisite of wilfulness could not be present; in effect they voted to reverse the conviction and to remand the case to the court of the first instance recommending the accusation to be dismissed. Justices Frankfurter and Harlan urged the reversal of the conviction and a new trial in the court of the first instance to ascertain whether the defendant relied indeed on the *Wilcox* precedent and was misled by it. "The Supreme Court 1960 Term", op. cit., p. 241 and p. 243. This view is clearly based on the doctrine of justifiable mistake of law caused by reasonable reliance upon a judicial decision. The only member of the Court who would have affirmed the conviction was Justice Clark, who held that *Wilcox* was overruled earlier and was not binding at the time when James committed the tax offense.

[20] Note, "Prospective Overruling", op. cit., p. 924.

The Justices' opinions seem to question this seemingly logical interpretation of the decision. The starting point for the six Justices who agreed that *Wilcox* should be overruled, was the factual situation in the *James* case. The law required an element of willfulness to be proved in such offense. Chief Justice Warren, joined by Justices Brennan and Stewart, argued that willfulness cannot be proven to the defendant who relied on a precedent binding at the time of the commission of the alleged offense. "We believe", says the opinion, "that the element of willfulness could not be proven in a criminal prosecution for failing to include embezzled funds in gross income in the year of misappropriation so long as the statute contained the gloss placed upon it by Wilcox at the time the alleged crime was committed. Therefore we feel that the petitioner's conviction may not stand and that the indictment against him must be dismissed"[21] (emphasis added). The quoted words seem to suggest that in a similar situation only a defendant indicted of an intentional crime may escape responsibility. It is a potential mistake of law caused by reliance on the defective precedent, which is a legal ground for dismissal. The specific character of the mistake of law seems to account for the acquittal although a mistake of law is usually irrelevant.[22] Moreover this type of mistake of law is presumed from the mere fact of the existence of a relevant precedent. It is not necessary for the defense to prove that the accused had actual knowledge of the precedent and relied on it.

At another instance Chief Justice Warren, concluding that the *Wilcox* case was wrongly decided, added: "Thus, we

[21] *James* v. *U.S.*, op. cit., pp. 221–222.

[22] In *James* the mistake of law is all the more relevant because it is not a mistake of criminal law but of tax law. The mistake of criminal law is but a consequence of the original mistake. A mistake of law other than criminal is often treated as a mistake of fact. G. Williams, *Criminal Law*, op. cit., p. 305 and passim; *James* v. *U.S.*, pp. 242–243.

believe that we should now correct the error and the confusion resulting from it, certainly if we do so in a manner that will not prejudice those who might have relied on it"[23] (emphasis added). Characteristically, Chief Justice Warren indicated that not only those must be protected who relied on the overruled precedent but also those who might have relied on it (potential justifiable mistake of law). In this context reliance ceases to be a factual question which must be proved because almost everyone who acted under the rule of the old law could, at least, have relied on it.

Speaking about the specific legal nature of James' alleged offense Chief Justice Warren stressed that such an offense does not include willfulness only but that a specific intent must be proven since the word "willfully" was used in the statute.[24]

Justices Frankfurter and Harlan dissented.[25] The element of willfulness was also in the center of their considerations. If however the decisive point is the evil motive on the part of the defendant and his possible reliance on *Wilcox* this fact must be examined. The defendant's possible legal misapprehension raises factual not legal questions which cannot be decided *in abstracto*.[26]

It would seem that the inconsistency of all these opinions stems from the fact that the problem is considered from the point of view of the moral guilt instead of the

---

[23] *James* v. *United States*, op. cit., passim. This view seems to be characteristic to the whole line of cases. As LaFave and Scott pointed out: "Courts never seem to ask in *stare decisis* cases whether the defendant actually had read or heard of the precedent and did in fact rely on it. The chance that he did seems to be enough." Under this doctrine a rather difficult and not yet dealt with question arises what should be the solution in cases in which defendants could not have relied on an overruled precedent.

[24] Ibidem, p. 221.

[25] Ibidem, p. 241 and passim.

[26] Ibidem, pp. 242–3 and passim.

l e g a l i t y o f t h e a c t. It is the Blackstone tradition[27] which makes it impossible to state point-blank that the new precedent does constitnte a new law which replaces the old law based on the ancient precedent. The fallacy of the argumentation in the *James* case was raised by some American authors, though it certainly was inadequately argued.[28]

The opinion of Justice Black introduces some interesting legal considerations. Justice Black was in general opposed to prospective overruling. He considered the retroactive operation of precedent as one of the most serious restraints on the law-making function of the court. In his judgment the purpose of this restriction was precisely this: to separate the court's function of the interpreter of laws from that of the law-making function of the legislator. Thus Black again drew attention to the constitutional objections to prospective overruling, objections dismissed years before (in 1932) *in Sunburst.*[29]

The constitutional objections to prospective overruling are, according to Justice Black, particularly valid in criminal law. "In the first place", we read in the opinion, "a criminal statute that is so ambiguous in scope that an interpretation of it brings about totally unexpected results, thereby subjecting people to penalties and punishments for conduct which they could not know was criminal under existing law, raises serious questions of unconstitutional vagueness. Moreover, for a court to interpret a criminal statute in such a way as to make punishment for past conduct under it so unfair and unjust that the interpretation should be given only prospective application seems to us to be the creation of a judicial crime that Congress might not want to create."[30]

[27] Compare the opinion of Justice Harlan (ibidem, p. 247) where he denies that the law has changed following the change in the judicial decisions.

[28] T. S. Currier, "Time and Change in Judge Made Law: Prospective Overruling", *Virginia Law Review*, 1965, Vol. 51, p. 1256.

[29] This case was discussed in Chapter 1,

[30] *James* v. *U.S.*, op. cit., pp. 224–225.

As the notable lack of unanimity in the *James* decision shows, both the institution of prospective overruling in criminal cases and its legal rationale are controversial issues even among the Justices of the Supreme Court.

A step forward toward the mitigation of the effects of breaking the principle *nullum crimen sine lege* was taken in the decision in *Bouie* v. *City of Columbia* (1964).[31] Resorting to analogy the South Carolina state courts convicted the defendants for an act which at the time it was committed was not an offense.[32] The Supreme Court of the United States reversed the decisions of the state courts on the grounds that *ex post facto* inflicted punishment is unconstitutional. The legal argumentation may be summarized as follows:

In giving retroactive application to its new construction of the statute on the ground of analogy the state courts acted in contravention of the Fourteenth Amendment due process clause. In the last case the defendants were not only deprived of their right to fair warning but were lulled into a false sense of security by a statute which on its face was precise. Further the retroactive expansion of punishability by applying analogy would have precisely the same effect as retroactive criminal legislation which is explicitly forbidden by the Constitution.

The legal reasoning in *Bouie* introduces at least two new elements:

(1) Judicial retroactive penalization is impermissible not only when certain conduct was formerly clearly held unpunishable but also when the law remained silent. The *Bouie* decision

[31] 378 US 347 (1964). The *Bouie* case was briefly discussed in Chapter 2.

[32] The decision which was passed in this case has a very interesting background. The defendants were Negroes from South Carolina who staged a sit-in demonstration in a drugstore which refused to extend service to Negroes. To manifest their protest the Negroes refused to leave the bar upon explicitly being asked to do so. The state courts convicted them *per analogiam* for a crime under Paragraph 16-386 of the South Carolina Code which holds criminal an "Entry upon the lands of other... after notice from the owner... prohibiting such entry...".

only constitutes a precedent for cases which involve analogy. One cannot escape the conclusion that the same reasons work against retroactive penalization on the grounds of common law.

(2) For the first time the Supreme Court of the U.S. based the prohibition of judicial retroactive penalization on constitutional grounds. Consequently the prospective limitation of precedents which create new offenses becomes a constitutional principle. Hence the implementation of this technique in similar cases is binding on courts both state and federal.

In spite of the obvious merits of the Supreme Court's decision in *Bouie* it should be pointed out that the decision does not take exception to the principle of the expansion of punishability as to include a new act *per analogiam*, but only restricts its retroactive effects.

The decisions under review covering the Type I situations reveal what follows:

(1) It is an established tradition in the American judicial decisions both state and federal that a certain type of conduct which was held innocent by an authoritative court decision remains unpunishable although a later decision made this kind of act punishable, provided that the commission of the act took place after the first and prior to the second decision. The later precedent is applied prospectively.

(2) The legal arguments underlying this practice are rather unconvincing and vague. Judges would usually refer to some general notions of justice and the justifiable mistake of law made by persons who acted in reliance on the binding precedent. The reasoning of the decisions focusing on the subjective culpability seems rather elusive since the courts do not go into the *bona fide* question; there is only a presumption of *bona fide*.

(3) The weakness of the legal argumentation stems from the reluctance to admit that the precedent does constitute the source of law, hence the change of the precedent entails the

change of law. The attempts to argue a case by the constitutional *ex post facto* laws clause, present in the earlier decisions, disappeared following the Supreme Court decision in *Ross* v. *Oregon.*[33]

Type II: As opposed to Type I, Type II is not uniform. For the convenience of description and analysis we will divide it into two categories. The Type II situations have one common quality: the operation of constitutional precedents in time. These precedents are called here for convenience's sake constitutional because they concern the constitutionality of the criminal legislation.

Category 1 is close to the situation under Type I. Its pattern may be put this way: a statute is declared unconstitutional; next, an act is done which has the features of the offense described in the statute; afterwards the court changes its opinion and declares the statute constitutional, overruling the first precedent. What is the status of the defendant under these circumstances?

Following a uniformly applied rule the defendant is acquitted. The new precedent is applied prospectively.[34] The legal reasoning underlying this type of decisions is not uniform.

In the earlier mentioned *Ingersoll* case the precedent was applied prospectively. The reasons for the decision were limited to the principle of a right and proper judgment.

In *State* v. *O'Neil*[35] there are interesting legal considerations concerning the issue under discussion. The majority of the judges declared that the defendant was in mistake of law. The court held that as a general rule a mistake of law does exonerate a defendant, however when he has justifiably relied upon a valid prior holding of the highest court of his state he should be exculpated. In the opinion of the majority

---

[33] 227 US 150 (1913).

[34] *Ingersoll* v. *State,* 11 Ind. 464 (1858); *State* v. *O'Neil,* 147 Iowa 513, 126 NW 454 (1910).

[35] *State* v. *O'Neil,* op. cit., p. 457.

of the judges the conviction was reversed because there was no element of guilt in the defendant's action.

In a separate opinion Chief Justice Deemer presented a different view: the judicial interpretation of a statute becomes a part of the statute and, if that interpretation is afterwards modified, it is subject to the same limitations as the legislative changes. It follows that an act which was innocent at the time of the commission of the alleged offense, cannot be declared criminal, because of the constitutional prohibition of *ex post facto* laws which also applies to a change of judicial precedent.[36] Furthermore Justice Deemer referred to the constitutional principle that cruel and unusual punishment shall not be inflicted.[37]

Observe that both here and in the decisions surveyed under Type I there are two competitive lines of argumentation: the objective one which only raises the question whether or not the law was changed in order to draw respective constitutional conclusions, and the subjective *bona fide* line[38] which tacitly assumes that there was no change of law.[39]

---

[36] Ibidem, pp. 459–460. As we know the United States Supreme Court dismissed this thesis in 1913 (*Ross* v. *Oregon*). But see| *Rhodes* v. *State*, 283 So 2d 351 (Florida, 1973).

[37] Ibidem, p. 460.

[38] It should be emphasized that the *bona fide* line is not homogenous. Some decisions accept *bona fide* of a defendant as a matter of legal presumption stemming from the mere chance of reasonable reliance (e.g., the majority opinion in *James* v. *United States*, op. cit.). Some other courts took the view that the reasonable reliance is a factual issue, which has to be examined in each case upon its evidence.

[39] Against the background of the presented decisions the stand taken by the New York Court in *People* v. *Berner*, 10 N.Y. S. 2d 339, 344, 170 Misc. 501, 506 (1910) is rather exceptional. Although the defendant acted in accordance with the local law he was nonetheless found guilty of an offense because the local law conflicted with the state law, and the former was declared invalid. The *bona fide* of the defendants, who acted in reliance on the local law, was barely accepted as an extenuating circumstance.

Category 2. The pattern may be put this way: (a) there is an act which constitutes a statutory offense; (b) the defendant is convicted; (c) the statute which provided the basis for the conviction is declared unconstitutional. The question arises whether the precedent which deemed the statute unconstitutional should be applied retroactively and what should be the scope of its application. Generally the courts make such precedents fully retroactive, that is, both when the decision returned under this statute is before the appellate court in direct review[40] and also when the decision is final. In the latter type of cases the precedent is applied retroactively on habeas corpus proceedings.[41]

Such cases were particularly abundant in 1939 as a result of the U.S. Supreme Court decision in *Lanzetta* v. *New Jersey* (compare Chapter 2) which declared the 1934 New Jersey Gangster Act unconstitutional on grounds of vagueness. The time which elapsed between enforcing the Gangster Act and voiding it was long enough to accumulate a certain number of final decisions. The *Lanzetta* precedent brought floods of petitions for discharge on habeas corpus. The convictions, as the pertinent decisions demonstrate, were reversed. (According to a rule laid down in 1879[42] habeas corpus applies to defendants convicted under an unconstitutional statute.) In the cases decided in the 1930's the courts, without engaging in general considerations on retroaction, usually based their decisions on statutes regulating habeas corpus.[43] This

---

[40] This type of retroactivity is nothing exceptional, it is rather a rule. Compare: *Partain* v. *State*, 77 Okla. Crim. 270, 141 P. 2d 124 (1943).

[41] Ex parte *Siebold*, 100 US 371 (1879); Re *Rose*, 122 NJ. L. 1507 (1939); Re *Miller* 122 NJ. L. 511, 6A 2d 389 and Re *Sterling* 122 NJ. L. 510 6A. 2d 390 (1939); Re *Burke*, 7 Cal. App. 2d 731, 41 P. 2d 322 (1935); Ex parte *Connollan*, 123 NJ. L. 229, 8A. 2d 345 (1939); *State* v. *Carr*, 151 Kan. 36, 98 P. 2d 393, 396 (1940).

[42] Ex parte *Siebold*, 100 US 371 (1879).

[43] Ex parte *Connolon*, 123 NJ .L. 229 (1939) is an interesting example of a case which followed the *Lanzetta* decision. The defendant was convicted

kind of judicial practice has been approved by the literature.[44]

The application of constitutional precedents aims at the protection of both defendants and convicts. In cases under Category 1 it is protection against *ex post facto* penalization; in cases under Category 2 it is a protection against penalization on the ground of an unconstitutional statute. This practice, although it is correct in its general outline, does have some faults. The prospective overruling of precedents which reinstate the constitutionality of the statute is based on "the principles of rightness and justice". This would seem a fragile base if this is to be the foundation of the principle of legality. It seems that the constitutional fair warning doctrine would be more proper to do the job. A statute declared unconstitutional by the court can hardly warn the defendant that a violation of this statute is punishable. On the contrary, declaring a statute unconstitutional assures the defendant that such acts which the statute held offensive remain unpunishable. Under the fair warning doctrine it is not the defendant who must prove that he acted in reliance upon a later overruled precedent but it is the prosecutor who must prove that the law binding at the time of the commission of the alleged offense contained the warning. The fair warning doctrine applied in this way could prevent judicial retroactive penalization in the same way as Article I Sections 9 and 10 of the United States Constitution bar legislative retroactive penalization.

---

in 1934 as "known to be a member of a gang" under Article 3 of the New Jersey Gangster Act. After four years spent in prison he applied for a writ of habeas corpus, pleading the unconstitutionality of the statute under which he was convicted. The state Supreme Court ruled the convict to be discharged and held that because of the unconstitutionality of the statute the defendant was "illegally restraint of his liberty".

[44] Note, "Prospective Operation of Decisions Holding Statutes Unconstitutional or Overruling Prior Decisions", *Harvard Law Review*, 1947, Vol. 60, p. 446; Currier, op. cit., p. 256 and passim.

CLOSING REMARKS

Let us now draw some general conclusions concerning the realization of the principle *nullum crimen sine lege* in the American legal systems.

I.

1. Punishment imposed on the grounds of the common law is the most flagrant and manifest form of offense to *nullum crimen sine lege*, although it is not the only form of violation of this principle in the American penal systems. The penalty is inflicted for acts not defined by statute. Moreover it is imposed without any legislative authorization, however general. The common law of crimes offends the principle *nullum crimen sine lege* by the bare fact of its existence constituting the extra-legislative source of criminal liability. As we noticed earlier the forms of penalization on the grounds of common law differ: punishments are imposed either on grounds of a specific precedent or on the basis of the general doctrine.

2. Penalization on the grounds of precedent, although offensive to *nullum crimen sine lege*, violates its safeguarding function to a relatively small extent. The punishable offenses are defined in advance, so that the accused has at least in theory the opportunity to find out about the illegal nature of his act. Retroactive penalization is excluded. The court follows criteria laid down in earlier decisions, so that the danger of an arbitrary judgment is eliminated. Common law lawyers even suggest that case law, being much more specific, is superior to Continental codified law. There is probably some truth in this statement.

The fundamental question now arises which of these two types of legal systems—the common law or the Continental law—is more likely to accomplish the realization of the principle of legality in the substantive criminal law.

Without any doubt Continental European systems have the advantage of having punishable types of conduct *exhaustively defined by statutes* which the courts are not allowed to overstep. On the other hand the principle *nullum crimen sine lege* implies a high degree of generality in defining punishable conduct and, in turn, weakens certainty of the law. Indeed the court is bound to move within a closed circle of statutory definitions. But even remaining within this circle, given the abstractness of statutory definitions, the court may declare some concrete acts punishable at its discretion. Are we thus to consider the restrictions put on the court to be somewhat illusory? Is not the illusory nature of the restrictions proved to some extent by the considerable differences in judicial decisions concerning the limits of penalization under statutes formally unchanged?

In place of the few abstract provisions contained in Continental penal codes, the common law systems contain numerous precedents defining punishable conduct much more specifically. Specific in content and narrow in scope, definitions of punishable conduct contained in precedents do not satisfy adequately the need for penalization. Therefore common law systems are supplemented by the idea of penalization based on general doctrines, a concept which provides the ground for the creative power of the judges. There is no question that the supplementary penalization introduces an element of uncertainty into the criminal law. The question arises, however, whether the margin of punishability on the ground of general doctrines permits a more serious departure from the principle of legality than does the high degree of abstractness in the Continental penal statutes.

It is hardly possible to solve this question *in abstracto*. It would take an extensive analysis of many factors inherent in both types of legal systems to give an exhaustive answer. Above all, an analysis of the legislation and of the general doctrines which serve as the basis for penalization would be necessary.

Let us put aside for a while the problem of punishability on the ground of general doctrines and concede for the sake of argument the existence of a common law system under which there is no punishment except in accordance with concrete precedent. True, such a system will have an extra-legislative basis of penalization and consequently, in a formal sense, *nullum crimen sine lege* will be violated. But does it follow that the principle of legality is offended? Not on the face of it, because punishable conduct would be precisely and adequately defined, in advance by law, though not by statute. Would it follow that such a system, due to its specific and detailed expression, would be a more effective safeguard of the principle of legality?

The issue is not as simple as it may seem.

First, as a distinguished Polish scholar Professor Władysław Wolter rightly indicated: "... a broader casuistry means that the diverse concrete reality is more extensively reflected, while at the same time it protects against an excessively arbitrary punishment. All this granted, casuistry, in the nature of things, contains more words ... and in each new word there is an inherent danger of an erroneous interpretation."[1]

Furthermore, the great mass of precedents which define punishable offenses turns the general assumption—that an ordinary citizen knows what sort of conduct is criminal—into more of a fiction than is the case under the Continental penal codes. Some other problems emerge too: the orders and prohibitions contained in judicial decisions are not formulated *expressis verbis* as they are in statutory enactments. The nor-

[1] W. Wolter, "Granice i zakres prawa karania" (Limits and Scope of the Right to Punish). *Państwo i Prawo*, 1957, No. 3, p. 246.

mative element of the decision has to be extracted from the judicial opinion and this is not always easy, as we have tried to demonstrate. T h e c o u r t which a p p l i e s t h e l a w has a considerable influence on defining the scope of the prohibition contained in the earlier decision, because, for example, it may distinguish the earlier case from the one at hand. Hence it does not follow that security and predictability are necessarily inherent in the specificity of case law. Moreover under the American *stare decisis* doctrine the court is free to depart from the precedent. Even assuming that departure from the precedent does not mean that the court might extend the scope of the criminal law, is there no danger that different treatment may be applied to similar acts?

Finally, in terms of the principle of legality, it is not a matter of indifference whether a legislative body by a properly promulgated statute declares an act indictable, or whether it is declared so by a judicial body as an incidental part of deciding the case before it.

3. The second manner of penalizing common law offenses—on the ground of general doctrines—effects a complete breach of the principle of legality. This form not only breaks the penalization monopoly of the statute but offends the most rudimentary principles of certainty and predictability in the criminal law. Conspiracy, contempt of court and the common law misdemeanors doctrine allow the courts to create new crimes. The vague and flexible formulas of these doctrines do not restrict the law-making function of the court, and simultaneously keep up the appearances that "old rules are applied to new facts". The latter is a stock argument of the advocates of the general doctrine commonly used to parry the objections against retroactive penalization.

The long-standing polemic between those who hold that punishability under the common law is tantamount to punishability based on existing precedents and the supporters of penalization on grounds of general doctrine, is in actual fact a dispute over the principle of legality, with the assumption that the principle *nullum crimen sine lege* is not binding.

II.

Derogation of the common law of crimes is a relatively simple operation, provided of course that the legislature entertains no doubts concerning its desirability.

As we mentioned earlier[2] this process is steadily developing. In effect well over half of the American jurisdictions formally recognize legislation as the only basis of criminal responsibility. It would be erroneous, however, to conclude that *nullum crimen sine lege* is fully effective under all these systems because the statute law itself, shaped under the predominant influence of the common law concepts often becomes the carrier of ideas, doctrines and institutions which leave ample room for the judges to define types of criminal conduct. Indirectly the statute delegates to the court the power to define punishable acts. Thus the officially declared exclusivity of the statute as the source of penalization sometimes, in fact, turns out to be illusory. This peculiar feature of the American statutory law can be understood only in terms of the role played in the whole system by the common law.

At the foundation of the European Continental legal systems lies the assumption of their completeness. The legislator builds a complete system by constructing abstract and hypothetical norms, in which his hypotheses are based on foreseeable fact-situations which are likely to occur in the future. The legal norms cover only the distinctive indicia of the type of conduct prohibited and stops at a rather elevated level of abstraction.

At the foundation of the common law systems, however, lies the assumption of their incompleteness. Legal norms grow up from

[2] Compare Chapter 4.

concrete legal controversies. In effect these norms are rich in content but narrow in scope.[3] Finally, these norms grow up from real situations which have occurred in the past and not from hypothetical situations which may occur in the future. Hence the "historicity" of the common law systems.

Yet the common law systems contain a general principle due to which, in spite of their incompleteness, they can meet the exigencies of life. What we refer to is the philosophy underlying these systems, i.e., the law-making power of the judges, which assures the common-law systems of a steady supply of flexibility and dynamism. Confronted with a new situation, a judge makes a new legal rule and decides the case. And so it has gone full circle: the casuistry and historicity of the common law systems is inherent in the fact that the systems are made in the process of deciding concrete cases. The common law systems are therefore by definition incomplete; the inevitable gaps are bridged by the judges who when confronted with new situations make new rules upon which the decision in the concrete case is based. Consequently, both the point of departure and of arrival is the law making power of the court. The elimination of this fundamental element does not seem possible without a more fundamental change in the system.

This general regularity effects the problem referred to, i.e., the breach of the principle of *nullum crimen sine lege* even where the common law has been replaced by statute. The casuistry characteristic of the common law became part and parcel of the statutory criminal law in American jurisdictions.[4]

---

[3] Some interesting deliberations concerning this issue are contained in the study by Professor R. David, *French Law: Its Structure, Sources, and Methodology*, Transl. by M. Kindred, Baton Rouge, 1972, p. 76ff.

[4] For some reasons for this state of affairs see A. A. Ehrenzweig, "Das Common Law", *Zeitschrift für Rechtsvergleichung*, 1960, No. 1.

Compare very interesting comments concerning casuistry and abstractness in defining criminal conduct in: G. O. W. Mueller, *Crime, Law and*

We will look in vain for synthetic and abstract norms (so characteristic of European codifications) in traditional American statutes. What we will find however are detailed common law rules in the statutory dress or provisions formulated in line with the same pattern.

Criminal statutes, large as they are in number, cannot be considered as consistent systems. An *ad hoc* response to an immediate demand, they are fragmentary and sometimes inconsistent and contradictory as a result of piecemeal amendments. This explains the present state of chaos in criminal legislation in many American jurisdictions. It is not only devoid of inner consistency but it lacks a clear, intelligible form.[5] Without independent ideas, incomplete and fragmentary, criminal statutes cannot rid themselves of dependence on the common law. The forms of the dependence vary. Frequently

---

the Scholars, Seattle, 1969, p. 161. See also "Introductory Statement of Advisory Committee" to Minnesota Criminal Code of 1963 in *Minnesota Statutes Annotated*, Vol. 40 at p. XII: "The statement of the offense should not be so general that a reading of the statute leaves unclear the prohibited conduct. At the same time it should not be so detailed that it runs the risk of omission of specific acts not thought of when the enumeration was made...".

[5] H. Wechsler, "The American Law Institute: Some Observations on Its Model Penal Code", *American Bar Association Journal*, 1956, Vol. 42, p. 321; F. Cohen, "Criminal Law Legislation and Legal Scholarship", *Journal of Legal Education*, 1964, Vol. 16, p. 263; F. A. Allen, "Book Review", *University of Chicago Law Review*, 1960, Vol. 27, p. 415; H. Packer, "Book Review", *Harvard Law Review*, 1964, Vol. 77, p. 791.

For the quality of criminal legislation in Connecticut and Michigan before law revision see: 1) R. M. Meyers, "Criminal Law: The Structure of Connecticut New Penal Code", *Connecticut Law Review*, 1970, Vol. 2, p. 661 ("We do not have a code; we have a series of separate and often inconsistent contradictory and in some cases irrational and archaic criminal sections"); 2) B. J. George, "A Comparative Analysis of the New Penal Laws of New York and Michigan", *Buffalo Law Review*, 1969, Vol. 18, p. 235, 236. The issue here is the traditional American statutory criminal law. The modern codification movement is discussed in short below in the later part of this chapter.

it is reflected in the adoption of the ideas, doctrines and institutions of the common law. In other words, some common law elements simply get a statutory dress. At times when questions emerge which are not regulated by statute, the statute refers explicitly or implicitly to the common law.[6]

This dependence also manifests itself in the very definition of criminal acts, thus breaking ground for the court to make new offenses under the guise of applying the statute. An illustration is furnished by conspiracy: the statutory law of the majority of jurisdictions still follows the common law concept of conspiracy, i.e., that an agreement to do certain non-criminal acts is punishable.[7] This is the law in many states, such as California, which long ago abolished the common law of crimes. Formally in these jurisdictions a person may only be held responsible for conspiracy under the statute. But the statute itself freshly delegates to the court the authority to make new offenses. The declared exclusivity of the statute as a source of penalization is futile if the statute itself adopts a common law doctrine which, by its nature, involves the law-making function of the court.

Statutory regulation of criminal responsibility for conspiracy is a typical, but certainly not the only, illustration of situations in which the formally eliminated common law comes back in statutory disguise. To illustrate: Paragraph 12-22-01 of the North Dakota Code holds that "Every person who willfully and wrongfully commits any act which openly outrages public decency and is injurious to public morals, although no punishment is expressly prescribed therefore, is guilty of a misdemeanor".

Here are some other examples:

Section 97-35-37 of the Mississippi Code Annotated defines as "vagrants" punishable under this Section: "(b) Persons

---

[6] W. R. LaFave and A. W. Scott, op. cit., p. 3.

[7] Compare Chapter 5.

leading an idle, immoral or profligate life who have no property to support them, and who are able to work and do not work" as well as "(k) Every able-bodied person who lives without employment or labor, and who has no visible means of support".

It should also be noted that similar provisions were still in force in the early 1960's in several American jurisdictions. Some of them were abolished by the legislator, some others have been invalidated by the courts on the grounds of vagueness as unconstitutional.[8] Another good example is Article 133 of the Uniform Code of Military Justice which provides: "Any commissioned officer, cadet, or midshipman who is convicted of conduct unbecoming an officer and a gentleman shall be punished as a court-martial may direct."[8a]

The above quoted provisions formally fix penalties for statutory offenses. In fact however, they amount to nothing more than a legislated version of the common law misdemeanor

---

[8] Compare, for example, Section 43 of the former New York Penal Law repealed since 1967: "A person who willfully and wrongfully commits any act which seriously injures the person or property of another, or which seriously disturbs or endangers the public peace or health, or which openly outrages public decency, for which no other punishment is expressly prescribed by this chapter, is guilty of a misdemeanor". See also: *Massachusetts General Laws*, Chapter 272 (1951), Para. 66, which punished by imprisonment: "idle persons, who not having visible means of support, live without lawful employment"; the statute was struck out on the ground of vagueness by the Supreme Judicial Court of Massachusetts in *Alegata* v. *Commonwealth*, 353 Mass. 287, 231 NE 2d 201 (1967). The general trend toward invalidation of criminal statutes of this type is discussed in: M. Budnitz, "Criminal Law—Statutory Offenses—Vagrancy Laws Invalid as Too Vague and as Improper Exercise of Police Power", *Harvard Civil Rights Civil Liberties Review*, 1968, Vol. 3; W. S. Davis, "Vagrancy-Loitering Laws: An Antithesis to Recent Jurisprudential Trends", *Tennessee Law Review*, 1968, Vol. 35.

[8a] Article 133 UCMJ, 10 U.S.C., Section 933 (1970). This provision has been recently upheld by the *U.S.* Supreme Court in *Parker* v. *Levy*, supra Chapter 2.

doctrine. They fail to define the elements of the forbidden act; they contain only a general instruction to punish acts or "statuses" offending some vaguely defined public interests. Again they bestow upon the judge, police and prosecutors the authority to define types of punishable conduct and invite highly arbitrary enforcement. The philosophy underlying these provisions is to sanction the law-making power of the judge; consequently provisions of this kind create a "general clause" to supplement the incomplete and inadequate legislative enactment. The pretense of the exclusivity of the statute as the only source of penalization is maintained but the deep rift in the rule is a matter of actual fact.

There is still another form of violation of the principle *nullum crimen sine lege*. What it comes to is this: the entire function of the statute is reduced to specifying the punishment. The criminal offense itself, however, is defined outside the statute. What we actually have in mind is a rather widespread legislative technique which designates the act by using a common law technical term. In such cases there is only one source to draw on for the definition of the offense, and that is the common law.[9]

By utilizing a common law term instead of a developed, self-contained definition of the offense, the legislator again puts into the hands of the judge the authority to define the criminal offense.

---

[9] Several examples of applying this technique have been given earlier; see Chapter IV, ft. 28 and accompanying text supra. The legislation of Maryland and West Virginia is rather typical in this respect. From the earlier judicial decisions see: *Commonwealth* v. *Webster*, 5 Cush. (Mass.) 295, 52 Am. Dec. 711 (1850); in this case the Massachusetts courts resorted to the common law for the definition of murder.

The history of criminal legislation of Louisiana furnishes a classical example of the application of this technique. See in particular: The Crimes Act of May 4, 1805. Compare: F. F. Stone, "The Reception of Law in Louisiana", in *Legal Thought in the United States*..., op. cit., pp. 139–140.

III.

The above remarks leave no doubt that it is not an easy task to make *nullum crimen sine lege* fully effective under American legal systems. The declaration that the statute constitutes the only basis of criminal responsibility, that is, that the common law of crimes is repealed, does not mean that the principle is effectively enforced. A necessary condition for the full operation of *nullum crimen sine lege* is the elimination from the statutory law of borrowed common law doctrines which are the carriers of judicial legislation. Moreover, to make the principle of *nullum crimen sine lege* function, complete and adequate statutory criminal law systems must be created which will no longer require broad, vague general clauses. Notably, the principle of *nullum crimen sine lege* was effectively adopted in Europe along with the sweeping tide of comprehensive codifications, which aimed at a broad and exhaustive reform of the criminal law. It seems then that what is instrumental for the successful adoption of the principle *nullum crimen sine lege* in American law is a general reform and codification of the criminal law. The question now arises whether there is actually a need in the United States for such a reform, whether the atmosphere favors a movement for codification and how advanced it is.

In fact, the American penal systems never underwent a general revision and reform. Today for the most part these systems are anachronistic both in regard to the general principles of criminal liability and to the shaping of criminal responsibility for specific crimes.[10] We mentioned earlier that

[10] See above authorities collected in ft. 5. "Viewing the country as a whole", Professor H. Wechsler wrote in 1956, "our penal codes are fragmentary, old, disorganized and often accidental with their coverage, their growth largely fortuitous in origin, their form a combination of enactment and of common law that only history explains". Wechsler, "The American Law Institute: Some Observations on Its Model Penal Code", op. cit., p. 321.

the existing technical arrangement of the laws is far from perfect, so the need for a reform is unquestionable. Therefore the codification movement which began around 1952 is extremely significant.[11]

It is submitted that the achievement of uniformity in the laws of the various states is an important reason for codification. Relationships among the states, highly complex and intensive at present, are seriously hampered by the differences in the existing systems. One also should bear in mind that the tendency toward reform and uniformity is not confined to the sphere of the criminal law. Keen attention is focused on the

---

W. R. LaFave and A. W. Scott in their outstanding recent criminal law treatise observe: "In many codes some of the most significant crimes (such as murder) are not defined, and it is not uncommon for basic doctrines concerning scope of liability to have little or no reflection in the statutes. Prior to the time that the work on the Model Penal Code began to be circulated, only two states, Louisiana and Wisconsin, had accomplished an overall reform of their substantive criminal law". W. R. LaFave and A. W. Scott, op. cit., p. 3.

It should be pointed out here that particularly subjective standards of criminal liability in American legal systems stand in marked contrast to the Continental European law. Liability without fault is still widely applied in American criminal law (strict liability, vicarious liability, felony murder rule, Pinkerton doctrine, corporate liability). Compare: F. B. Sayre, "Public Welfare Offenses", *Columbia Law Review*, 1933, Vol. 33; *Model Penal Code*, Tentative Draft No. 4, Philadelphia, 1955, pp. 141–145; H. M. Hart, "The Aims of the Criminal Law", *Law and Contemporary Problems*, 1958, Vol. 23; F. B. Sayre, "Criminal Responsibility for the Act of Another", *Harvard Law Review*, 1930, Vol. 43; W. R. LaFave and A. W. Scott, op. cit., pp. 223, 545ff; F. J. Frederick, "Foreseeable Death in Felony Murder", *University of Pittsburgh Law Review*, 1956, Vol. 18; N. Morris, "The Felon's Responsibility for the Lethal Acts of Others", *University of Pennsylvania Law Review*, 1956, Vol. 105.

[11] 1952—the year when the Model Penal Code project was commenced may be accepted as the starting point of the codification movement. See: H. Wechsler, "Codification of Criminal Law in the United States: The Model Penal Code", *Columbia Law Review*, 1968, Vol. 68, p. 1426. As to the history of the Model Penal Code see also: G. O. W. Mueller, *Crime, Law and the Scholars*, op. cit., pp. 151ff.

civil and, in particular, on the commercial law. The ratification of the Uniform Commercial Code by many states including the State of New York is the measure of its success. The need for an inclusive and coherent system of laws is widely understood, and the movement to codify the law and make it more uniform is by no means limited to one sphere.

Shifting back to the criminal law, let us point to some additional factors which have been essential in stimulating the reform and codification movement. American legal literature specifically cites as one of these factors the spread of humanitarianism after the Second World War.[12] This could hardly leave the criminal law untouched. Another factor has been America's increased involvement in international affairs and the development of comparative law. This popularized the idea of reform and codification, particularly as the American criminal law systems became more exposed to world public opinion.[13]

Although there is much in favor of codification, the goal is neither simple nor easy to accomplish, given the actual conditions, primarily because the reformers must start out on the basis of the law now in force.

It seems impossible to create a code which would reflect the existing casuistic fabric of the law in its entirety. The selection, choice and abstraction of the legal principles central to some problems is bound to be difficult since the job is to be done by people for whom casuistry is second nature. The skepticism and mistrust of abstract and synthetical rules[14] which is natural with common law lawyers must be reckoned with. Failure of legal scholarship to provide the philosophical ground

---

[12] A. P. Murrach, S. Rubin, "Penal Reform and the Model Sentencing Act", *Columbia Law Review*, 1965, Vol. 65, p. 1168.

[13] Ibidem, p. 1167.

[14] L. B. Schwartz, "The American Penal System: Spirit and Technique", *Annals*, 1962, pp. 6–8.

for codification is another handicap.[15] There is no deeply ingrained tradition of theoretical study in the field of criminal law in the United States, while studies in the "General Part" of the criminal law[16] are practically neglected. It is enough to point out that there are only very few comprehensive works in American literature dealing with the fundamental problems of criminal liability.[17]

Despite the serious drawbacks the social need for reform has sustained the movement for codification. What is known as the Model Penal Code has been conceived and drafted under the auspices of the American Law Institute and has become the turning point in the history of the American codification movement.[18] In 1953, the American Law Institute began to publish tentative drafts[19] and in 1962 the Proposed Official Draft, the finished, final form, was published.[20]

The Model Penal Code is not the result of official government sponsored initiative. It is a collaborative effort of legal scholars, judges and lawyers drawn from various backgrounds and different regions of the United States. An embodiment of the codification philosophy, the Model Penal Code contains a number of original ideas. However, since

---

[15] F. Cohen, op. cit., p. 263.

[16] L. B. Schwartz, op. cit., p. 7.

[17] Among these few existing Professor Jerome Hall's *General Principles of Criminal Law* (First ed., 1947, Second ed., 1960) should be mentioned first of all.

On the present situation in the American criminal law scholarship see generally: G. O. W. Mueller, *Crime, Law and the Scholars,* op. cit., pp. 133ff.

[18] W. R. LaFave and A. W. Scott, op. cit., p. 3.

[19] See: The American Law Institute, *Model Penal Code,* Tentative Draft No. 1, Philadelphia, May 1, 1953. All together there were thirteen Tentative Drafts of the Model Penal Code published from 1953 to 1962. H. Wechsler, "Codification of Criminal Law in the United States: The Model Penal Code", op. cit., p. 1426.

[20] The American Law Institute, *Model Penal Code,* Proposed Official Draft, Philadelphia, May 4, 1962.

the Code was meant to be followed either wholly or in part by the states, it is firmly entrenched in the common law tradition. It is criticized by legal scholars for its inconsistencies and compromises, although some inconsistency is inevitable in a work which makes concessions to various conflicting tendencies.[21] It offers alternative solutions to highly controversial questions, leaving the ultimate choice to the legislatures. In this respect the Model Penal Code exemplifies a characteristic American approach. Technically, however, the Model Penal Code measures up to the Continental penal codes. It regulates all the fundamental substantive criminal law issues, clearly distinguishing and separating "General Provisions" (Part I), which cover questions usually dealt with by European codes in their "General Parts", from "Definition of Specific Crimes" (Part II). It also includes Parts III and IV under the headings: "Treatment and Correction" and "Organization of Correction". The Model Penal Code breaks with the traditional dependence of the statutory criminal law on the common law both in respect to general principles and to the definition of specific crimes. The "General Part" also governs liability for all crimes not specified in the Code.

Both the development of the tentative drafts and the publication of the Model Penal Code in its final form were positive catalysts in the codification movement.[22] Even while the work on the Model Penal Code was still in progress, and to a greater degree when it was completed, the codification of the states' criminal law was accelerated. No less than twenty-five American jurisdictions have already accomplished their criminal law revisions process and have enacted criminal codes properly

---

[21] Compare: G. O. W. Mueller, *Crime, Law and the Scholars*, op. cit., p. 159ff.

[22] H. Wechsler, "Codification of Criminal Law...", op. cit., p. 1427; A. P. Murrah, S. Rubin, op. cit., pp. 162ff; W. R. LaFave and A. W. Scott, op. cit., p. 4; G. O. W. Mueller, *Crime, Law and the Scholars...*, op. cit., p. 162f.; B. J. George, op. cit., p. 233ff.

so called (Arkansas, Colorado, Connecticut, Delaware, Florida, Georgia, Hawaii, Illinois, Kansas, Kentucky, Louisiana,[23] Minnesota, Montana, New Hampshire, New Mexico, New York, N. Dakota, Ohio, Oregon, Puerto Rico, Pennsylvania, Texas, Utah, Virginia and Wisconsin).[24]

In eighteen other jurisdictions, including seventeen states and the federal jurisdiction, criminal law revisions have been completed; however new criminal codes have not yet been enacted.[25]

In the majority of remaining jurisdictions criminal law revisions are also either under way or at least contemplated.[26]

The work undertaken by the American Law Institute has not only been an impetus to reform, but in the majority of jurisdictions it has become very influential in shaping the content and style of the new penal codes.[27] As Professor Andenaes correctly pointed out, commenting on the Study Draft of the Federal Criminal Code: "Through these Codes and the present Study Draft, American draftsmanship in criminal law has reached a level far higher than previously".[28]

Bearing in mind that the Model Penal Code is not law but a proposed draft promoting the idea of codification, it is nevertheless suggested that it stands as an indicator of the existing codification tendencies.

What is the impact of the codification movement on the

[23] Criminal law revision in Louisiana resulting in the enactment of the new criminal code in 1942 should be considered separately.

[24] The American Law Institute, *1975 Annual Report*, p. 23.

[25] Ibidem (the status of substantive penal law revision reported as of April 1975).

[26] Ibidem.

[27] Compare: citations in ft. 22, supra.

[28] J. Andenaes, "Comment Comparing Study Draft of Proposed New Federal Criminal Code to European Penal Codes", in *Working Papers of the National Commission on Reform of Federal Criminal Laws*, U.S. Government Printing Office, Washington, D.C., 1971, Vol. III, p. 1451.

principle *nullum crimen sine lege*? Taking as our point of departure the provisions of the Model Penal Code (an approach, it seems, fully substantiated) the answer is that in this area too the codification is truly progressive. First Section 1.05(1) of the Model Penal Code introduces a formal definition of crime, clearly stating that there is no crime except in accordance with the Code or another statute.[29] Considered in the American context this provision eliminates common law crimes.

As we know, so far well over half of the states have abolished the common law of crimes. Section 1.05 of the Model Penal Code ostensibly points the direction for the reform to follow for the states where the common law still provides an independent basis for criminal responsibility.[30]

The special significance of the Model Penal Code also lies in the fact that through its general principles of criminal liability and its definitions of specific offenses the legislative monopoly of defining criminal conduct has been accomplished. Consequently the Model Penal Code eliminates many disguised forms of the violation of *nullum crimen sine lege* which were

---

[29] This provision runs as follows: "No conduct constitutes an offense unless it is a crime or violation under this code or another statute of this state". The terminology used in this phrase needs some explanation: the word "offense" is a general term accepted by the MPC to define any kind of breach of the penal law. All "offenses" fall into two classes: "violations" (less serious breaches of law punishable, in principle, only by fines) and "crimes". "Crimes", in turn, fall into three categories: felonies, misdemeanors and petty misdemeanors (Section 1.04 of the MPC).

[30] Following the example of the Model Penal Code the states of Wisconsin, Illinois, Connecticut, Kentucky, New Hampshire, Pennsylvania and Delaware have abolished common law crimes in their new penal codes. The only exceptions from this general trend among states which have enacted new penal codes are, so far, the states of New Mexico, Florida and Virginia. The 1975 Arkansas Criminal Code was not available to this writer at the time of sending the present study to print.

discussed previously. The new definition of conspiracy contained in the Model Penal Code breaks with the tradition of punishing for an agreement to commit a non-criminal act.[31]

By removing the judicial power to make new offenses under the guise of conspiracy, the Model Penal Code has destroyed the most frequently utilized weapon to attack the *nullum crimen sine lege* principle. Several modern criminal codes, such for example as: Colorado, Connecticut, Georgia, Illinois, Kansas, Kentucky, New Hampshire, New York, New Mexico, Oregon, Pennsylvania, Virginia and Wisconsin criminal codes following the example of the Model Penal Code, restricted the objects of criminal conspiracy to acts punishable *per se*.[32]

The Model Penal Code curtails the list of possible objects of criminal conspiracy excluding not only acts not criminal *per se* but also minor offenses. The scope of conspiracy is also further restricted by the introduction to its definition of several other new elements.[33] Perhaps in its future development the

---

[31] Section 5.03(1) of the MPC runs as follows: "Definition of conspiracy. A person is guilty of conspiracy with another person or persons to commit a crime if with the purpose of promoting or facilitating its commission he:

(a) agrees with such other person or persons that they or one of them will engage in conduct which constitutes such crime or an attempt or solicitation to commit such crime; or

(b) agrees to aid such other person or persons in the planning or commission of such crime or of an attempt or solicitation to commit such crime".

[32] Comp.: Chapter V, ft. 50–52.

[33] Under Section 5.03(1) MPC (quoted in ft. 31) violations punishable only by fines (comp. MPC Section 1.04(5)) are eliminated from the list of conspiratorial objects.

Concerning other elements restricting the scope of conspiracy in the Model Penal Code the following should be mentioned:

a) specific intent aimed at the commission of a crime (Section 5.03(1)); the same requirement is present in several modern state criminal codes; comp. criminal codes of Connecticut, Illinois, New Hampshire, New Mexico, New York and Wisconsin (see Chapter V, ft. 80);

American law, following the European example, will refrain from treating conspiracy as a catch-all crime and restrict the responsibility for conspiratorial relationships to the most serious crimes.

Considerable progress toward the effective adoption of *nullum crimen sine lege* is accomplished through the definition of specific crimes in the Part II of the Model Penal Code. We will not find there provisions like Section 12-22-01 of the North Dakota Code which leaves to the court the power to decide what constitutes a crime. Neither will we find provisions tacitly referring back to the common law for the definition of the offense. The Model Penal Code uses its own complete definitions of crimes, in which the balance between descriptive and evaluative elements meets the standards of an average Continental codification. In this sphere too recent state codifications seem to follow the example of the Model Penal Code.

The new codifications show considerable progress in respect to the implementation of the principle *nullum crimen sine lege*. In effect, the tradition of excessive flexibility in the administration of the criminal laws has suffered a severe blow which may not be welcomed without reservations in all quarters.[34]

---

b) Section 5.03(5) provides that: "no person may be convicted of conspiracy to commit a crime, other than a felony of the first or second degree, unless an overt act in pursuance of such conspiracy is alleged and proved to have been done by him or by a person with whom he conspired"; the same is true for the majority of modern criminal codes;

c) Section 1.07(1) (b) and Section 5.05(3) exclude a simultaneous conviction for conspiracy to commit an offense and for its commission; comp. also: criminal codes of Illinois and Oregon (see Chapter V, ft. 65).

[34] A. H. Sherry, "The Politics of Criminal Law Reform. The United States". American Journal of Comparatire Law, Vol. 21 (1973). p. 204f. ("The general attitude of prosecutors towards comprehensive criminal law revision is one of apprehension, mistrust and instinctive unwillingness to reexamine the whole body of the law".)

BIBLIOGRAPHY: MOST IMPORTANT SOURCES

Aigler, R. N., Legislation in Vague and General Terms, *Michigan Law Review*, 1923, Vol. 21.

Allen, C. K., *Law in the Making*, 7th ed., Oxford, 1964.

American Jurisprudence, A Modern Comprehensive Text Statement of American Law State and Federal, 2nd ed., Rochester and San Francisco, 1965.

Amsterdam, A. G., "Federal Constitutional Restrictions on the Punishment of Crimes of Status, Crimes of General Obnoxiousness, Crimes of Displeasing Police Officers, and the Like", *Criminal Law Bulletin*, 1967, Vol. 3.

Von Bar, C. L., and others, *A History of Continental Criminal Law*, Boston, 1916.

Beccaria, C. B., *On Crimes and Punishments*, transl. by H. Paolucci, Indianapolis and New York, 1963.

Bentham, J., *An Introduction to the Principles of Morals and Legislation*, New York, 1948.

Bishop, J. P., *A Treatise on Criminal Law*, 9th ed., Indianapolis, 1923.

Black, H. C., *Black's Law Dictionary*, 4th ed., St. Paul, Minn., 1968.

—*Handbook on the Law of Judicial Precedents*, St. Paul, Minn., 1912.

Blackstone, W., *Commentaries on the Laws of England*, Philadelphia, 1898.

Brownlie, J., Williams, D. G. T., "Judicial Legislation in Criminal Law", *Canadian Bar Review*, 1964, Vol. 42.

Cardozo, B., *The Nature of the Judicial Process*, New Haven and London, 1964.

Carson, B., *The Law of Criminal Conspiracies and Agreements as Found in the American Cases*, Philadelphia, 1887.

Clark and Marshall, *A Treatise on the Law of Crimes*, 6th ed., Chicago, 1958.

Covington, H. C., "The American Doctrine of *Stare Decisis*", *Texas Law Review*, 1946, Vol. 24.

Cross, R., *Precedent in English Law*, 2nd ed., Oxford, 1968.

Currier, T. S., "Time and Change in Judge Made Law: Prospective Overruling", *Virginia Law Review*, 1965, Vol. 51.

"Developments in the Law—Criminal Conspiracy", *Harvard Law Review*, 1959, Vol. 72.

Esmein, A., *A History of Continental Criminal Procedure*, Boston, 1913.

O. Fischl, *Der Einfluss der Aufklärungsphilosophie auf die Entwicklung des Strafrechts*, Scientia Verlag, Aalen, 1973.

Fordham, J. B., Leach, J. R., "Interpretation of Statutes in Derogation of the Common Law", *Vanderbilt Law Review*, 1950, Vol. 3.

Freund, P. A., *The Supreme Court of the United States*, Cleveland and New York, 1964.

—"The Supreme Court and Civil Liberties", *Vanderbilt Law Review*, 1951, Vol. 4.

L. M. Friedman, A History of American Law, New York, 1973.

Glueck, S., Hall, L., *Criminal Law and Its Enforcement*, Boston, 1958.

Goodhart, A. L., "Case Law In England and America", in *Essays in Jurisprudence and the Common Law*, Cambridge, 1931.

—"Determining the *Ratio Decidendi* of a Case", in *Essays in Jurisprudence and the Common Law*, Cambridge, 1931.

Gray, J. C., *The Nature and Sources of the Law*, 2nd ed., Boston, 1963.

Haddad, J. B., "Retroactivity Should Be Rethought: A Call for the End of the Linkletter Doctrine", *Journal of Criminal Law, Criminology, and Police Sciences*, 1969, Vol. 60.

Hall, F. W., "The Common Law: An Account of Its Reception in the United States", *Vanderbilt Law Review*, 1951, Vol. 4.

Hall, J., *General Principles of Criminal Law*, 2nd ed., Indianapolis, 1960.

Hall, L., "Strict or Liberal Construction of Penal Statutes", *Harvard Law Review*, 1935, Vol. 48.

Harno, A. J., "Intent in Criminal Conspiracy", *University of Pennsylvania Law Review*, 1941, Vol. 89.

Holmes, O. W., *Common Law*, Boston and Toronto, 1963.

Jackson, R. M., "Common Law Misdemeanors", *Cambridge Law Journal*, 1937, Vol. 6.

Kenny, C. S., *Kenny's Outline of Criminal Law*, by J. W. C. Turner, Cambridge, 1952.

Kessler, N., "Common Law Offenses and Penalties in Pennsylvania", *Temple Law Quarterly*, 1960, Vol. 33.

Kline, S., Hitchler, W. H., "The Common Law Misdemeanor Doctrine", *Dickinson Law Review*, 1955, Vol. 59.

LaFave, W. R., Scott, A. W., *Handbook on Criminal Law*, St. Paul, Minn., 1972.

Lobingier, C. S., "Precedent in Past and Present Legal Systems", *Michigan Law Review*, 1946, Vol. 44.

Maestro, M. T., *Voltaire and Beccaria as Reformers of Criminal Law*, New York, 1942.

Marx, K., *Das Kapital*, Dietz Verlag, Berlin, 1968.

Markson, D., "The Punishment of Suicide: A Need for Change", *Villanova Law Review*, 1969, Vol. 14.

Michael, J., Wechsler, H., *Criminal Law and Its Administration*, Chicago, 1940.

Mueller, G. O. W., *Crime, Law and the Scholars, A History of Scholarship in American Criminal Law*, Seattle, 1969.

—"Liberalism and Conservatism in American Criminal Law", *Duquesne University Law Review*, 1965, Vol. 3.

Murrah, A. P., Rubin, S., "Penal Reform and the Model Sentencing Act", *Columbia Law Review*, 1965, Vol. 65.

Note, "Acts Not Formerly Criminal at Common Law, Held Punishable as Injurious to Public Morals", *University of Pennsylvania Law Review*, 1955, Vol. 103.

Note, "Blasphemy", *Columbia Law Review*, 1970, Vol. 70.

Note, "Common Law Crimes in the United States", *Columbia Law Review*, 1947, Vol. 47.

Note, "The Objects of Criminal Conspiracy", *Harvard Law Review*, 1955, Vol. 68.

Note, "Prospective Operation of Decision Holding Statutes Unconstitutional or Overruling Prior Decisions", *Harvard Law Review*, 1947, Vol. 60.

Note, "Prospective Overruling and Retroactive Application in the Federal Courts", *Yale Law Journal*, 1962, Vol. 71.

Note, "The Void for Vagueness Doctrine in the Supreme Court", *University of Pennsylvania Law Review*, 1960, Vol. 109.

Opałek, K., Wróblewski, J., *Współczesna teoria i socjologia prawa w Stanach Zjednoczonych* (Contemporary Jurisprudence and Sociology of Law in the United States of North America), Warszawa, 1963.

Patterson, E. W., *Jurisprudence, Men and Ideas of the Law*, Brooklyn, N. Y., 1953.

Paulsen, M. G., Kadish, S. H., *Criminal Law and Its Processes*, Boston and Toronto, 1962.

Perkins, R. M., *Criminal Law*, Brooklyn, N. Y., 1957.

Plucknett, T. F. T., *A Concise History of the Common Law*, 5th ed., Boston, 1956.

Pollack, B. F., "Common Law Conspiracy", *Georgia Law Review*, 1947, Vol. 35.

Pope, H., "The English Common Law In the United States", *Harvard Law Review*, 1910, Vol. 24.

Pound, R., "Common Law and Legislation", *Harvard Law Review*, 1908, Vol. 21.
—"The Development of American Law and its Deviation from English Law", *Law Quarterly Review*, 1951, Vol. 67.
—*The Spirit of the Common Law*, Boston, 1963.
Radbruch, G., *Einführung in die Rechtswissenschaft*, II Durchgearbeitete Auflage, Stuttgart, 1964.
Radzinowicz, L., *A History of English Criminal Law and Its Administration*, Vol. I, *The Movement for Reform*, London, 1948.
Salmond, J. W., "The Theory of Judicial Precedents", *Law Quarterly Review*, 1900, Vol. 16.
Salmonowicz, S., *Prawo karne oświeconego absolutyzmu. Z dziejów kodyfikacji karnych przelomu XVIII i XIX wieku* (The Criminal Law of Enlightened Absolutism). Toruń, 1966.
Sayre, F. B., "Criminal Conspiracy", *Harvard Law Review*, 1921, Vol. 35.
Schwartz, L. B., "The American Penal System: Spirit and Technique", *Annals*, 1962.
Scott, A. W., "Constitutional Limitations on Substantive Criminal Law", *Rocky Mountain Law Review*, 1957, Vol. 29.
Smith, J. C. and Hogan, B., *Criminal Law*, 3rd ed., London, 1973.
Sobel, N. R., "The Anticipatory Offenses in the New Penal Law: Solicitation, Conspiracy, Attempt and Facilitation", *Brooklyn Law Review*, 1966, Vol. 32.
Stallybras, W. T. S., "Public Mischief", *Law Quarterly Review*, 1933, Vol. 49.
Stephen, J. F., *A History of the Criminal Law of England*, London, 1883.
Sutherland, J. G., *Statutes and Statutory Constructions*, 3rd ed., Chicago, 1943.
Thompson, J., "Common Law Crimes Against Public Morals", *Journal of Criminal Law, Criminology and Police Sciences*, 1958, Vol. 49.
Wechsler, H., "Codification of Criminal Law in the United States: The Model Penal Code", *Columbia Law Review*, 1968, Vol. 68.
Williams, G., "Common Law Misdemeanors", *Law Quarterly Review*, 1952, Vol. 68.
—*Criminal Law, The General Part*, 2nd ed, London, 1961.
Wolter, W., "Granice i zakres prawa karania", (Limits and Scope of the Right to Punish), *Państwo i Prawo*, 1957, No. 3.
Wright, R. S., *The Law of Criminal Conspiracies and Agreements*, Philadelphia, 1887.
Yawn, M. T., "Conspiracy", *Military Law Review*, 1971, Vol. 51.

Bei Fragen zur Produktsicherheit wenden Sie sich bitte an:
If you have any questions regarding product safety,
please contact:

Walter de Gruyter GmbH
Genthiner Straße 13
10785 Berlin
productsafety@degruyterbrill.com